The Workhorse
of Helmand

The Workhorse of Helmand

A Chinook Crewman's Account of Operations in Afghanistan and Iraq

Michael Fry

Pen & Sword
MILITARY

First published in Great Britain in 2022 by
Pen & Sword Military
An imprint of
Pen & Sword Books Ltd
Yorkshire – Philadelphia

Copyright © Michael Fry 2022

ISBN 978 1 39907 551 0

The right of David Tremain to be identified as Author of this work has been asserted by him in accordance with the Copyright, Designs and Patents Act 1988.

A CIP catalogue record for this book is
available from the British Library.

All rights reserved. No part of this book may be reproduced or transmitted in any form or by any means, electronic or mechanical including photocopying, recording or by any information storage and retrieval system, without permission from the Publisher in writing.

Typeset by Mac Style
Printed in the UK by CPI Group (UK) Ltd, Croydon, CR0 4YY.

Pen & Sword Books Limited incorporates the imprints of Atlas, Archaeology, Aviation, Discovery, Family History, Fiction, History, Maritime, Military, Military Classics, Politics, Select, Transport, True Crime, Air World, Frontline Publishing, Leo Cooper, Remember When, Seaforth Publishing, The Praetorian Press, Wharncliffe Local History, Wharncliffe Transport, Wharncliffe True Crime and White Owl.

For a complete list of Pen & Sword titles please contact

PEN & SWORD BOOKS LIMITED
47 Church Street, Barnsley, South Yorkshire, S70 2AS, England
E-mail: enquiries@pen-and-sword.co.uk
Website: www.pen-and-sword.co.uk

Or

PEN AND SWORD BOOKS
1950 Lawrence Rd, Havertown, PA 19083, USA
E-mail: Uspen-and-sword@casematepublishers.com
Website: www.penandswordbooks.com

In memory of

Flight Lieutenant Geraint 'Roly' Roberts RAF

Kabul, Afghanistan

11 October 2015

'Sefyll yn hawdd'

Contents

Acknowledgements		xiii
Chapter 1	Moving Home	1
Chapter 2	How Did I Get Here?	13
Chapter 3	A Series of Strange Events	23
Chapter 4	Iraq, it's like Afghanistan but flat	36
Chapter 5	Fly, Sleep, Rinse and Repeat	46
Chapter 6	Without Firing a Shot	59
Chapter 7	A Funny Thing Happened on the Way to the Hindu Kush	82
Chapter 8	Fighting Season	91
Chapter 9	Send Fat Cow, Over	100
Chapter 10	Black Cats Aren't Always Lucky	109
Chapter 11	Boom, Boom, Shake the Room	123
Chapter 12	Groundhog Month	132
Chapter 13	Maps, Windows and Lightning Strike at Inopportune Moments	149
Chapter 14	A Brief Glimmer of Normality	165
Chapter 15	Thanks, Bob	170
Chapter 16	Frenchie the Bullet-Magnet *Extraordinaire*	181
Chapter 17	It's Been Emotional	192
Epilogue		195
Glossary		198

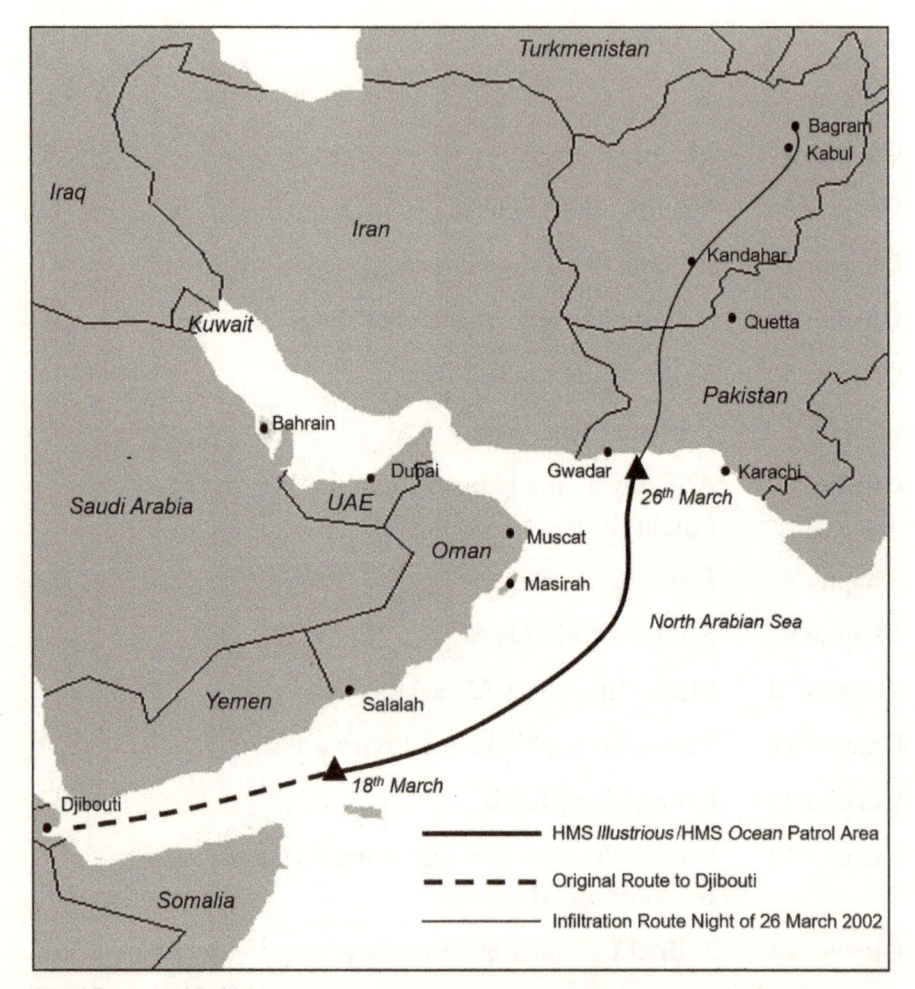

Patrol Route and Infiltration.

Iraq.

Provinces within Regional Command (South) shown in grey.

Regional Command (South).

Helmand.

Acknowledgements

What started out as a lockdown project came to life with the support of many. Firstly, my thanks go to those mentioned in the book, and also to Zoe, for their support and agreement. Thanks also go to Rob and Colleen (and Cookie), for being the canaries in the cage and for the encouragement to keep writing. To Frenchie go thanks for providing so many incidents to chronicle, yet ensuring we survived, as they do to all those from the Chinook Force who shared the experiences described within. I'd like to acknowledge Padre Tudor, for providing a light to all of us in the darkest of times; Boeing, for making an awesome aircraft that always got us home; Henry and the team at Pen & Sword, for working quiet miracles; and for flapjacks and coffee after a long walk on a cold day. Thanks also to Guy VDB for showing me what people leadership really is. But most of all, I need to thank my children, despite the gaps in their childhood whilst I was away, for the love I received from them each time I returned. There are others I want to thank, but they don't like attention, which I respect (no names, Woody, Andy …).

Whenever possible, I have identified the source of photographs, but I apologise to anyone whose images I have failed to credit.

Chapter 1

Moving Home

HMS *Ocean*
11 Nautical Miles off the Pakistan Coast
26 March 2002

As I stepped out through the metal hatch on to the blacked-out flight deck, leaving the red glow and air conditioning of flight operations, the first things to hit me were the humidity and blackness of the night. I closed the hatch behind me, dropping the latch into place with a heavy clunk, pausing to allow my eyes to adjust to the dark. Across the deck, towards the stern of the carrier's flight deck, I could make out the shadowy outline of the two Chinook helicopters.

Flight decks are hazardous places even in daylight, and so it was with no small degree of caution that I started making my way towards the nearest helicopter, ZA 679. As I got closer I sensed, rather than saw, ground crew moving around, and I eventually negotiated the tie-down chains securing the aircraft to the deck and dumped my flight bag on the seat just inboard of the rear loading ramp.

I heard a clunk behind me and saw one of the ground crew fitting the M60 machine gun to a mount on the sill of the ramp, before fitting the can containing a 200-round belt of ammunition. As I looked forward I could see Roly and Bungle checking the port and starboard miniguns at the front of the cabin.

'Where are the other two?' I asked, referring to the pilots.

'Over at the ISO collecting weapons,' replied Roly, smiling as always.

I retraced my steps, off the ramp and across the flight deck to the shipping container, where the squadron armourers had set up shop several weeks earlier. I nodded to our pilots Morris and Phil as we passed and greeted the ground crew, who handed me a 9mm pistol, two magazines, an SA-80 A2 rifle, six magazines and a bayonet. I thanked the guys and checked the chambers on the weapons, clearing them as safe before heading back to the aircraft, trying not to trip over any tie-down chains and face-plant the deck, or drop any guns or ammunition.

By now the guys had turned on the aircraft battery and there was a dim blue light emanating from the cabin; blue light is common in military aircraft as it doesn't affect night-vision goggles. I checked the pistol was clear once more, loaded a magazine and placed it in my drop leg holster, along with the second magazine. I went through the same process with my rifle, placing it behind the seat, and stowed the other five magazines in my chest webbing. The bayonet was for clearing a path through minefields rather than leading some vainglorious charge against the enemy, and I secured it to the chest webbing.

I grabbed a torch, clipped my flight bag to the seat and started a walk-round of the aircraft, checking panels were secure and covers had been removed. After five minutes or so I arrived back at the ramp and found a group of people huddled together ready to board. We had several passengers that night, some of our own ground crew and an advance party from 45 Commando. The other aircraft had a similar number, and although the Chinook is capable of taking many more troops, both aircraft carried two large internal fuel tanks, each of which was effectively a five-foot cube and cut down the space within the cabin significantly. What we lost in cabin space we gained in range, and the four and a half tons of fuel in the internal tanks, together with the three tons in the main aircraft tanks, would allow us to reach Kandahar; that was the theory, anyway.

However, that did mean the aircraft would be heavy when we left the deck; the maximum weight on wheels for the Chinook was 22.7 tons, and with the fuel, passengers and full ammunition load we would be significantly above that, closer to 24 tons. Morris had spent several hours poring over performance graphs with a furrowed brow, but it was what it was; with some last-minute changes that had come in the previous day we needed every kilo of fuel to make it across Pakistan and reach the first available fuel at Kandahar, some 500 miles away.

I gave the passengers a thumbs-up, and they filed onboard, found a space and settled in as best they could; nobody was expecting a comfortable ride and they filled any remaining space like a tide washing in. We had loaded the baggage and equipment and prepared the aircraft during the day, making the most of the time and daylight to ensure we had only last-minute pre-departure checks to do on the blacked-out deck.

'Helmets!' came the loud call from the cockpit, and I retrieved my flying helmet and slipped it on, hearing the intercom crackle into life as I plugged into the system. In the cockpit Phil and Morris were ready to start, powering up the AC systems so Morris could start punching our route into the GPS.

I scanned the back of the aircraft to ensure it was clear of people, checked the hydraulic pressure on the gauge mounted at the ramp and flicked the intercom to talk.

'Clear start APU.'

'Roger' was the reply from Morris, and a second later, the auxiliary power unit started up with a high-pitched whine. Low-pressure warning lights came on across the cabin as systems activated, and I walked outside to watch the engine starts, relieved when the rotors started to turn and the downwash provided a welcome respite from the humidity. With both engines running and the rotors now turning, I pulled out the chocks from the back wheel and climbed back onboard, lifting the ramp to the horizontal, as I heard the APU wind down, no longer needed now the main generators were producing AC power.

As Roly ran through the arming-up checks with Phil, I put on my safety harness and knelt on the ramp to load a belt of ammunition into the M60. I also flipped down my Night Vision Goggles (NVG) and turned them on, checking the green images on both tubes. At a nod from Roly I killed the cabin lights and settled on to the ramp, legs astride the M60, boots dangling in free air. Once we lifted off the deck, we would be over Pakistan within minutes.

I heard Morris on the radio talking with the flight controller and saw the ground crew run in and remove the tie down chains. I gave Roly a thumbs-up and heard Nick in the second aircraft key his mike twice to let us know he was ready. Our call signs for the mission were Vortex 36 and 37.

'Vortex, on deck,' called Morris.

'Vortex, Clear take-off port,' replied FLYCO.

I sensed the downwash as the other aircraft lifted to the hover, and then felt our own back wheels leave the deck. As we slid to the left and cleared the deck, I saw the other aircraft drop its nose and follow us, the wake of the ship showing up brightly on the NVG below us. Morris's hard work with the performance data had paid off, and although the heavy aircraft sank towards the blackness of the sea for a second, causing some consternation, it quickly recovered, and we climbed away from the water, much to the relief of all on board.

'Vortex, airborne port,' Nick called, letting the ship know we were clear of the deck.

We continued to climb as we headed for the shore, well aware of a range of mountains just inland of the Baluchistan coast. Facing backwards as I sat on the ramp, I saw the bright glow of the ship's wake arcing against the dark sea as she turned towards the west; her job done now that we had launched, she would start the long voyage back to Portsmouth, stopping in Oman to disembark the remaining members of 45 Commando. As we came in over the coast, a moonscape of rocky ground slowly gave way to barren, jagged peaks.

'Vortex, feet dry,' informed the ship that we had coasted in and were now over dry land.

'Copy feet dry. Good luck and Godspeed,' replied the controller.

With that, we were now no longer the Royal Navy's problem. Far behind us, HMS *Ocean* slowly faded into the distance. It was shortly after 3.00 am, we were on our own and sneaking across Pakistan in the dark on our way to Afghanistan.

A few days earlier, we had been ordered to make our way from HMS *Ocean* to Bagram, a disused Russian airbase just north of Kabul, where we would be supporting 45 Commando, Royal Marines. There had been much planning, and we had sought diplomatic clearance to cross Pakistan and refuel at a CIA-operated site in the desert just north of the Afghanistan/Pakistan border. However, the day before we were due to depart, the CIA closed the refuelling site, leaving us with major adjustments to make to our fuel load in order to reach Kandahar. Pakistan had also revoked our diplomatic clearance after a major bomb attack in Islamabad a week earlier. So our transit over Pakistan that night was 'on the QT', and we had mitigated that as best we could by following the routes used by the US Navy's Fifth Fleet aircraft on their nightly missions over Pakistan and into Afghanistan. However, the limited guidance we had received from the UK Operations Centre in Bahrain had been clear: do not land in Pakistan for any reason – which was not the best advice for two helicopters operating at the very limit of their capabilities.

As if we hadn't had enough issues to juggle, the intelligence community provided us with an updated threat assessment which served as a stark reminder of what we were up against: if captured, we would be tortured into revealing addresses of family members so they could be attacked in the UK and to serve as a deterrent to further British military involvement in Afghanistan. This had vexed all of us; we had signed up for the job, but our parents, children and wives had not. We conferred with RAF Odiham to find out what the plan was if we went down over Pakistan or Afghanistan and quickly learned there was no plan. To their credit, Odiham worked quickly and soon had a plan to pick up families and take them to a place of safety if we went down. Satisfied that our families would be safe, we went back to the task in hand.

Luckily, the transit across Pakistan, although tense, was uneventful, other than an inability to contact the US AWACS which was meant to act as top cover for our mission. However, the radios were quiet, and so was the intercom – apart from occasional chatter regarding fuel or navigation each of us was alone with our thoughts; even Roly, who was usually talkative during long transits, was silent.

As the sun rose, the rocky grey landscape gave way to a desert plain of red-hued sand dotted with small clumps of green spinifex which seemed to extend for infinity; it was stunningly beautiful, and I was admiring the view as Morris interrupted the silence.

'Welcome to Afghanistan,' he said flatly. We had crossed the border, and by now had descended to low level and were skimming the desert at 50ft. Despite there not being a soul in sight, I gripped the M60 a little tighter and felt a little more alert.

Eventually, a faint grey outline of mountains appeared on the horizon, and as we approached Kandahar the tempo of activity increased and intercom chatter picked up. As we crossed the fence we armed down the counter-measure system and flared to a slow hover-taxi down the runway past a clutch of derelict buildings and damaged aircraft. It was clear the fighting for the airfield had been ferocious. As we turned off the main runway, I saw a small tent site and a fuel truck ahead, and we landed, ground-taxiing forward before braking in a spot alongside the fuel truck. The other aircraft taxied in and stopped behind us.

The APU started, with its high-pitched whine, and I dropped the ramp and set foot on Afghan soil for the first time. Within minutes, we had shut down the aircraft and gathered by the ramp, as Roly helped the US Marine hook up the fuel hose and begin pumping fuel into the near-empty tanks. The passengers emerged from their resting places to gaze at the desert landscape and a prominent peak in the distance. There was nervous laughter as people realized that, although we were in Afghanistan, we had made it off the deck and across the chaos of Pakistan safely.

I walked down the taxiway a few yards, putting a respectful distance between myself and the fuel truck, and lit a cigarette. I didn't really know what to expect from Afghanistan, but it was a relief to be out of the confines of the ship, after ten weeks of boredom. As I smoked I watched the engineers checking out the aircraft, like expectant parents, and admired their courage and dedication. I have always been in awe of how parental they are with aircraft, as to a lesser extent are the crews; not one man jack of them would let us fly an aircraft they wouldn't fly on themselves. Right now they had a chance to play their part, and not one inch of that aircraft went unchecked.

I stubbed out my cigarette and rejoined the group, but the chitchat was short-lived as the refuel was complete, Roly helping the Marine pull the heavy hose clear of the aircraft. It was time to start up again, and with everyone back onboard, the tanks full and the rotors turning, we taxied out and lifted to the hover. With Nick's aircraft leading, our nose pitched forward and we accelerated down the runway, arming up as the concrete gave way to desert and we settled in at 50ft and turned to the north.

By now we had a slight problem; our analogue fuel gauges were pinwheeling through the numbers and not giving any useable reading for fuel contents. We informed the other aircraft, which had the same issue, but it was manageable, and we continued towards Bagram.

Afghanistan is a stunningly beautiful country, and if I thought the sunrise over the red desert an hour or so earlier had been a memory that would stay with me forever, I would add the next hour, as we climbed from the desert floor and weaved between snowcapped peaks, with green rivers snaking through pine forests and rocky valley floors below. This was Oruzgan Province and would be the main area of operations for Australian Special Forces in the years to come. Although too early in the season to be obvious on that morning, the green valleys were mainly given over to opium production; two months later, they would be red ribbons of poppies.

Occasionally we would skirt a village and see local Afghans looking curiously but with no obvious displays of hostility at the helicopters passing over, or pass turbaned figures on remote mountain tracks. With no real idea what to expect, in our minds everyone was potentially Taliban or Al Qaeda, and the M60 would quickly be trained at them; most just ignored us as they went about their business.

By early afternoon fatigue had set in, we were starting to feel tired and it was a relief when we approached Kabul, buoyed by the knowledge that Bagram was only 20 or so miles beyond, across a mountain pass. However, we still had to cross a sprawling city surrounded by mountain peaks which left us exposed to small arms fire from any of the many buildings in our path.

We did receive some ground fire, but thankfully it was from young kids with slingshots, a few small rocks pinging off the belly of the aircraft as we passed overhead. The people of Kabul, repeatedly invaded by foreign powers and let down by successive regimes, eyed us cautiously. We waved as we passed overhead, and a few waved back, mainly kids. It wasn't a policy we'd decided on, it just seemed like the logical thing to do.

Like a shadow, we passed over sleepy districts, busy streets and parks, then with approval from the American air traffic controller, crossed the extended centre line of Kabul International Airport and climbed up over a saddle between two mountains.

As we descended from the saddle, Bagram was laid out ahead of us in the Charikar valley, a green belt of vegetation snaking through low ground between towering peaks capped with the late snow of spring. A long runway stood out, cleared of vegetation but surrounded by partially collapsed buildings and abandoned equipment. The years had not been kind to Bagram since the Russians had left in 1989.

We armed down for the final time, and as we hover-taxied down the runway, I unloaded the M60 and looked at the abandoned Russian aircraft lying in rusting heaps at the side of the taxiways. We were aware that Bagram had been heavily mined, knowledge underscored by seeing a mine-clearing vehicle recently abandoned and sitting near the runway with its flails blown off.

We turned into a makeshift parking bay on what had once been a taxiway and shut the aircraft down. As the APU wound down, I removed my helmet and saw figures emerging from behind the fuel tanks, cramped and squinting; they had obviously been asleep for much of the second half of the journey. A couple of vehicles approached, and the engineers, assisted by the Marines, loaded bags and equipment into the back of them.

Even in mid-afternoon, Bagram was cooler and less humid than the North Arabian Sea, and I reached for my windproof smock and put it on, zipping it up and feeling a bit warmer as I made out the figure of our squadron boss striding towards the aircraft. A man of few words, he had flown into Bagram a week earlier, direct from the UK, and we hadn't seen him since before Christmas.

I walked up the cabin to where the rest of the crew were gathering belongings and equipment and called out quietly, 'Boss is inbound.'

They nodded, and a few seconds later, he strode up the ramp and stopped.

'I've managed to get us some tasking for tomorrow,' he said, and then turned and pointed at a collection of aged olive-green tents across the taxiway. 'The engineering line is just over there.'

With that, he turned and headed over to the other aircraft, leaving us to exchange glances and raise eyebrows. We had just flown almost 1,000 miles, from a ship, across Pakistan and Afghanistan, and although we weren't expecting a parade, a 'How did it go?' or 'Good to see you' would have been nice. But it wasn't to be; as I said, a man of few words.

We gathered the last of our kit and walked over to the tents, where the engineers had started unpacking tool chests and aircraft logbooks. It was minimalistic, but the main party would start arriving from the UK over the next week, bringing in more equipment. A young marine walked us to the place that would become home, a draughty tent at the end of a short row, on dusty ground which had been bulldozed to clear the topsoil (and any mines that may have been buried near the surface) into a wide berm some 6ft in height; our tent was next to the berm.

'Don't go on the berm, or off the taxiways or hard standing, guys. The Russians littered this place with AP mines as they left,' the marine advised and left us to it.

There was just dusty ground, and no liner. It was going to be a cold night once the sun dropped behind the mountains and the cooler air sank down to the valley floor. We set up our 1940-vintage issue camp beds and threw sleeping bags on top. Bergens were placed between the beds, and it was a snug fit for the nine of us. Our engineers had moved in next door.

What sets the UK military apart from its US counterpart is the ability to accept that you're going to turn up under-equipped every time; that and the cunning to procure a more comfortable existence by any means, fair or foul. This was that task we set about, and Bungle had pulled out a gas stove and began boiling water for a brew, as Stan, Morris and I built a bench of cardboard boxes filled with water bottles, and a wooden duckboard. Phil and Roly disappeared with one of the engineers in a Land Rover and returned half an hour later with a vehicle full of the much more comfortable US Army-issued cot beds, which were quickly assembled to replace the rickety British versions, which later lay abandoned in a neat stack at the far end of the tent. I didn't ask how they had acquired the cots, but I believed Roly's involvement suggested some level of subterfuge and probably a very confused American.

Over our time at Bagram, the British forces were known as 'the Flintstones' or 'the Borrowers' by the US forces, either because we turned up with nothing and dug holes, or because we 'borrowed' everything we needed; and the term 'borrow' was used loosely and normally indicated a more permanent arrangement. But that first afternoon, we managed to make ourselves more comfortable, and as we sat drinking tea on our new bench there was a last nugget of joy when the engineers managed to hook up some lights in their tent and ran the cable through into ours to banish the growing evening gloom.

It was as we gathered over tea, in a dusty area off the southern taxiway at Bagram, that the boss returned, this time with a few more words. As a pilot, he was a phenomenal set of hands and had won the Distinguished Flying Cross during the first Gulf War, dropping in the SAS Bravo Two Zero patrol behind Iraqi lines, as well as many others. As a Squadron Commander of a front-line squadron of 200 aircrew and engineers, he was less gifted. He just wasn't a natural people person and came across as aloof and distant, a great shame given his prowess as a pilot.

He updated us on the operations and kept referring to Afghanistan as 'South Armagh with teeth', which I would reflect on in later years and chuckle at the naivety of. He did, however, lay out two basic rules of operation which made a lot of sense. Firstly, we would operate everywhere as a pair, the second aircraft to provide support or pick up the crew if the first went down. After the intelligence brief we had received before leaving the ship, none of us rated our chances of fighting off Al Qaeda for long as particularly high; we were aviators, not infantrymen. Secondly, we should be on the ground for no more than 90 seconds, again a good decision as Al Qaeda and the Taliban (or

AQT as they were now known colloquially) possessed mortars and were allegedly skilled with them.

As he was wrapping up, a young marine approached and told us the camp commandant wanted to brief all new arrivals, so we followed him over to a patch of dirt, where a strange-looking tattooed guy in combats stood with a small horseshoe shaped crowd around him, including several Colonels, an RAF Wing Commander, several other officers, senior NCOs and a few young marines.

'Right, I'm Staff Sergeant Smith and I am the Camp Commandant,' he began, and off he went, running us through the camp rules, using the f-word as a comma. Toilets were a long plank over old oil drums, which collected deposits. Every Thursday, the drums had diesel added to them and were set fire to – 'Thursday is shit-burning day' was his briefer description. We would be issued with a 24-hour ration pack each evening, and a trailer of hot water was available to heat up the boil-in-the-bag meals. Junior ranks would be allocated guard duty.

At the end of the briefing, a young marine innocently asked for clarification on something he hadn't understood.

'Come and see me later, and I'll fuck you off then,' replied Smith, before turning around and walking off, leaving the audience silent and with raised eyebrows. He would be an unending source of irritation and mirth, occasionally at the same time.

As darkness fell, ten ration packs were dumped at the entrance to our tent, and we each took one and wandered over to the trailer to heat up our dinner. As I stood chatting with Roly and Bungle, waiting for the water to boil, a group next to us were grumbling about the chicken and herb pasta. Although several varieties of ration pack are available, someone in the UK had sent a complete load of Menu H, and Menu H only; chicken and herb pasta had been on the menu for days and would be for some time to come.

After dinner, we joined the others on the bench outside the tent; the early evening temperature had dropped significantly, and we'd each donned additional layers to stay warm. As we drank tea and chatted about what had been a very long day, there was a whining sound which steadily increased in volume.

'That sounds like a mortar,' said Roly, and seconds later there was an ear-splitting explosion a few hundred yards away. We hit the ground, as three or four more explosions shook the place. We lay prone for another thirty seconds or so, waiting for the silence to be split again, but it was all quiet now.

'Welcome to Afghanistan,' muttered Morris, as he made his way to the tent.

Whatever levity a full stomach and an evening brew had provided had been extinguished by the mortars, and I found my cot and climbed into my sleeping bag. After a day of intense activity, I fell asleep quickly and slept through until morning.

As I rose the following day, the sun had just cleared the high mountain peaks, and Bungle was, as ever, brewing tea. He shook a cup at me, and I nodded, climbed out of my sleeping bag and joined him on the bench, where he handed me a steaming mug of Earl Grey. Bungle and his stove would be one of the few constants in life over the next few days.

I washed as best as I could with some wet wipes I had bought from the ship, and boiled some breakfast in a bag before having a quick walk around the camp, catching up with some of the engineers. Our armourer 'Scoff' was a notorious snorer, and they hadn't slept as soundly as we had.

The bench had become a focal point for our community, and as I returned to the tent, the rest of the guys were gathered around it. Morris told us the boss was on his way and was going to brief us on today's tasking.

The man of few words arrived and told us he'd be flying our aircraft today; we would be going down to Kabul to pick up aid, and then flying up to Nahrin, a small town north of Bagram and roughly halfway to the border with Tajikistan. A 6.6-magnitude earthquake had struck the area about the time we were leaving the ship and destroyed a lot of buildings.

A few hours later, we departed Bagram to the south, dropping down into Kabul, flaring over the runway and taxiing on to the ramp in front of the main terminal. An RAF fire tender sat at the edge of the ramp, along with several 4WD vehicles and a truck; there were also a lot of cameras.

There had been little visible sign of the UK contribution since it was announced in Parliament, and with the additional three Chinooks yet to arrive from the UK, and only an advance party from 45 Commando behind the wire at Bagram, we were the international press's first news story of Operation Jacana.

As we shut down, the truck swung around and came to a halt at the back of the aircraft. Surrounded by a huddle of journalists, a loading party began carrying blankets and tents up the ramp. Bungle and I stacked them in a neat pile and secured them with a cargo net. The engineers had removed the ferry tanks, no longer needed for short hops across the mountains, the previous evening, and we had plenty of space now for cargo. As the empty truck pulled away, the puffa-jacketed NGO crowd began emerging from the 4WDs and walked over towards us.

Over the years I had come into contact with NGO people repeatedly, and although I didn't doubt their sincerity, they always blurred into a homogeneous group of North Face-sporting enthusiasts with shiny new vehicles and a room at the best hotel in town. They had descended on Kabul en masse and were accompanied by several diplomats, including the German ambassador and his bodyguard. They filed on and found seats in front of the cargo. Once they were on, I watched the journalists make their way over to the other aircraft and get onboard.

We departed Kabul to the north, with a flurry of camera flashes from the puffa-jacketed day trippers. We climbed as the mountains got higher until eventually we were at 16,000ft, where the thin air left you short of breath if you moved too quickly. This was the Hindu Kush, and the mountains were spectacular. Eventually we began to descend, and twenty or so minutes later, we let down into a green valley and made an approach to a field on the edge of town, where we landed and shut down.

The puffa-jacket mob departed to do some good, and with the help of Sevvy and Stan on the other aircraft, we carried off the blankets and tents and stacked them against a stone wall. Nobody seemed too interested in them, and no one was there to collect them.

As Bungle lit his stove, I did a quick walk around but found my checks on the aircraft hampered by a cameraman following me and sticking a camera in my face every time I touched or looked at anything.

'Do me a favour, mate. Take that camera and bugger off,' I told him quietly, and with a crestfallen look he set off after the puffa jackets. I am not sure if Bungle had witnessed the exchange, but he was giggling as I sat down next to him.

Our communication with family members had been limited to a weekly 20-minute phone call on board the ship, and we hadn't told them we were leaving to go ashore in Afghanistan. However, as Bungle pointed out, they would know where we were by the evening news. As I sipped my tea, I realized how crazy life had become, and I reflected on how I came to be drinking Earl Grey in a field in the Hindu Kush.

Chapter 2

How Did I Get Here?

As for many people, my world changed on 9/11. I was on an exchange with the 5th Aviation Regiment of the Australian Army, based in Townsville in northern Queensland. To be honest, the guys on C Squadron had been excellent hosts, and I'd had a great time in what is a stunning part of the world. I'd even managed to get back to New Zealand, my home country, for a week.

We had deployed two aircraft to RAAF Fairbairn in Canberra at the beginning of September, to conduct mountain flying and run trials of new equipment in the Snowy Mountains. The trials had been successful, and we departed Fairbairn at 8.00 am for RAAF Amberley, where we would overnight before carrying on to Townsville the following day.

At 10,000ft over the New South Wales hinterland, the aft gearbox detected metal shards within the oil and set off a warning. These shards, or 'chips' as they are known, can signal the breakdown of gears, so it is a warning which demands urgent action in the form of getting on the ground.

We were spiralling down, losing height and looking for a suitable landing point, when I spotted a large field next to a farmhouse. I pointed it out to Dirk, the aircraft captain, and he set up for an approach, as the non-handling pilot let the other aircraft know of our situation and our intention to land.

The second aircraft remained in orbit overhead until we were safely on the ground, and then informed us they would head on and wait for us at the planned fuel stop at Tamworth. Once on the ground, we shut down the aircraft and gathered at the ramp. Luckily, we had half of the engineering complement onboard, and they were soon poking about in the gearbox and checking oil samples.

Sure enough, metal shards were recovered from the gearbox, but not enough to raise real concern. The engineers required 40 litres of jet oil, and they would drain and flush the gearbox to remove any further debris.

This involved myself and Jimmy, one of the Aussie guys, borrowing the farmer's 4WD and driving 40km to the airport at Armadale to pick up the oil. This we did, and returned in the late afternoon, to the relief of both the engineers and the farmer.

The drain and flush was a success, but it was dark by the time the engineers had finished. We started up the aircraft and lifted for the short transit to Tamworth, where we taxied in next to our playmates and left for a motel which had been booked by the other crew. As we drew up in a taxi, the other crew met us and informed us that the kitchen was closing, so now was the best time to grab some dinner.

I was sharing a room with Jimmy, and we dumped our bags in our room and made our way to join the throng in the motel restaurant. The US Army exchange pilot, a CW4 by the name of Mike, was as noisy as ever; a great guy and built like the tank with which he shared a name. Mike was in full flow as we ate and washed dinner down with a couple of beers.

About 10.00pm Jimmy and I went back to our room and I opted for the first run at the shower. I had just got my hair wet when Jimmy called me to come and look at something on the TV. I wrapped myself in a towel and left the bathroom, to see a plane striking one of the World Trade Centre towers. We watched in horror, trying to make sense of it. I left to get back in the shower and had just got wet, when Jimmy called again.

'Mate, you're not going to believe this, but a plane has just hit the other tower.'

We watched TV for some time, as reports of other plane crashes started to come in, and it was very late by the time we got to sleep.

The next morning, I walked into breakfast with Jimmy, and at a table on his own, in silence, was Mike. Usually so gregarious, he was distant and obviously stunned by the attack on his country, and although we greeted him we left him to his thoughts.

A little later, I went for a last smoke and found Mike sat on the floor in the sun with his back against a wall. I sat down next to him and asked how he was. He was silent for a few moments and then spoke quietly.

'You'll come with us, won't you, Mick?' he asked.

'Not much choice, mate,' I replied. 'It's a long walk to Townsville otherwise,' I joked, trying to lift his mood.

'No, I mean to Afghanistan. When we go and get these bastards. The British, they'll come with us, right?'

'I expect so, Mike. That seems to be how it works,' I replied, without any idea of how prescient that conversation would turn out to be. He nodded, crushed out his cigarette and got up and walked off.

Clutching our bags, we headed back to the airport. By now the airspace over Australia was closed to commercial flights, and the radios were unusually silent as we flew north to RAAF Amberley, arriving in the early afternoon.

We gathered in the beer garden of the Sergeants' Mess and watched the news on TV. By now the name Osama bin Laden was in the public domain; I had heard the name previously from attacks on the USS *Cole*, and these attacks on the US seemed to fit with what I knew of him. What none of us knew – and this was the subject causing the most debate that afternoon – was how George W. Bush and the USA would react to the attacks.

The following day, we arrived back at Townsville and I was informed I was returning to the UK a few days later. I was unsurprised, and on 15 September I found myself at Cairns Airport boarding a flight for Heathrow via Singapore. It was the first commercial flight from Cairns since the attack and was mainly full of Japanese tourists heading home to a very different world.

Arriving back at RAF Odiham I noticed more activity than normal. As I walked into the squadron and climbed the stairs, the flight commander's office was the second door I passed.

'Welcome back, don't get too comfortable. We're deploying,' he shouted, and I recalled the conversation with Mike.

I found the guys in the crewroom, caught up with events and learned that two crews had already deployed to Salalah in Oman to join HMS *Illustrious*, and that we would be replacing them just after New Year. *Illustrious* had been in the Gulf for a major exercise in Oman which had been extended whilst the MoD tried to figure out what was coming next.

I was in the process of a divorce and had moved into the Sergeants' Mess at Odiham. In early October I was driving down a dark lane on the way to Reading to visit my son, when the news came on the radio that the US had attacked targets in Afghanistan.

In the meantime, we had a lot of training and preparation to get through, to enable us to operate off a carrier and deploy ashore if needed. Sure enough, by December we had deployed to RFA *Argus*, a Royal Fleet

Auxiliary ship, off the south coast and spent several days practising ship-landing approaches; as we left the squadron for the Christmas break, we had practised just about every skill in the manual and considered ourselves ready for whatever might come our way.

We had absolutely no idea that the operation on which we were about to deploy would last twelve years and cost the lives of almost 1,000 British troops, one of our number amongst them. Thousand more would be injured, and two Chinooks would be so badly damaged they would be blown up *in situ*.

We flew out of RAF Brize Norton on 19 January on an RAF VC10 that had passed its 'best-by' date before I was born, landing at Salalah in the dark, transferring by bus to the port and boarding HMS *Illustrious*. We met up with the crews we were relieving who, despite Christmas alongside in Kenya, had had a pretty quiet time and were glad to be heading home. Over a few beers we exchanged news and caught up with the usual squadron gossip: who was promoted, who was posted where. They had an early start the next day and so, by the time I got up for breakfast, they were already boarding the VC10 for Brize Norton.

I knew all of the crew well; unlike our predecessors, who had been drawn from both 18 and 27 Squadrons, we were all from 27 Squadron and used to living and working together. As an initial foray into the post-9/11 world, the squadron had thrown some pretty big characters together.

Our boss, Dave, was an experienced Squadron Leader and a great guy. A natural leader, he was a superb pilot and knew how to lead his guys but also made time for fun. He worked us hard and made sure we were all prepared for any deployment.

His deputy was a big, silver-haired navigator known as Morris. He had come to the Chinook from the Wessex, and we had gone through the Chinook course together. He was a great guy but wasn't scared to be forceful when he felt things needed to be said. Highly experienced, he'd been awarded the Queens Commendation for Bravery in the Air during his time in Northern Ireland and was well respected.

Ricky was another navigator, who had joined us from another flight. Highly experienced in helicopter tactics, Ricky could be a bit quiet, which sometimes led you to wonder what he was thinking and whether he was happy or sad; sometimes it wasn't immediately obvious.

DC and Nick were the other two pilots. DC was a very experienced pilot and had been an instructor when Morris and I had gone through conversion to the Chinook. With a great sense of humour and sharp banter, DC and I got on well; he would later become godfather to my son.

Nick was a former navigator who had crossed over to pilot. He'd had a hard time the year before, but had got himself back together and was firmly in 'the circle of trust' now he was back to his old self.

Stan was a commissioned crewman and ran the rear crew on the squadron. A jovial northerner, he had a gift for making complex issues simple with a touch of self-effacing humour. Faced with a strawberry daiquiri in a hotel bar, he had informed all present that he wasn't sure whether he was supposed to drink it or dip bread in it.

Bungle was the voice of reason amongst the crewmen; an experienced instructor, he had come to the Chinook from the Puma. He didn't own a TV, was a prolific reader of books and knew pretty much everything. Tall and well built, he was the guy you wanted on your pub quiz team, but on the ship he did perplex people who didn't know him by cutting about in a sarong.

Roly was an ex-air traffic controller who had re-mustered to aircrew. He was from North Wales and very proud of it. We knew each other well, as his mother had been my father's cancer nurse a few years previously. Despite his unending banter, Roly was precise; he set high standards in everything he did.

Lastly, there was Sevvy. A larger-than-life character from Nottingham, he was a great guy at heart but, as the saying went, if you went to Tenerife on holiday, Sevvy had been to Elevenerife. Sevvy was marmite; you either loved him or you hated him, but it was generally accepted that his heart was in the right place.

Whilst Stan was accommodated with the pilots in the officer's wardroom, Sevvy, Bungle, Roly and I were in a Petty Officers' Mess. A clutch of bunks buried in the depths of the ship, the mess had its own bar and washrooms. The ship's company made us very welcome and kept us from getting into too much trouble.

The days and weeks that followed were monotonous, with limited flying and very little to do other than watch DVDs or sleep. The Fleet Air Arm held a morning meeting at 8.00 am, and after a short update we'd try and figure out how to fill the rest of the time until dinner. Occasionally, the ship's company would hold events that broke the monotony, such as the weekly quiz night, held via CCTV and open to much cheating. Another evening, they projected 'Gladiator' on to the island superstructure, and we all lay on the flight deck watching Russell Crowe emerge from the 30ft screen.

However, with so much time on our hands and no sign of anything meaningful to do, conversation invariably steered to when we would be going home. This seemed to elicit very little response from the UK, and more than one person commented that Odiham had probably forgotten we were out there. The silence from Odiham did little to dampen the rumours, and it seemed that each morning someone had a scoop on when and how we would be escaping the ship.

Odiham hadn't forgotten us completely, however, and as *Illustrious* headed through the Strait of Hormuz to put alongside in Dubai for a few days, we flew off the carrier and headed for Bahrain. The aircraft had been at sea for several months and being too large for the hangar deck had been open to the elements; not being designed for the salty maritime environment, they now needed to be swabbed out to prevent corrosion.

We spent a few days in Bahrain as replacement aircraft arrived by C17, and the outgoing cabs were disassembled and loaded into the huge cargo bay. With the replacements now in-theatre, the engineers rebuilt the aircraft and fitted the blades; once complete, we took them for an air test to ensure they were fully functional. It was during one of the air tests that an oil hose came loose and dumped all the oil from the aft gearbox into the cabin. DC and Ricky were twelve miles out to sea, with Sevvy on the ramp clutching the emergency dinghy as DC put out a 'Mayday' call and headed for Bahrain with a gearbox in serious danger of running dry and seizing, with catastrophic results. A C17 on approach to Bahrain, flown by a former Chinook pilot, heard DC's distress call, overshot his approach and circled above the helicopter until it was safely on the ground, before landing in Bahrain to face the wrath of the airfield operations department.

It was a great opportunity to relax, away from the grey environment and boredom of the carrier. A few days later, with some dodgy suits from Ali the tailor and some 'legit' DVDs, we departed Bahrain and met up again with *Illustrious*, threading through the Strait of Hormuz under the cover of darkness.

In early March, HMS *Ocean* arrived to replace *Illustrious*, which had been in the Gulf region for seven months. We spent the day cross-decking equipment on to *Ocean* and in late afternoon we bade farewell to the crew who had done so much to make us welcome. With a 140-knot fly-past of *Illustrious* to thank the guys, we flew the short mile and landed on the deck of HMS *Ocean*, shutting down just in time to see *Illustrious* turn and head back on a well-deserved trip to Portsmouth.

The marines of 42 Commando also went back aboard *Illustrious*; HMS *Ocean* had bought out replacements from 45 Commando who would remain aboard for the foreseeable future. On their way out from the UK, the marines had sparked a diplomatic incident, accidentally invading La Linea in Spain by landing on the wrong beach during an amphibious exercise in Gibraltar, only to be turned around by a solitary Spanish policeman, who pointed out their error with a wry grin.

Sadly, joining *Illustrious* on the return to Portsmouth were Dave and DC. Dave was due for a posting and had been ordered back, and DC had injured his leg running on the flight deck. Morris would replace Dave as the boss, and Odiham informed us they were sending out a replacement for DC. Both were popular members of the team and would be very much missed.

In early March we were following the coast of Oman and Yemen en route to Djibouti for an exercise with the US Marines near the border with Somalia. In the evening Sevvy had turned up with a DVD he'd picked up in Bahrain, and we settled in to watch 'Black Hawk Down' which, in retrospect, wasn't the best viewing as we steamed towards Somalia with two helicopters.

Later in the night, I was woken from my sleep and felt the ship suddenly turn back to the east; US special forces in Afghanistan had engaged Al Qaeda forces fleeing Afghanistan in a mountainous region on the border with Pakistan, as part of Operation Anaconda, and the fighting, at altitude, had been bitter. Al Qaeda seemed far more determined to dig in and fight to the death than first imagined. The US had requested support from the Royal Marines, as mountain warfare specialists, and a debate was scheduled in Parliament for 18 March to consider the request.

Onboard, the activity kicked up a gear; the marines from 45 Commando were training intensely on deck, and we dusted off maps and charts of Pakistan and Afghanistan and started planning a route to Bagram, which had been taken over by a force from the Special Boat Service (SBS) just before Christmas and was now ramping up as a major US and UK military hub for special forces operations.

Both the SBS and SAS had been heavily deployed to Afghanistan in late 2001 and had been heavily involved both in the battle of Tora Bora and in quelling the uprising at Qala-i-Jangi fort, when several hundred Al Qaeda prisoners revolted and took over a weapons cache. The US military had also moved into Bagram, and it was becoming the centre point for what the US had termed 'Operation Enduring Freedom'.

Aboard the ship, as we contemplated our impending relocation to Bagram, we were conscious that we'd had very few opportunities to fly over the last three months, instead performing mainly deck landings, air-tests and a transit to Bahrain. From the limited information we were getting from the regional HQ in Bahrain, this was not going to be an operation for the 'slightly rusty', so we arranged to spend a day and evening at Masirah Island doing some low-level overland flying by day and night to get back up to speed. We flew ahead of the ship as it followed the coast of Oman, and with our night flying complete, we coasted out and met HMS *Ocean* as she continued east towards the Gulf of Oman.

An awkward realization dawned as the days went by: filling the Chinooks with fuel tanks and taking minimal support crew, we could just about make southern Afghanistan at the limit of our range and payload. We had more engineers than we could carry, and there were many marines from 45 Commando onboard. Pakistan was in an awkward position at the time, and seeing British marines and military equipment disembarking at Karachi or Gwadar would have inflamed tensions. Likewise, very few of the mainly Islamic countries in the region were keen to accept an aircraft carrier full of soldiers heading for Afghanistan. Only Oman stepped up, and so, after launching us from the edge of Pakistan's territorial waters, HMS *Ocean* would steam to Oman, where 45 Commando would disembark and board RAF transport planes to Bagram. It was a longer logistics chain than I think many initially imagined, and it delayed the arrival in country of the bulk of 45 Commando.

Even for us, the numbers required a sharp pencil to make them work, and there were virtually no options if we had a mechanical issue which required a precautionary landing. A lot of additional fuel was required, and we would need two ferry tanks, but these would make us very heavy and cut down our payload. Added to this, a pump failure in one of the ferry tanks would make life very interesting; we could use internal system pressure to suck the fuel from the tanks, but at a very reduced rate, and it would be a race to draw that fuel before the other tanks ran dry.

In the middle of this intensive planning, DC's replacement arrived via Muscat. Phil was a newly qualified captain, and with Morris as navigator he would be leading two helicopters across Pakistan and Afghanistan with two crews who had been stranded at sea for almost three months. Capable as he was, he was understandably apprehensive as he joined in with the planning.

Our departure was set for the early hours of the 26th; on the evening of the 24th the Captain of *Ocean* put the quarterdeck out of bounds so we could have a few drinks as a group before we left. It seemed to bring home the fact that we were finally leaving the ship, but also that we were heading to Afghanistan and God knows what. At the end of the evening, there were just Phil and I sat on the deck with a bottle of Australian Shiraz.

'Are you scared?' Phil asked tentatively.

'Of what comes next?'

'Yeah.'

'I am a bit apprehensive,' I replied.

'Me too,' said Phil, almost relieved to have voiced his concern.

'That's all right then,' I said as I got up, nodded to Phil and headed off to bed.

The next day, we loaded all the baggage and equipment on to the aircraft and ran a good check of all the systems we could, particularly the ferry tank hoses and fittings we would be relying on that night. The miniguns were checked, and we fitted our NVGs to our helmets and stowed a bag near the front ferry tank. We would be 'sanitized', wearing no rank and carrying no personal documents other than our dog tags. Our passports and other documents were all collected into a small bag that could be forced into the fuel tank if we went down.

In the early afternoon we had an update brief, and as it went on someone asked about our escape and evasion plan. Roly was our Combat Survival Instructor and he stood up and cleared his throat.

'If we end up on the ground, we will destroy any personal or classified documents and gather at the ramp with weapons and go kits only. If there is any sign of enemy activity, I will shoot Bungle in the leg and we'll all run like fuck. By the time he's finished talking, we'll be miles away'.

We all laughed, even Bungle, and it punctured the tension perfectly. After we'd finished chuckling, Roly ran through the actual escape and evasion plan. Nobody was laughing by the time he was finished; it was not a particularly happy story.

Where we were headed, there were very few people on the ground who wouldn't enjoy seeing members of the British military kneeling in front of a black flag and a guy with a sword taking aim at the back of their necks. Even if we managed to evade the enemy, it was inhospitable terrain, and across the border in Afghanistan it was littered with landmines from the Soviet occupation.

After the update brief we retired to our bunks to get some sleep. A meal had been booked for midnight, and we had eight hours available for some rest. But I couldn't sleep, and after a couple of hours' tossing and turning I got up and walked around the ship, with no particular destination in mind. I am not religious in any way, but I found myself in the ship's chapel, which was quiet and empty. I sat there for some time, and phrases like 'valley of death' ran through my head, so I decided I would just fear no evil and went up to the quarterdeck for a smoke. Afterwards I went back to my bunk and managed to nap for a couple of hours.

We ate at midnight. At what had become known as 'the last supper' the chefs in the HMS *Ocean* mess knocked out a reasonable steak and chips, and with full stomachs we gathered in the briefing room for a final mission brief. As we were coming to the end, the Ship's Executive Officer entered and told us in no uncertain terms that Pakistani ships were starting to take an interest in our presence as we approached their territorial limit, and we needed to get off on time. As soon as we were clear, *Ocean* would leave the area quickly, en route to Oman and then Portsmouth. He wished us good luck and was gone as quickly as he had arrived. We gathered our remaining belongings and headed up into the red-lit area of flight operations, checking out one last time as we each headed for the flight deck.

Chapter 3

A Series of Strange Events

As I sat in the field drinking my tea I was bought back to the present by the approach of a small group heading towards us from the direction of the village. Four US Army soldiers laden with heavy rucksacks and headed by a bearded Major looked at Bungle and me, dropping their packs to the floor.

'You guys heading for Kabul? Can we get a ride?' he enquired.

'Just the four of you?' I asked. We had some spare seats, but I just wanted to check he didn't have a platoon behind him in the village. He just nodded.

'Hop on and make yourself comfortable,' I replied, making possibly the best decision I would make that day.

As they disappeared, two Norwegian soldiers arrived with a similar request and received the same response. They were mine-clearing specialists, and I was keen to get any military guys home who had been up here doing the hard yards.

Bungle and I finished our tea and had headed down to talk with the others, when two figures appeared walking purposefully towards us. As they drew closer, it became clear that one was a British Army General. A lean figure, he had an intensity in his eyes that instantly made you listen.

'I have a casualty I need you to take to Kabul. He'll be here shortly,' said the General.

'OK, Sir,' said Stan. There didn't seem to be another answer.

With that, the General turned and walked off briskly back towards the village. Bungle and I went back to the aircraft and told Roly what was going on, and together we cleared space for a stretcher near the ramp. As we were busy lifting seats, the boss walked over.

'There's a thunderstorm developing over that high ground,' he said, pointing at a dark patch of cloud rolling up the valley. 'We need to get going soon. I don't fancy spending the night here.'

He was right, and we told him about the General and the casualty. He nodded and then added that he needed to get here soon or none of us were going anywhere. As he spoke, we saw the first of the puffa-jacket crowd bumbling up the track from the village.

The puffa jackets started to make their way onboard and joined the Norwegian and US army guys already seated. They told us that the German Ambassador wasn't back yet but was on his way. By now the boss was eager to get going, asking me every few minutes if everyone was onboard. The cameramen were also back and getting in the way as they filmed every single movement we made.

After a few minutes, a vehicle drew up and some guys pulled out a stretcher from the rear. As they carried it onboard and placed it on the floor, I saw a young Afghan kid with bandaged wrists and scorching around one ear.

'Mohammed, 13-year-old male, lost his hands digging in the rubble looking for his sister,' one of the guys carrying the stretcher told me, before getting in the vehicle and taking off down the track.

The US Major appeared next to me. 'Need a hand? We're a surgical team,' he said, and I was immediately glad I'd agreed to take them to Kabul.

I nodded, and they repositioned themselves at the back with the stretcher in between them. Within seconds they had an IV line into Mohammed and were assessing his injuries, despite being confined to a small working area by the throng of cameramen filming their every move.

By now the boss was losing patience, and for good reason; the black clouds were getting closer, and the lower part of the valley was disappearing into the gloom.

'Let's start the APU. Those not onboard will get the message,' he said.

Unfortunately, the area directly under the APU was full of journalists filming Mohammed and the surgical team.

'If you're getting on, get on. If you're not, fuck off!' I shouted, and from the look on my face the journalists realized their ride was going and headed over to the other aircraft, whose rotors were already turning. As I put on my helmet, the APU whined into life.

Sure enough, the German ambassador then appeared up the track, and he and his bodyguard ran up the ramp and into a now crowded cabin. As they threaded their way through the stretchers, bags and people, the bodyguard managed to catch the IV line in his pistol holster and was literally dragging the catheter out of the kid's arm. Morris, with an angry look on his face, stopped him, and the Major unhitched the line and pushed the hapless bodyguard up the cabin.

As I looked back I now saw a fresh problem about to severely test the boss's patience as he sat in the front looking at the weather, unaware of the three-ring circus at the back of the aircraft. A large, bearded Afghan had appeared at the ramp and was refusing to let them take Mohammed. He was the kid's father and he wanted $5,000 in cash so he could bring his son back from Kabul after he'd got out of hospital. This discussion went back and forth until the Head of the Red Cross promised to get the boy back to Nahrin after he had been released from medical care. The father nodded and then without a further word walked on and took a seat next to the Major.

With the matter resolved, we started the engines and rotors quickly, and I was about to lift the ramp when another Afghan appeared at the back holding a bag. He motioned at the stretcher, handed me the bag and then ran off back down the track. Being new to Afghanistan, I was understandably nervous about a random Afghan handing me a bag and running off, so I opened it and looked inside; the only contents were the boy's hands.

I was stunned for a few seconds, and then I handed the bag to the Major. As he checked the contents, we locked eyes and he gave me a questioning look, shrugged his shoulders and went back to working on the boy.

Within a few moments, the ramp was up and we were lifting, hugging the valley floor as we picked up speed and then climbing away just in time towards the narrow slice of ridgeline not yet shrouded in dark, heavy cloud. As we crossed the Hindu Kush, the Major and his team continued to work on the boy despite a considerable amount of turbulence; I even saw the Major quietly open the bag and assess the condition of the hands. As we descended into the Charikar Plain he motioned me over.

'He'll be OK. I'm not sure about the hands, they'll have to assess that when they get him into theatre,' he shouted.

I nodded in acknowledgement as he continued, 'Tough day, eh?'

I nodded again and thanked my lucky stars that he and his team had turned up looking for a ride. We were now on approach into Kabul, and Roly had radioed ahead to arrange an ambulance. We taxied in and I dropped the ramp as the ambulance pulled up clear of the still turning rotors.

Without being asked, the Major and his team picked up the stretcher and started to carry Mohammed off the aircraft, accompanied by the father.

'We'll take him to the hospital and hand him over,' he said. 'Thanks for the ride.'

We shook hands, and the team walked over, placed the stretcher in the ambulance and climbed in with it. I would find over the coming years that places like Afghanistan and Iraq attracted some of the best human beings on the planet, particularly in the field of medicine.

As the ambulance drove off, we shut down, the rotors slowing to a stop. As I took off my helmet, the puffa-jacket crowd filed past and returned to their 4WDs, no doubt heading off to their hotels and compounds for a feel-good gin and tonic. Last off were the two Norwegians, who stopped to thank us for the ride before wandering off into the airport complex.

As we went to start up, Roly caught my eye and nodded, and I nodded back. He grinned, and shortly afterwards we were airborne on our way back to Bagram for chicken and herb pasta. That evening, I sat and smoked for a while, reflecting on what a weird day it had been. I had no idea that the next day would be even stranger.

* * *

The sun was out at Bagram as we briefed for a theatre familiarization mission with the boss; usually a familiarization consists of a navigation exercise to view key areas and landing sites, as well as practising theatre-specific skills such as dust landings. Today, this was to be combined with a re-supply mission for the CIA at Gardez. We would fly south to Gardez, drop off supplies at a fort and then route back north via the area of the Takur Gar, where Operation Anaconda had been fought a few weeks earlier, before heading back to Bagram.

With the brief complete, we headed over to the aircraft early to load the supplies. As we walked out across the taxiway, three Afghans were pushing a wheelbarrow along its edge collecting rocks and debris that had gathered over the years. It was backbreaking work, and as the sun climbed in the sky I admired their work ethic.

As we got to the aircraft, a flat-bed truck was parked at the back with two of the weirdest-looking guys I'd ever seen standing around it. To say they looked out of place in Afghanistan would be an understatement; outside of Palo Alto, I can't imagine any place they would have fitted in.

The first was short, with thick glasses, wearing a fishing waistcoat over a heavy-metal T-shirt and carrying some kind of carbine. The second was tall, skinny and resembled Shaggy from Scooby Doo, also wearing a heavy-metal T-shirt. I confess to thinking it was no wonder the CIA didn't see 9/11 coming if these were the guys on the front line.

'You the guys taking us to Gardez?' Shaggy asked.

'Yep, right aircraft. You've got some freight to go as well?' Roly asked, as he studied the two strange life forms in front of us.

The shorter one nodded and dropped the tail gate on the truck. A healthy stack of MREs sat on the bed with a 45-gallon drum of fuel. We humped the MREs onboard, making a stack as we'd done the previous day with the tents and blankets, and threw a cargo net over it. The fuel drum we lashed near the ramp so we could undo it quickly at Gardez, given that we only had 90 seconds on the ground.

As we finished, Shaggy came back on with armfuls of shopping bags containing frozen steak, and several cartons of 7UP, which we stuck next to the MREs.

By now the pilots had turned up, and with Shaggy and his mate onboard, beaming from behind their Oakleys and stroking their carbines, we started up and headed south, initially towards Ghazni, before running into Gardez from the west. An adobe fort, very much in the Beau Geste style, stood in a dusty desert plain, surrounded by a horseshoe of low hills to the west and an open plain to the east stretching towards the line of high mountain peaks that separate Afghanistan and Pakistan.

A couple of vehicles were parked at the edge of an open area near the fort, and we shot an approach to them, landing in a cloud of fine dust that filled the cabin. As I dropped the ramp, Roly had already removed the cargo net and untied the fuel drum. We turned it on its side and rolled it down the ramp and gently towards the vehicles. A huge guy with a thick red beard and sunglasses stormed up the ramp and looked at the stack of MREs.

'You can keep that shit!' he shouted over the noise, then picked up the bags of steak and the cartons of 7UP and was gone.

I lifted the ramp, Roly threw the net back over the MREs and we lifted, all within 90 seconds, which as just as well; everyone for miles would have seen the dust cloud we'd kicked up. We cleared the cloud and accelerated through the horseshoe low and fast. As I looked to our left, plumes of earth were erupting from the ridge.

'Mortars, left 9 o'clock,' I called, and the boss did his magic, jinking the aircraft hard a few times before we zoom-climbed clear up to 2,000ft. In the cabin Shaggy and Scooby were high-fiving each other, and Bungle and I gazed at each other in disbelief.

We tracked north through the mountains, easing through valleys and passes over desert plains, pine forests and grey rocky slabs, before descending into the Charikar Plain and landing at Bagram. We taxied in and parked up, shutting down and letting Shaggy and Scooby off. Without a word, they got in a 4WD and disappeared.

In the cabin, Roly, Bungle and I took stock; we'd had another crazy day, but before us was the best part of a ton of MREs, so we'd solved the Menu H problem. When the engineers appeared to check the aircraft over, we told them about the MREs, and they smiled and ran off to get the Land Rover.

We collected our stuff and walked over towards the line. In the distance, I saw the guys with the wheelbarrow were still clearing the edges of the taxiway. It was as we were leaving the line that we heard a bang in the distance; they had found a mine, and the next wheelbarrow crew would be a lot more cautious.

That night, we heated up a delicious 10-man tray of steak and vegetables from the MRE and, with the engineers, we ate like kings. Roly, in an effort to build a bridge, went to seek out Staff Smith and see if he and his guys wanted any MREs.

'Fuck off!' was his only response apparently, and Roly returned with a shrug as if to say, 'I tried.'

The following morning, we slept late, since we would be retracing the route from the previous day that evening as our night familiarization. News from the outside world was in short supply, but as we had breakfast we heard the sad news that the Queen Mother had died the previous day; there would be a memorial service in one of Bagram's few remaining hangars.

We duly attended the very respectful memorial service and walked back to our tented camp, gathering for a brew whilst we waited for the boss to arrive. I felt a bit down; it was Easter Sunday, and I hadn't spoken to anyone back home for days, but I was sure that after our playdate with the journalists at Nahrin a few days earlier, most of our friends and family would know by now exactly where we were. I also thought of my son eating his Easter eggs and probably wondering where I was.

The boss arrived, and we huddled together in the tent to brief that night's sortie. For most of us, that's where things started to unravel.

The brief followed the usual format, until we got to the illumination data. Night Vision Goggles are not magic 'see in the dark' devices. They work by amplifying ambient light, which in places like the UK is fine, since other than in the Scottish Highlands there is usually considerable ambient light from towns and cities to augment the light provided by the moon. In Afghanistan, however, there was very little ambient light, and in the deep valleys, often bathed in shadow during the day, we would need the precious amount of light afforded by the moon and stars. It was quite simple; without ambient light, even with NVG, all you got was a fuzzy dark green picture which was insufficient to navigate through mountain ranges and desert plains, especially given the probability of enemy activity. That's why the illumination data provided by the meteorologists was so important.

Nick was leading the brief, and when he got to the illumination data he referred to the briefing pack we had received from the Meteorology Officer on HMS *Ocean* and briefed moonrise at just before midnight.

'No, that's wrong, Nick,' stated the boss firmly.

'But this is the data I got from the ship,' replied Nick, puzzled.

'The local data says moonrise is just after 7.00 pm, so we'll plan to lift then.'

'Er, that's quite a bit different from the data I have,' Nick continued.

'We'll go with my data, Nick, and we'll lift from here at 7.00 pm,' the boss said, firmly bringing the issue to a close. Nick nodded his assent, but we all exchanged glances as Nick continued to the next section of the brief. We would be routing via Kabul on the way back to pick up some spares that had arrived on a flight from the UK.

We filed out of the tent after the brief for a brew, and I joined Morris for a smoke. We were a little peeved at the heavy-handed way the boss had dealt with Nick, but it wasn't a major issue. We finished our cigarettes and rejoined the others for coffee at the makeshift bench.

Just after 6.00 pm we were at the aircraft and prepared for the sortie. I was conducting a walk-round by torchlight. It was pitch black. I fitted my NVG to my helmet, and walked off the ramp to check the focus, but it wasn't much better, just an abstract collage of dark green shapes on a slightly less dark green background.

But 7.00 pm came and went, and it was still as black as a witch's cat. There was no sign of the moon, and the boss was getting slightly frustrated.

'We'll slip by 30 minutes,' he said.

At 7.30 pm it was still pitch black, but the boss claimed he could see some light over the top of the mountains and told us to start up. With the rotors turning, I stepped back on to the ramp and stowed the chocks. It was still dark, apart from an occasional flash from the direction of the saddle separating us from Kabul. To add to the poor light levels, there was now an unforecast thunderstorm on the high ground we'd have to cross after departing Bagram. I informed the boss of the thunderstorm moving in behind us and he acknowledged it.

'Let's go for a circuit here at Bagram and see what the light levels are like,' he said. 'If we aren't happy, we'll land on and wait a bit.'

Shortly afterwards, we lifted to the hover and, as a pair, taxied out to the main runway. We transitioned from the hover into forward flight and climbed to fly a racetrack-pattern circuit back to the runway. As we flew along the downwind leg, it was still pitch black.

'37 from 36, I'm not happy with the light levels and landing on,' called Nick over the radio.

'Poof!' muttered the boss over the intercom, and then transmitted to Nick on the radio, '37 copy, we'll continue as a singleton.'

In the cabin, Roly and Bungle snapped round to exchange glances, and they then looked at me. Nick had a very valid point: in the space of ten seconds the boss had called him a poof behind his back and broken his own rule of only travelling as a pair. I could imagine Morris quietly smouldering in the left-hand seat.

'We'll go via Kabul on the way outbound,' called the boss, as he pressed the transmit button and let Bagram tower know our intentions. We banked towards the south and climbed up the saddle, with lightning flashing all around us.

We negotiated the thunderstorm, weaving across the saddle before descending thankfully towards Kabul; the light levels were still very poor outside of the lightning flashes, and it was a relief to see the lights of the airport.

We landed and taxied to the ramp. Roly said he'd go and find the spares, and as he unplugged from the intercom I dropped the ramp and he walked past me, giving a shrug. We sat there with the rotors turning for a few minutes in complete silence; nobody wanted to speak, but eventually I could hold it in no longer.

'Boss, I think we should go back to Bagram,' I offered.

There was a long, excruciating silence before the boss replied, 'Why do you say that?'

'This not the sortie we briefed earlier,' I said. 'The light levels are poor, we've just flown under an unforecast thunderstorm and we are breaking your own rule by operating as a singleton.'

Silence. There was no response at all for several minutes, and eventually Roly reappeared at the back of the aircraft. I cleared him on, and he ran up the ramp past me and plugged back into the intercom system.

'Nobody knows anything about these spares. What's the plan?' he enquired as he refastened his monkey harness.

'We're going back to Bagram,' said the boss flatly.

With that, we taxied out and returned to Bagram in an uncomfortable atmosphere of formality; when something needed to be said it was said, but other than that nobody spoke.

We shut down the aircraft and headed for the tent to debrief. It was still pitch black, with no sign of the moon, and the thunderstorm had rumbled its way further down the high ground. Nick and his crew were already in the tent, and we joined them, with people clearing a space to sit down.

Nick started to speak as formation lead, but the boss stopped him; it was clear he wanted to run the debrief. He seemed to be of the opinion that we didn't want to go flying, and that somehow we should have been more enthusiastic despite the poor light levels. The fact was that other than two hours at Masirah a week or so earlier, we'd had very little opportunity for night flying, and what little we'd done was in the form of deck landings over the ocean. It was akin to spending months finger painting and then attempting a Sistine Chapel fresco. Most of all, there was no acknowledgement that the illumination the boss had come up with was completely wrong.

It was a very tense debrief, and as everyone paused for breath Roly, without meaning to, lit the touch paper.

'Boss, can I just add at this point that I don't agree with you calling Nick a poof for making a safety decision,' he interjected.

Nick's crew, who had been unaware of this up to now, all began asking what he was talking about. At that point, the boss had had enough and raised his hand.

'All the officers, outside now.'

This was very unusual; we flew as a crew and debriefed as a crew, and in all my years on the Chinook Force before and after that point, this was the sole occasion on which the officers were pulled aside for a separate debrief.

The guys filed out of the tent, leaving Bungle, Sevvy, Roly and myself alone in the tent, looking at each other in bewilderment.

'He's wrong,' said Roly, 'and this is wrong too.'

After five minutes or so Ricky came back into the tent and went and sat on his cot bed without speaking.

'Has he gone?' Sevvy asked.

Ricky nodded, and we all left the tent to join Morris and the others. Morris was visibly angry, and his hand shook as he lit a cigarette.

'What the fuck just happened?' asked Roly.

It took Morris several seconds to calm himself enough to speak. He took a drag on his smoke and exhaled long and hard, as if to expel some anger whilst he formulated his words.

'Basically he accused us all of cowardice and told us we weren't up to the job and he was going to send us home as the new guys arrive,' he said, still seething with rage.

'Good,' said Roly

We chatted for a while, and Morris drifted off to one side whilst he calmed down. The storm arrived quickly with Morris but subsided just as quickly; a little while later, he had calmed down significantly, was 'back in the room' and joined us on the bench.

The evening's events had clearly frustrated all of us, but at the same time we were now almost twelve weeks into an eight-week deployment, with the last two weeks having been pretty intense.

It was about midnight by the time we'd all calmed down and headed back to bed. As we crossed the few yards from the bench to the entrance to the tent, Nick nudged me and pointed to the mountains. A bright glow was bathing the snowy peaks as the moon rose behind them; Nick's illumination data had been spot-on.

* * *

By now we were into our fourth month of a two-month deployment, the focus was on the incoming crews and we saw very little of the boss. Two of the three additional Chinooks had arrived by C17 into Kabul, and the engineers were reassembling them for the flight up to Bagram. The first crews were arriving, and we were flying down to Kabul to pick them up and fly them to Bagram.

We headed off an hour early; we'd heard rumours of a shower facility at Kabul and, having cleaned ourselves with wet wipes for over a week, it was with some excitement that we packed towels and wash kits for the trip to 'Kabvegas'. By now our waving had paid off, and instead of using slingshots, the kids would wave excitedly back as we passed overhead.

On our infrequent visits to Kabul we'd never felt particularly welcomed by the British unit there. There were some good reasons for that: they were on a peace-keeping operation and wore green combats, while with our steadily thickening beards, matted hair and dirty desert combats, it was clear we were different. I sensed a them-and-us attitude at Kabul, as if they didn't want the dirty oiks from the north coming down and screwing up their comfortable life.

We shut down, and along with some of the engineers headed off to find the showers. A few blocks back from the ramp, we found them: a strange green hexagonal tent with a zip-up door on each segment, plastered in 'ship routine' signs. For the uninitiated, ship routine involves turning on the shower for a few seconds to get wet, then turning it off and soaping up the whole body, before rinsing it off quickly. This is fine if you shower regularly, but when you're living on a bare desert floor and haven't seen running water in over a week it just doesn't work the same way.

Before anyone could speak, we'd all zipped into a segment and were getting clean; it was bliss. After a minute or two we heard a loud voice yelling, 'Who's running that shower?' which was very quickly followed by,

'Fuck off!' from our armourer. A few seconds later, I heard a commotion as the RAF Regiment Warrant Officer unzipped his segment.

'Was that you?' he bellowed.

'Sounded like it was coming from over there' replied Scoff, pointing in a random direction.

Realizing he was unlikely to make much headway with the scruffy bunch in his showers, he shouted, 'Ship routine!' and walked off. At least we knew who to tell if one of the signs fell off. He was still watching from a distance as we unzipped after our showers, together with an RAF Regiment Group Captain. I was just relieved the military still had that level of resource to throw at a tented shower unit.

We wandered back to the flight line, and it was great to see a collection of friendly faces; the remaining crews from the UK had arrived and there were some really good friends amongst them. I stood smoking with Morris, and one of our very experienced Squadron Leaders walked over to say hello. A pilot with thousands of hours across several helicopter types, he was much respected on the squadron. As he drew closer, he stopped and looked at us.

'What the fuck have you guys been through?' he asked.

We looked at him quizzically.

'You all look completely empty, ready to go home,' he said.

We told him about the previous night, and he shook his head; he just couldn't believe some of the decision-making and was amazed that anyone would accuse any of us, especially Morris, of cowardice.

We flew the guys up to Bagram and walked them over to some newly erected tents, before leaving them to sample the Staff Smith arrival brief in all its 'f–ing' glory. We caught up for a little while and then went back to our own tent.

Despite all our colleagues arriving, some of whom were best friends, we felt uncomfortable outside our own bunch. The engineers who had flown off the ship with us were the same; for some inexplicable reason we had collectively withdrawn into our own small group. Even now, some years later, that bond is still very strong, and at the annual Chinook reunion those who flew off the ship on 26 March 2002 always manage to end up around a table at the end of the night.

The days that followed were very quiet for us, the focus being on helping the new guys get up to speed, and although it was good having a calmer tempo after our first week of mayhem at Bagram, it gave us too much time to think. I became quite withdrawn and was quite relieved when Stan told me I was going home the next day.

I was up early, packed my things into my Bergen and headed off to the flight line. An aircraft was flying to Kabul to pick up some equipment and would drop me off for my flight back to Brize Norton. It was a sunny day, and I took a last look at Bagram as we approached the saddle; the next time I would see it would be ten years later, arriving on a civilian flight from Dubai into a huge complex, very different from the wrecked site we'd arrived at and more like a small American town.

The crewman on the flight to Kabul was a mate of mine from the squadron, and as I picked up my Bergen and rifle and walked down the ramp, I slapped him on the shoulder.

'Try not to get shot, mate. I owe you a beer,' I shouted over the noise of the rotors.

We both laughed, but a week later a young marine with a belt-fed machine gun tripped on the ramp and fired several rounds between his legs. He was shaken but uninjured, though poor Keith used up one of his nine lives that day at Bagram.

There were no flights until the following day, so I found an empty tent and went to sleep. The following morning, I went to find some breakfast and bumped into an old mate who was on the same flight that evening.

It was already dark when we checked in and I handed over my Bergen and a small bundle containing my rifle and pistol. In the lounge where we gathered there was a booking-out desk, so the administrators could check who was in and who was out of theatre. I was pretty sure they didn't have my details and I walked past as well. As we came through a door, a medic was handing out some forms. These were questionnaires asking if you were depressed, had suicidal thoughts or flashbacks. I put mine in my pocket and walked out and up the ramp of the C17. The huge jet's massive cargo bay was half empty. As soon as we took off, everyone unrolled sleeping bags and stretched out, myself included. For me, it was just a sense of relief, and I slept for hours, until a shake from the crew announced our descent into Brize Norton. It was 7 April and a beautiful spring day.

Chapter 4

Iraq, it's like Afghanistan but flat

RAF Odiham
United Kingdom
January 2003

As 2002 drew to a close the drumbeat of war became louder, and it was clear Iraq was next. I followed both the news and intelligence briefs closely but I couldn't understand the urgency; there was no doubt the world would be a better place without Saddam Hussein, but why now? He'd been left in power at the end of the last Gulf War, and it seemed an odd point in time to oust him. I was sceptical about the case for war and the mountain of WMDs he was allegedly sitting on, and operations in Afghanistan had been successful but were far from complete. Why now?

As December drew on, we began contingency planning for a 'fast run' to the Eastern Mediterranean in case there was a need to deliver aircraft for operations in the Middle East. With Turkey reluctant to become embroiled with a war in Iraq, plans were being drawn up to use Jordan as a possible jumping-off point.

A 'fast run' is the term used for a rapid deployment over long distances, with pre-positioned crews to take over an aircraft and keep it running in excess of the standard crew duty periods. In this manner, helicopters could be deployed up to 2,000 miles with just short stops for refuelling and crew swaps, as had been done in 2000 to Sierra Leone for Operation Barras, the SAS raid on the West Boys camp at Gberi Bana to free members of the Irish Guards taken prisoner whilst on patrol. Several aircraft had slipped out of Odiham and self-ferried to West Africa for the assault.

Over the Christmas break we were warned off that we would be ferrying two aircraft to Akrotiri in Cyprus in early January, but instead of a reactive fast run it would be pre-planned; we would overnight in Nice, arriving in Cyprus after two long days of flying.

We departed Odiham on 9 January 2003 and settled into a long transit across the Channel and through France. By mid-afternoon we were a couple of hours out from Nice, and we arrived there in early evening. We made our way to the hotel and, after a good dinner and a glass of wine, were ready for bed. It was the end of a long day, and tomorrow would be even longer, as we crossed from one end of the Med to the other.

The next day, we left Nice and headed east for our first fuel stop at Naples. The second would be at Heraklion in Crete, before arriving in Cyprus just after dark. The morning was largely uneventful, and it was almost a relief to fly in over the Italian coast and approach the US Navy site at Naples.

'There are some isolated thunderstorms over the mountains, might get a bit bumpy,' Danno informed us as we finished the refuel.

We departed Naples and climbed into the valleys running through the Apennine Mountains between rolling hills and sprawling villages, climbing as we went. For once the weather forecast had been accurate, and we skirted heavy showers and dark black clouds as we fought our way through the reduced visibility. Eventually, we had slowed to 30–40 knots and were hover-taxiing over the highest ground en route and considering a return to Naples, when we started to descend into lower cloud, and the visibility slowly improved.

Relieved to have made it through the bad weather, we prepared to coast out south of Brindisi, checking our fuel burn and endurance. We were all good, and would cross the Adriatic at its narrowest point, turning south to hug the Greek coast around to Crete.

We had been over water for a few minutes when we were surprised to see the second aircraft suddenly turn back towards the coast, and heard them transmit a Mayday call.

'2 from 1 – you OK?' asked Danno, as we banked sharply to follow them.

'1 from 2, we've just had a large UFCM,' replied Chris, the captain of Number 2.

UFCM stands for 'uncommanded flying control movement', and translated meant that the autopilot had started ignoring Chris's inputs and begun doing its own thing.

Within a minute or two we crossed the beach and saw Chris bring his aircraft down gingerly over a ploughed field. We approached the same field and landed alongside, the wheels settling into the mud as Danno lowered the collective.

As we saw the rotors on the other aircraft slow, we knew this wouldn't be a quick fix, so we shut down and slogged through the mud to meet the other crew. Chris explained what had happened, and he and Danno were debating possible causes when an Italian Military Search & Rescue helicopter flew low overhead. As we looked up, we also saw a fixed wing maritime patrol aircraft circling us at height.

'Chris, you did cancel the Mayday when you landed?' asked Danno.

Chris looked sheepish as his co-pilot ran to the cockpit to radio the Italians and apologize for not updating them when he'd landed. They were cool, and just relieved to hear we were OK, the winchman probably most of all; it was a cold day, and I wouldn't have fancied getting in the water.

As the helicopter flew back to base, I saw a quad bike heading our way at speed; the rider had a rifle slung over his back as he bounced across the ruts.

'Ah, looks like the landowner is inbound. I'll take care of this one,' I said.

I had spent six months in Italy a few years earlier and spoke some very basic Italian.

Along with our RAF Regiment contingent, who we had brought to guard the aircraft overnight at Nice, we walked towards the quad biker, who had dismounted and now approached with a heavy-looking rifle in hand.

'*Buongiorno Signore, come stai*?' I asked.

Clearly pissed off was the answer, as he waved his arms excitedly and spoke in rapid Italian, pointing at his neatly ploughed field which now contained two twenty-ton helicopters and a handful of foreign oiks dressed in green traipsing through the furrows.

'*Mi dispiace, veniamo dal cielo con problem*,' I offered, guessing he had already figured out we had come from the sky with a problem.

I am not sure if it was the absurdity of the situation, or my shocking Italian, but he started to laugh, and the next thing he was shaking our hands.

With the rifle now propped against the quad, he produced a flask of coffee and offered us some. We'd made a mess of his field, so I wrote down the address for the Station Commander at Odiham and handed it to him.

'*Per il tuo reclamo*,' I added. I have no idea if he understood, or ever claimed, but he nodded and headed off on his quad bike.

By now, Chris and Danno were on the phone to Odiham, and the engineers were crawling over the aircraft trying to trace the issue. It was now mid-afternoon, and darkness wouldn't be too far away at this time of year.

Eventually, Odiham informed us they were sending down some parts from the UK, and told us we should find somewhere to stay. We agreed to take the good aircraft, which was slowly sinking in the mud, to Brindisi, leaving the stricken one *in situ*, with the two RAF Regiment guys to keep an eye on it.

Darkness was creeping across the field as we started up and lifted out of the mud, flying north to Brindisi, where Danno had booked us into a hotel. For a few hours we were the most unpopular group in Brindisi, firstly for leaving heavy clods of earth across the runway as we landed, and shortly afterwards for leaving muddy boot prints across the hotel's marble lobby as we checked in.

Having showered, changed and washed off our boots, we gathered and headed out to see what Brindisi offered; the answer being not much in mid-January. After a bowl of mediocre pasta and an obligatory glass of grappa, we were back at the hotel. I had a quick nightcap with Snods, then headed off to bed.

It was two days before the other aircraft joined us at Brindisi and we were ready to depart for Akrotiri. The quad bike farmer had become good friends with the RAF Regiment guards and appeared regularly with pasta, pizza and bottles of red wine.

This time, we left Italian airspace without any dramas, entering Greek airspace and starting a descent into Corfu to take on fuel for the transit to Crete, as per the flight plan we'd filed several weeks earlier. As the bowser pulled up, I connected the hose and started pumping fuel into the tanks, checking the gauge to make sure they were fully topped up.

I'd just disconnected the hose and handed the invoice to the refueller as Danno and Chris returned from operations looking slightly bewildered.

'All filled up. What's the score?' I asked.

'We're not allowed to leave,' replied Danno.

'What? Because we're a couple of days late?' I questioned.

Danno shook his head. The civil aviation ministry in Greece had changed its rules on 1 January and now visual flight between islands was only permitted if there was an instrument flight route above it. No such route existed between Corfu and Crete.

'It's with the Air Attaché in Athens at the moment,' Chris said.

'But we're here for the night,' added Danno.

I could see their frustration; we were now approaching five days into a two-day transit. We headed off to the hotel, managing a very mediocre meal in an empty taverna that evening.

The next morning, the issue had been resolved. Obviously, the Air Attaché had whispered in the right ear, and we departed Corfu and skirted southern Greece before setting up an approach into Heraklion a few hours later.

After the previous few days, with every passing minute at Heraklion I expected some further calamity or delay; but if the gods were not quite smiling on us, they'd at least finished laughing at us for now, and we departed on schedule. Next stop Cyprus!

It would be a good three-hour transit to Akrotiri, over water and in fading light, scheduled to land just after dark. About an hour or so out of Akrotiri, we changed radio frequency for the last time to Nicosia.

'RAFAIR, be aware I have multiple contacts on your track, not under my control and advise a track further to the south.'

'Probably the US Navy,' said Danno.

We were in international airspace and didn't have the fuel to divert south, so continued tracking towards Akrotiri. As a precaution, the co-pilot checked our IFF setting, and switched on our radar warning receiver as an extra sensor for any aerial activity.

A few minutes later, our radar warning receiver began to melt with noise and warnings; we were being tracked by something fairly significant. The noise escalated in pitch, and it was clear we had been locked up by an airborne radar.

'What the fuck?' called Danno.

Over the radio I heard him transmitting to any jets in the area, to let them know they were locking up a friendly.

'RAFAIR, airborne call sign Buddy Spike, Buddy Spike,' he called.

By now I had dropped the ramp just in time to see two US Navy Prowler aircraft descending to take up positions either side of our formation of two aircraft.

I looked out from the ramp and, unsure what to do in a situation like this, just waved. A minute or so later, both aircraft peeled away and the chaos from the RWR slowly subsided. We'd had enough excitement for the week, and it was a relief for all when, 30 minutes later, we saw the runway lights at the British base at Akrotiri laid out before us.

We landed, taxied in and were marshalled to an unused dispersal, where we shut down; we'd got there, albeit four days late. The aircraft would be heading to Jordan the next day, and as we gathered our stuff together, engineers from 7 Squadron who had flown out by C130 were already onboard to prepare it for its next task. It was 8.00 pm as we waited for a bus to the mess; it would be a very quick brandy sour and a few hours' sleep, since we would be on the 0430 VC10 back to Brize Norton.

Those who wanted a war got their way, and before long Iraq was under US control, with the UK administering the area around the southern city of Basra. Our deployment date to Iraq had been set for 9 August. Despite my scepticism, I now had a date to work to and got stuck into the pre-deployment training.

The weeks flew by in a blur of training sorties, ground briefs, administration and medicals, and before I knew it I was stood in the dark outside the squadron lines, chatting with the other aircrew as we waited for the bus to take us to Brize Norton for our flight to Basra.

Whatever my thoughts on the war, I would leave them behind now and concentrate on supporting the guys on the ground and making sure we all came home together. If I am honest, it also felt good getting back on the horse, so to speak, after Afghanistan.

Basra Airport, Iraq
Operation Telic
July 2003

The summer of 2003 ushered in a heatwave across Iraq, and even for a desert country with a harsh climate it was unseasonably hot. The Chinook has an operating range of -30° to +55° Celsius, but there were regularly days when we couldn't fly as temperatures soared into the high fifties.

The British had been given the provinces of Al Basra and Maysan in south-east Iraq as an Area of Responsibility (AoR), encompassing the second city of Basra and smaller cities such as Um Qasr and Al Amarah. Both provinces shared borders with Iran, and the Shatt al-Arab waterway, formed by the confluence of the Tigris and Euphrates Rivers, ran down from the north, bisecting Basra to form a littoral border with Iran to the south as it emptied into the Persian Gulf. Around the Shatt al-Arab were extensive marshlands, and the Marsh Arabs were no fans of the regime, having been gassed by Saddam Hussein in reprisal for an attempted uprising at the end of the war in 1991. The border was ill-defined, moving as water levels changed, and it was an easy point of entry for smuggled weapons from Iran.

Delayed leaving Brize Norton the previous day, the VC10 had been forced to overnight in Bucharest before arriving in Basra in mid-afternoon on 10 August, just as the heat of the day reached its peak. In the days before we had left, the UK had recorded some of its highest temperatures ever, the mercury rising into the high thirties, but even that did little to prepare us for the wall of heat as we left the VC10 and negotiated the steps on to a concrete apron that reflected the heat for the full blast-furnace experience.

There was the normal administration and form-filling on arrival, and as we left the air terminal, with its marble floors and rows of fridges full of water bottles we were met by the guys we would be replacing and a 4-ton truck for our baggage. Throwing our bags on to the truck, we walked the 200–300m to a large four-storey office block, which had previously housed the airport administrators and would be home for our stay.

The ground floor of the building was unusable; in the process of taking the airfield earlier in the year, the Black Watch had fired a Milan anti-tank missile into the building, and the subsequent explosion and fire had rendered the entire floor a charred, blackened mess. We were on the top floor, and as the truck arrived, we collected our bags and carried them up what seemed like an endless stairwell, sweating profusely with each step. By the time we reached the landing on the fourth floor, we were all emptying the fridges of water.

The accommodation was OK. Large offices now accommodated bunk beds, with five or six people to a room; there was a cheap electric fan next to each bed which did nothing to cool the hot, heavy air, but at least kept it moving. I threw my stuff on the top bunk and sat on the bottom bunk, as Sparky did the same at the adjacent one.

'It's too hot, Mick, it's too hot!' he gasped as he sat down and took another gulp of water. We both chuckled and went off to check out the other rooms and figure out who was where. When most people think of deserts they imagine a dry heat, and this was the case a lot of the time; but occasionally the wind would drive up from the south carrying moisture from the Gulf, and then Basra would become a humid hell which consumed what seemed like a pint of sweat for every few steps.

Later that day, we were led over to the flight line and shown our working area and where to find all the support we would need over the coming days when we started flying. The following day, we'd need to zero our rifles on the range; this was a legal requirement before leaving the base and involved check firing and ensuring the sights were still aligned, so if we did have to open fire we would be firing aimed shots in accordance with international law. We had done this before leaving the UK, but the second zeroing ensured sights had not been knocked around during the flight to Basra.

In the early evening we walked up to the mess tent for dinner; in a collection of tents with the walls rolled up, the chefs were knocking out meals in unbearable heat, and I admired the quality of the food given the conditions they were working in. We sat on folding benches at folding tables and ate off paper plates with plastic knives and forks. As was the case everywhere in Basra, an array of large fridges hummed as they struggled to keep their packed shelves of water bottles cool.

Although I couldn't fault the quality of the food, the options were often very 'pub lunch', and many of us lost weight as the heat, along with endless water consumption, killed appetites for a roast dinner or pie and chips.

I was very fortunate and slept well that night, and every other night at Basra, despite the heat; overnight temperatures hovered in the mid-forties, and many struggled to sleep, resorting to dragging their mattresses up to the roof to take advantage of whatever light breeze they could find, as they tossed and turned under the stars. For me the heat had the opposite effect, and I drifted off quickly with the fan moving warm air over me.

In those early days at Basra there was no range available, so the following morning we ate breakfast at the mess tent, signed out weapons and climbed aboard a 4-ton truck for the 15-minute drive to a nearby range. It seemed surreal to be in a slow, open-topped truck limping down a six-lane highway trailing smoke, as Iraqi taxis overtook us, their drivers and passengers staring at us with curiosity and probably a degree of pity.

We arrived at the range and zeroed our weapons; most required little or no adjustment, and were quickly in the truck and heading back down the highway. About halfway into the journey one of the tyres blew, and we pulled into the side of the road to change it. Acutely aware that we were a vulnerable target, we fanned out to form a perimeter whilst the driver and two helpers changed the large tyre. Iraqis drove by, slowing down to see what was happening, but generally it was inquisitiveness rather than anything more sinister.

Once the operation to oust Saddam Hussein and the Ba'ath party was complete in early 2003, life in Basra was generally quiet; there were notable incidents, but compared with later years when the airfield would be repeatedly attacked with rockets, most Iraqis were busy negotiating fuel queues and complaining about power cuts and shortages of essentials. The euphoria of liberation was still subsiding, and anger at a lack of progress had not yet stoked the fires of insurgency that would come later.

The tyre was changed, and with some relief we boarded the truck and completed the remainder of the journey back to the airport without incident.

Later that day, I completed my day Theatre Qualification (TQ), performing a number of exercises that would be needed to operate in Iraq, such as dust landings; the outgoing crew indicated key points such as the base at Basra Palace, the PoW camp at Um Qasr and the field hospital at Shaibah, a former RAF airfield from the 1930s.

Basra Palace had been one of Saddam's holiday homes in the south. Just ten minutes flying time from the airport, the palace sat on the waterfront of the Shatt al-Arab, and Saddam's former yacht now lay there semi-submerged, guarding the entrance to an ornate clutch of buildings spread over several acres at the southern end of the city. The palace now housed a British battalion, and a helicopter landing site had been cleared in the grounds.

Two and a half hours later, we landed back at Basra airport. I was soaked in sweat from the 50° heat. I was drinking litres of water a day but remained careful not to drink too much. Several military personnel had been hospitalized after drinking an excessive quantity of water and thus effectively washing out all the minerals in their body, something which was almost as dangerous as dehydration or heat stress.

With the debrief complete I was now day-qualified in Iraq, and I trudged across the sand, taking a short cut back to the office block and stopping to sit down outside. As I smoked, I began to reflect on how I had ended up in Iraq as part of an occupation following a war I never really believed in.

Chapter 5

Fly, Sleep, Rinse and Repeat

Southern Iraq
Operation Telic
September 2003

An hour north of Basra by Chinook lay the town of Al Amarah, where UK forces had a Forward Operating Base (FOB) at a former Iraqi army barracks. The resident battalion when we arrived was 1st Battalion, the Parachute Regiment (1 PARA), and we had two Chinooks based there on a cleared patch of dirt across the road from the camp. Facilities were basic, and although there was some air conditioning in the small building near the gate that doubled as an Ops Room and accommodation, the generators would cut out about midday as they overheated.

One of the Chinooks was designated as an Incident Response Team (IRT), mainly for Casualty Evacuations (CASEVAC), and in addition to the crew we carried a number of medics, who shared our small building, separated by a curtain.

The second aircraft was on call for short-notice tasking by the resident battalion. Most of the time this meant runs to the various Patrol Bases dotted around Maysan, but more regularly to the checkpoints on the border with Iran which were frequent flashpoints.

On the whole, life at Al Amarah was a lot more uncomplicated than Basra, and the long hours of reading or sunbathing were interrupted infrequently, though often at short notice. Most CASEVACs were heat-stress victims, and we would get the stretcher onboard and climb to 5,000ft as we tracked south to Shaiba and the hospital. En route we would drop the ramp and cock the aircraft a few degrees off to get a strong breeze through the cabin; together with the water the medics poured on to the victims, this would assist in lowering their body temperature.

Tragically, we did have one death at Al Amarah when a young soldier on guard duty collapsed due to the heat and was placed by his colleagues in an air-conditioned room to cool down. Unfortunately, this was just before midday when the generators invariably overheated and shut down. Private Jason Smith was found a few hours later with late-stage heat-related damage. The alarm was raised and we ran to start the aircraft, but it was too late, and he died of hyperthermia.

1 PARA were relieved by the Argyll and Sutherland Highlanders during August, and we were called to the Operations Room one evening. There was intelligence that a leading insurgent was hiding in a small town north of Al Amarah.

The plan was that a ground party would travel up by road and secure a road junction near the house in which the insurgent was believed to be hiding, controlling access to the town, and a small force would assault the house. With the insurgent in custody, we would land, take him onboard and fly him south to the PoW camp at Um Qasr. The assault party would regroup at the road junction and drive back to Al Amarah.

I was crewed with Shippers, a Royal Navy exchange pilot who had left the military to start a civil aviation career on 9/11 and subsequently applied to the RAF as work dried up. The co-pilot was a young guy called 'D Squared', a talented pilot who had not long joined from RAF Shawbury but was already showing a boatload of potential. The other crewman was Matt, a Welshman with a PhD in sarcasm and a laid-back manner; we got on very well.

About 4.00 am we landed at the road junction in a cloud of dust that enveloped the vehicles and broke the silence of the night. I scanned the area east of the road with the M60, as Matt dropped the ramp and the Scottish soldiers led a plasticuffed figure up the ramp and deposited him in a seat, taking the seats on either side of him. We lifted and departed to the south, blasting the vehicles in sand and hot air as the assault force climbed in for the drive back to Al Amarah. The mission had gone like clockwork, and as the night sky began to lighten with the approaching dawn, we climbed up to 5,000ft for the hour-long transit south.

As dawn broke, the radio chatter got very busy; it was clear something was happening in the area, and I turned up the volume to listen. Over the radio we heard the other aircraft get airborne from Al Amarah, and as the CASEVAC aircraft guessed, there must be a casualty; a radio message confirmed there had been a major contact at Al Sharq, south of where we had picked up the insurgent and just off the highway the vehicles would be taking on their route back to Al Amarah.

It transpired that after we had departed, the vehicles had headed off down a main highway towards Al Amarah, but as they approached the town of Al Sharq they had been diverted off the main highway and through a built-up area, where they had been ambushed. Fusilier Russell Beeston had been fatally wounded and several of his colleagues had been injured.

We were still speeding south and a few minutes later we changed frequency as we entered Al Basra Province, descending slowly as we approached Um Qasr. As we approached the PoW camp to land, we heard the other aircraft switch on to our frequency as they sped towards the hospital at Shaiba; they were really shifting, and we guessed there were some urgent cases onboard.

Half an hour or so later, we taxied in at Basra, as the other aircraft landed behind us and followed us into the parking area. We would shut down, refuel and have breakfast before heading back up to Al Amarah, and I went over to the other aircraft to find my mate Fudgey and discover what the hell had gone on.

They had picked up the casualties, some of whom were quite badly injured. Fudgey, who despite the appearance of a mild-mannered janitor, had a wealth of combat medic experience, had helped treat the guys. His shirt was covered in bloodstains as we walked over to the mess tent and ate breakfast, and afterwards we sat outside so I could have a smoke.

It was just after 6.00 am, and we just stared into space for a little while. It had been a long night for both of us, I having met the troops at the road junction to pick up a detainee, and a much longer one for Fudgey, who'd had to contain the fallout from a major firefight and fatal shooting as best he could.

The silence was broken as our operations clerk approached us from a night manning the radio and let out a sigh.

'All right, guys. You wouldn't believe the night I have had,' he said.

I looked at Fudgey, his shirt covered in bloodstains, and back at the ops clerk squinting through his glasses.

'You're right, mate, I wouldn't believe it,' I replied as I chuckled to myself, and Fudgey and I started to trudge back towards the flight line.

* * *

In late September I was crewed up with a pilot known as 'the Vicar' due to his strong religious beliefs and also as a play on his name. A lovely guy and a fairly capable pilot, he was just a bit too vague and, dare I say it, nice to be flying 18-ton combat helicopters around southern Iraq in 2003.

Fortunately, Matt and I were crewed together and kept the Vicar on the straight and narrow, most of the time at least. However, there were a few funny incidents during that time, which Matt and I still laugh about over a beer.

The first involved a flight north along the Iraq/Iran border with the Vicar flying. Down the back and sitting on the left, I was not expecting to see Iranians, and so it was a little disconcerting to see watch towers passing by us as we flew north.

'You happy with the Nav, Vicar?' Matt enquired.

'Yeah, sure, Matt. Why?'

'Just that we seem to be in Iran, Vicar.'

'According to the grid ...' he responded, as Matt cut him off.

'The Iranian border is on our left, mate. I'm pretty sure it should be on the right?'

'Coming left.'

The Iranian border guards were pretty good about it, all things considered, and waved as we passed by on our way back into Iraq. To be fair to the Vicar, I don't think we were the first or last.

A few days later, we were flying Jeremy Greenstock around southern Iraq, whilst the UK's Special Adviser and his team identified reconstruction projects. We would fly from power station to bottling plant, then sit on the ground whilst they walked around bombed-out ruins admiring the RAF's handiwork and promising millions to rebuild them.

To keep us safe during all of this, whilst we sat, shut down, on some Iraqi car park, they left a young lance corporal from one of the Scottish regiments. A good guy, he was pretty effective at yelling in Arabic and keeping the hordes of curious kids away from the aircraft.

It was, therefore, something of a surprise to turn around whilst off to one side of the car park having a cigarette and see the Vicar leading a crocodile of Iraqi children towards the aircraft, like Moses leading the Israelites to the promised land.

'What the actual fuck?' I muttered to myself as the young lance jack shrugged his shoulders and pointed to the Vicar.

I started walking back towards the aircraft, stubbing out my smoke as I went. I didn't seriously think any of the kids were wearing S-vests, but kids have hands like pockets and you never know what they might pick up in an aircraft full of loaded weapons.

'We need to get them off now.'

He nodded, and we started ushering off the kids, with Matt doing a quick visual check as they left the aircraft to confirm they weren't carrying anything they shouldn't be. As they stepped off the ramp, the soldier directed them away and back towards the nearby housing estate.

Despite the news that we, as taxpayers, had just spent £92m on repair projects that day, it was a relief to get Mr Greenstock and his entourage onboard and head back to Basra. Each time I looked at Matt he'd just laugh, as we thought back to the day we'd had. By complete coincidence, we were now finished flying with the Vicar, and went back to flying with the Cloggy exchange pilot, Roel.

* * *

Days became weeks and weeks became months as we rotated between Basra and Al Amarah, picking up and dropping off troops at the various sites. Three times a day we operated what was known as 'the bus run', which departed Basra Airport and stopped at Basra Palace, before flying north to Al Amarah, then completing the trip in reverse. One of the highlights of our route was flying over the top of Al Qumah, the alleged location of the biblical Eden at the confluence of the Tigris and Euphrates Rivers. In 2003 there was just a small town nestled at the junction of the two rivers, but in it was a small municipal park which we'd christened the Garden of Eden.

In early September we had to take a small party up to Baghdad. It was great to see a different patch of desert, and I was surprised by how green it was in the area around the capital. The airbase was huge, and a hive of activity as the US military went about the business of delivering liberty.

A couple of weeks later, we went to Talil to the west of Basra. I was flying with our exchange pilot from the Royal Netherlands Air Force, whom I knew well and enjoyed working with. On the edge of the base is a ziggurat marking the birthplace of Abraham, as close as I got to tourism in Iraq.

These missions were great at breaking the monotony of bus runs to Al Amarah, but after a few hours' relief we were soon back at Basra. By now we had moved out of the office block and into a tented camp built across the road by the Royal Engineers. It was pretty swish, with plastic flooring and air conditioning, and was set out in neat lines, each row having its own wash tent.

On 25 September we were scheduled to take over an aircraft rotors-turning at Basra and fly the afternoon bus run. The aircraft arrived and taxied in, and as the ramp dropped and the crewman gave us the thumbs-up, we braved the burning downwash and engine outflow to board. As soon as I walked on, I knew something wasn't right; there was an acrid smell in the cabin. I looked at Matt and made a sniffing motion, and he nodded. As the crew carefully climbed out to be replaced by us, one at a time, we plugged into the intercom.

'Guys, there is a funny smell in the cabin,' I said.

'Yeah, I caught a whiff of something on the way in. What is it?' replied Shippers, the aircraft captain.

'Not sure. Smells like electrics,' I said.

'Yeah, it does,' added Matt.

'What do you want to do, Mick?' asked Shippers.

'Let's slip five minutes and get the engineers out,' I suggested, and moments later I heard Shippers requesting an engineering presence at the aircraft.

I got out a spare headset and plugged it into the intercom, as Terry, one of our engineers, was cleared in by Matt and walked up the ramp. I offered him the headset, and he pulled it onto his head.

'Terry, we've got a strange smell in the cabin; it smells electrical but I don't recognize it,' I explained.

'Yeah, mate, I noticed something too when I came on,' he nodded. 'Give us five minutes and we'll have a look around.'

He removed the headset and, as one of the engineers walked around the outside of the aircraft looking for anything out of place, Terry and his mate started removing grey soundproofing panels and checking various components. After a few minutes they conferred, and Terry came up the cabin and put on the headset.

'Mick, there's definitely a smell of something, but we've checked all the usual suspects and we can't find anything. You can either take it, or shut down and we'll do a more extensive inspection.'

We were already running late, and the smell had become less noticeable. I discussed it with Shippers, and we decided to take the aircraft. Terry gave me a thumbs-up and removed the headset, and with his colleagues he left via the ramp, passing our passengers waiting at the rear.

We loaded up and set off for Basra Palace, where the majority of the passengers got off, leaving just seven for Al Amarah. We lifted from the pad, crossed the palace buildings and accelerated up the Shatt al-Arab waterway, before zoom-climbing up to 4,000ft on our way north. By this point the 130-knot wind passing through the cabin had long since got rid of any smell.

Two thirds of the way to Al Amarah I was struggling with a microphone failure on my helmet. It wasn't uncommon in the desert, as sand and dust got into everything, and electrical wiring was particularly susceptible to damage. I could hear the intercom but if I wanted to talk I had to use the microphone on the spare headset I had got out for Terry.

As I was grappling with this, Matt came on the intercom from the back of the aircraft near the ramp.

'Er, Mick ... look over your left shoulder,' he said, and I immediately turned to see flames and a thick trail of black smoke.

'We've got a small fire in the electronics shelf,' I said into the headset microphone and tossed it aside as I reached for the fire extinguisher and emptied it into the flames. The smoke continued, so I reached into the cockpit to grab the second extinguisher and emptied that into the fire too.

By now, Shippers was descending, and I heard the non-handling pilot, D Squared, selecting all the equipment linked to that particular shelf to 'OFF'. Matt had got the passengers to pass the remaining fire extinguisher from person to person until it reached me, and I held it in reserve in case it was needed later. The flames had gone and the smoke trail had lessened, but there was still a thin stream of it coming from the shelf.

The pilots had been through the immediate actions for a cabin fire, and Shippers was setting up for an approach to land.

'I'm going to land at CONDOR,' he stated, as an airfield opened up ahead of us, and we landed, running on and slowing to a stop, whereupon we rapidly got the passengers clear of the aircraft and shut it down.

CONDOR was a disused Iraqi Air Force airfield sitting in the desert between Majar Al Kaber and Qalah Salih, about 12 miles south of Al

Amarah. There was a huge runway, but most of the hardened aircraft shelters had been destroyed by aerial bombing in the First Gulf War; in fact, 27 Squadron, which had been equipped with Tornado GR1 bombers before disbanding in the defence cuts and reforming with Chinooks, had executed several raids on the airfield where we now stood.

We gathered by the ramp with the sat-phone, and I lit a smoke. Shippers had diligently put out a Mayday call as I had been emptying fire extinguishers into the source of the fire, but we were unsure if anyone had heard it. The sat-phone had pre-programmed numbers for the operations cell at Basra, and we dialled them, only to find they were all switched off. So we dialled the one number we knew off by heart and with relief heard a voice answer:

'27 Squadron Operations, Duty Authorizer speaking.'

Ignoring the irony of being able to get hold of someone 3,000 miles away in the UK more easily than anyone in Basra, we explained what had happened and asked them to contact operations in Basra.

As we hung up we heard aircraft noise, and an Army Air Corps Gazelle helicopter appeared from the north and approached the runway, landing a hundred yards away and shutting down. As the rotors slowed to a stop, a stout Staff Sergeant emerged and walked towards us.

'We heard your Mayday call. Everything OK?' he asked as he approached us.

'We're OK. We had a fire but got on the ground all right,' replied Shippers.

'What do you need? I can relay to Al Amarah,' he enquired.

'Engineering support and some force protection. We still don't know what caused the fire,' Shippers answered.

We got a thumbs-up as the Staff Sergeant walked back to the Gazelle and the rotors started to turn. Within a few minutes they were gone, becoming smaller as they flew north towards Al Amarah.

With help on the way we felt a bit happier, but that would be short-lived. One of the passengers now appeared, a Major from the Black Watch.

'Gents, we're not in a great spot here,' he informed us in a strong Lowland accent. He turned and pointed to a group of buildings a few kilometres away in the distance.

'That's Majar Al Kaber.' he said. 'We've already seen signs of activity over there since we arrived. They know we are here.'

Most of the UK population had heard of Majar Al Kaber in 2003, as in June that year a large mob had attacked the police station and murdered six members of the Royal Military Police; one of our own aircraft, flown by VDB, had been repeatedly hit trying to fly in reinforcements, with many of its systems disabled and several casualties onboard as a result of heavy fire from the ground. In short, we were a sitting duck in an unfriendly neighbourhood.

As the Major spoke, we glanced around and saw all the passengers were already on the ground in firing positions with weapons at the ready. Matt and I unclipped the two M60 machine guns from the aircraft and set them up facing the town, with a couple of belts for each weapon. We also collected water bottles and passed them out to the passengers as they lay on the hot sand.

There was a cloud of dust as vehicles manoeuvred outside the town, and we could see a white pick-up in the distance; it didn't approach, but it was clear its occupants were watching and waiting. It was a tense thirty minutes or so, before a Chinook appeared on the horizon and flared to land in the area behind us recently vacated by the Gazelle.

The Chinook settled and, with the rotors turning, the ramp dropped and twenty or thirty troops emerged and set up a defensive perimeter. Our head crewman, Spud, was at the ramp, and I headed over to speak with him; shouting over the noise, I filled him in on what had happened.

As we were talking, one of our young engineers named Tom walked gingerly past me in heavy body armour and towards our aircraft, accompanied by a second engineer. Spud motioned to me and I leant in to listen to what he had do say.

'We're good for fuel, so we'll remain in mutual support until you can lift.'

I nodded and walked back towards our aircraft, as Spud raised the ramp and they lifted and took off, climbing to 1,000ft and setting up in a racetrack pattern above us.

I walked on to the aircraft and up to the cabin, where Tom was investigating the source of the fire; by now the sun was setting, and he had to use a torch to inspect the damage. After a few minutes he switched off the torch and waved us over.

'OK, so it looks like the CPU for the infra-red jammer overheated and caught fire. All the wiring back there is burned through. It's OK and will be fine for a trip to Al Amarah, but I don't know which systems have been affected, and we won't be able to turn on any of the counter-measures,' he told us, shining his torch on a molten mess of black plastic and burned wiring to reinforce his diagnosis.

On one hand, with the angry residents of the Majar Al Kaber neighbourhood watch committee gathering in pick-up trucks and carrying God knows what, we really needed the counter-measures, but ultimately we were far safer just getting out of there.

Decision made, Shippers and D Squared climbed into the cockpit, and Matt and I refitted the M60s as they ran through the start. It was now completely dark and, operating on NVG and careful not to switch on any of the affected equipment, we started up. Once we were ready to depart, under the direction of the Black Watch Major, the troops got out of fire positions a section at a time and boarded the aircraft. With a last headcount and check that we had everyone on board, Shippers let the other aircraft know we were about to lift.

We lifted into the hover and transitioned almost immediately, speeding down the runway and climbing rapidly to fall into formation behind the other aircraft. Both aircraft were continuing to climb when lines of heavy tracer began to zip past us into the sky. We climbed to 4,000ft, still seeing tracer as we raced away from Majar Al Kaber; whatever they were firing at us that night, it was pretty bloody big.

We arrived with a sigh of relief at Al Amarah and shut down. We caught up for a brew with the other crew and thanked them for coming to get us. Snods and I didn't always get on, but he took Matt and I to one side and gave us a well done, which we appreciated.

Our Mayday had caused some comedy which we had been unaware of as we sat on the ground at CONDOR; in the Chinese whispers as information was being relayed, our landing had escalated to everyone at a CSE show in Shaiba being told we'd lost a Chinook at Majar Al Kaber and had pretty much emptied most of the aviation personnel in Iraq before the correct information had started to emerge. In Al Amarah the boss had decided to launch, and the crew had sprinted to the aircraft; however, our sole navigator, a jovial Geordie called Chunks, had tripped and face-planted into the diesel-soaked earth around the landing pad; having removed his broken glasses, he had arrived at the aircraft looking like a Geordie version of Al Jolson.

* * *

The remaining time in Iraq was quiet, with steady but repetitive tasking, and in early October it was a joy to see 18 Squadron arrive to take over. After running our replacements through their TQs, we packed up and boarded the VC10 back to the UK. As we descended through the clouds above Oxfordshire and approached Brize Norton, I was in sensory overload at how green the countryside was, having seen little but the brown hues of desert for months.

I didn't know it at the time, but that was my one and only visit to Iraq. Afghanistan was about to loom back over the horizon.

Over the next 24 months I attended the Central Flying School and became an instructor, taking some time out to teach at the Defence Helicopter Flying School in Shrewsbury. But after a while I was itching to get back to Odiham; throughout this time there was increased preparation across the military for a new deployment to southern Afghanistan.

Although I was under no illusions about where I would be going and what lay ahead, talking to the crews from 27 Squadron who had just returned, over a beer in the mess bar, it was clear the Taliban had not got the memo from George W. Bush about the war being over in Afghanistan, and the fighting was vicious, particularly in areas such as Sangin, Musa Qaleh and Nowzad.

The new ops flight I would be joining, C Flight 27 Squadron, were currently preparing to deploy, heading out to Kandahar in early October. I wouldn't be joining them for their first stint, as I had to convert back to the Chinook and complete a 'conversion to instructor' or 'C2I', which would take until December. Although experienced on the Chinook I would have to refresh during an abbreviated conversion course lasting three months, and then transfer my instructional qualification across types.

By November, C Flight were approaching the halfway point in their tour of Helmand, and I had completed both the refresher and C2I and had reclaimed my old locker on 27 Squadron. A Flight would be deploying just before Christmas, and I tacked on to their pre-deployment training, as I would be joining them in Afghanistan in early January. I'd deploy with them to gain the experience of operations in Helmand, so I could work C Flight up for their next deployment the following July.

The ops flights, as they were known, had been formed to undertake a number of roles in a set sequence; this involved being on standby for operations worldwide, manning long-term operations in Bosnia,

Northern Ireland and the Falklands, collective training and then back to standby. Initially, there had been three ops flights, which had grown to four. However, with the intensity of operations in Afghanistan and the harmony guidelines from the government, outlining target times on operations and at home, the Chinook Force found itself stretched.

By reducing the number of crews to what was required in Helmand, the Chinook Force managed to free up enough crews to form a fifth ops flight, bringing the deployment frequencies back to a manageable level; hence the formation of C Flight. Added to this, the six months away from Helmand weren't spent at Odiham. The Chinook Force had a number of other commitments both at home and abroad.

As the UK prepared for Christmas, I continued working through the pre-deployment training with A Flight, making the most of the short days to maximize NVG training, particularly operating in pairs. I also sat in on intelligence briefs and training sessions to make sure we were all up to date on actions if we were shot down or had to land in enemy territory.

As Christmas approached, the annual tradition of 'exchange drinks' came around; this was one of the few occasions in the social calendar when the Officers' Mess was opened up to Senior Non-Commissioned Officers (SNCOs) and vice versa. For the aircrew these were fun occasions, some of the few events at which pilots and crewmen could share a beer without having to go off-base.

This year, there were mixed feelings at exchange drinks. Odiham had found operations in Helmand were going to be much more kinetic than many had predicted, and at the back of our minds we were all aware that C Flight were deployed, and not to a particularly safe place.

However, there was also celebration. The operational honours and awards list had been made public that day and several 18 Squadron aircrew had been listed as recipients of gallantry awards. These included Major Mark Hammond RM, an exchange pilot from the Royal Marines, Flight Lieutenant Craig Wilson and Flying Officer Chris Hasler, who were awarded the Distinguished Flying Cross (DFC), and several other crews from both 18 and 27 Squadrons who had been mentioned in dispatches.

Chris Hasler was particularly interesting; a Canadian who had moved to the UK to join the RAF, he was the first Flying Officer to be awarded the DFC since the Second World War. He would, in turn, join C Flight, and he and I would trade friendly banter for years to come.

As the awards hit the press, it was becoming clear that the operation in Afghanistan was hotting up, and the fighting was of an intensity not seen since the Korean War. It was clear that the Governor of Helmand had hijacked the British strategy in the province and tied Commanders to a doomed policy of dispatching under-supported units to Platoon Houses across the most contested towns. Once *in situ*, these units became a magnet for Taliban attacks and many spent weeks under siege, the troops sleeping a couple of hours at a time in fire positions, with constant shortages of ammunition, water and food and the very real threat of being overrun.

The shortage of Chinook helicopters was also being raised at a senior military level, and the media were quick to put the issue into the public domain. This would be a contentious matter for several months and although resolved publicly, operationally it would place a strain on the campaign for Helmand for years.

It had been a busy but very satisfying year, and I took advantage of heading off on Christmas leave just as C Flight returned to the UK. I caught up with Dave Winters and the Ruffler before they, too, headed off to spend some much deserved time with their families.

From the debrief I received, it appeared we were facing an enemy willing to stand and fight to the death and who were learning quickly how to react to a helicopter-equipped force, even watering down the area behind them when they launched Rocket Propelled Grenades (RPGs) to suppress any giveaway dust clouds.

Chapter 6

Without Firing a Shot

Kandahar
Regional Command (South)
Operation Herrick
January 2007

'Ladies and gents, we have just entered Afghan airspace and will shortly be starting our descent into Kandahar. Please don your body armour and helmets, before returning to your seats. The cabin will be blacked out for our landing.'

In the cabin of the Tristar there was a flurry of activity as 150 or so passengers retrieved their body armour from the overhead lockers and shrugged into it, donning their helmets and squeezing back into seats clearly designed for 1980s holidaymakers rather than military personnel dressed in bulky Kevlar. Moments later, all the lights went out and we sat in the pitch black, hearing the flaps motoring and the gear drop down and lock. With a bump, the Tristar hit the runway and braked sharply, before taxiing for several minutes; it was too dark outside to see very much. Eventually, we came to a halt and the engines wound down. Everyone stood up and began to shuffle towards the exits.

As I left the aircraft, the first thing I noticed was the smell. All military bases have burn pits where everything is disposed of, including plastics which have an acrid smell that claws at your nostrils; it would be the same at every base across Afghanistan, and that aroma would stay with me forever and transport me back to Helmand in an instant.

As usual, the administrators were out in force and there were several forms to complete before I managed to escape the arrival hall and be reunited with my baggage. There to meet me were two of the crewmen from A Flight, Vinny and Stuart. It was after midnight, and I am sure they had other places to be, but it was good to see friendly faces as they helped me, my bags and my weapon bundle into a Land Rover in a parking area thronged with people and mostly in darkness apart from vehicle headlights.

We drove for five minutes or so through the unlit airfield, before entering a small town of electrical wiring, tent lines and temporary buildings. Kandahar had grown a lot since my last visit in 2002. Stuart pulled up outside a long single-storey hut at the edge of a gravelled parking area. Vinnie turned and put his finger to his lips, and I nodded; many of the crews flying tomorrow morning would be asleep, and we needed to be quiet.

I followed them into a narrow corridor, and halfway down Stuart opened a door and pointed to a bed in a dark room. As I squinted in, I could make out other beds and people sleeping so I placed my bags down at the end of the bed, took off my windproof smock and boots and lay back on the bed; unpacking could wait until morning.

It had been a long day, and it was clear that a lot had changed since I had left Afghanistan, but in a way it was nice to be back. I was really tired, but it took me quite a while to get to sleep – partly due to the new and strange environment, but mainly due to Ned's snoring in the next bed.

I chuckled to myself; I liked Ned. A new crewman on the Chinook Force, he was a genuine person, a 'proper northerner' who had actually transferred from the Royal Marines. He had been one of the young marines in 45 Commando at Bagram back in 2002, and finding myself in the next bed to him as I arrived back in Afghanistan seemed a very strange coincidence. However, after an early morning departure from Odiham and an eight-hour flight from Brize Norton, even Ned's snoring couldn't keep me awake for long, and I drifted into a deep sleep.

I stirred a few times as I heard people moving around, but it was about 8.00 am by the time I woke. Ned and a couple of others were lying on their beds with earphones in, either watching movies on laptops or listening to music. As soon as I sat up, they removed the earphones and everyone started talking. I got up a little fuzzily and began to unpack. As I was slipping my empty Bergen under the bed, Stuart walked in.

'You're probably a bit late for breakfast, mate. Grab a shower and we'll go down to Timmy's,' he told me, in a thick Scottish accent.

We went into the corridor and through a doorway at the end, where there was a line of sinks and several shower cubicles. The abundance of steam suggested there was no shortage of hot water.

'This is all right, eh?' I said, and Stuart nodded.

Things had come a long way since the early days of operations from Bagram.

Once I had showered and changed I joined Stuart and several other members of the flight in the car park and we walked down a road, past neat rows of buildings and tents, with Stuart pointing out landmarks as we went.

I hadn't been sure what Stuart was referring to when he mentioned 'Timmy's', but as we crossed the road I saw the familiar sign of a Tim Hortons coffee shop. As we made our way up some wooden steps on to a covered boardwalk I made out a Subway, a Pizza Hut and several other fast food outlets serving military personnel from converted shipping containers. I felt pretty sure that Thursday wasn't shit-burning day at Kandahar.

We ordered coffee and toasted bagels and took seats at a table overlooking a hockey pitch, where some Canadians were playing a hotly contested match.

'The Americans and Canadians have built most of this. British have put in fuck-all apart from an EFI,' said Stuart, referring to the expeditionary forces offshoot of the NAAFI which provides shops and cafés for British Forces deployed overseas on operations.

As I ate my bagel, the guys filled me in on the work side of things. The British had pulled out of Musa Qaleh in the north as part of a Taliban ceasefire, but the Taliban had immediately reoccupied the town and dug in defensively. In Sangin things were also dire; re-supplies to the beleaguered garrison in the district centre were a delicate operation involving Apache gunship escorts and fast jet cover, and even then there was a high likelihood of taking fire.

Any missions into the Sangin Valley were 'an adventure', and the Taliban were very keen to hit either an Apache or a Chinook. A wooded area a kilometre or so north of the garrison known as 'Wombat Wood' gave cover to the Taliban, and small arms, heavy machine gun and RPG fire would erupt from the trees whenever a helicopter was inbound.

After coffee, Stuart took me up to operations, where I caught up with the flight commander, read the theatre orders and grabbed a locker. I also went to see the 'squippers' and was fitted for my Mark 60 jacket, a new piece of equipment.

The MK60 was a combined life jacket, body armour and load-carrying waistcoat that had only just been introduced; it was so new that many people hadn't seen it prior to arriving at Kandahar. A heavy canvas waistcoat, it contained a Kevlar plate at the back, along with an attachment for the monkey harness. At the front was a double zip, with a second Kevlar plate which fitted between the inner and outer zip. Attached to the front were a number of pouches containing survival equipment, as well as reconfigurable magazine pouches. Leg straps attached to the back fed between the legs and fastened at the front, designed to stop the jacket from slipping up if the harness arrested your fall.

Overall it was a great improvement, but it was very heavy. A long flying day, weighed down with an MK60 jacket, helmet and NVGs in high temperatures, was fatiguing, and hard on the knees when kneeling on the vibrating floor picking up an underslung load.

The following day, I would be doing my TQ with Dougal and would also be conducting an air-to-ground gunnery shoot to qualify in-theatre. As well as being the crewman leader, Dougal was also an experienced QHCI and had instructed me when I had initially converted to the Chinook years earlier.

I caught up with Dougal for a brief chat about the following day, and Stuart gave me the tour of operations, walking down the flight line to visit the engineers who had established themselves in a temporary heavy fabric hangar at the centre of a cluster of shipping containers.

There was a bustle of activity as the engineers worked on an aircraft in the hangar as well as running to and from the tasking aircraft on the line. At the rear of the hangar, the line had set up shop and the aircraft logbooks sat on a row of folding camping tables. The afternoon was taken up with studying maps and getting a feel for the local area, pinpointing landing sites and forward operating bases.

The south of Afghanistan was under Regional Command South (RC South), the UK, Canada and the Netherlands being the lead nations, with support from a number of others including the USA and Australia.

The Province of Nimruz lay at the western end of RC South, next to the Iranian border. Consisting mainly of open desert, and sparsely populated, Nimruz was one of the quieter provinces, and apart from ranging patrols near the border, military activity was fairly light by 2006.

At the eastern end lay Kandahar province, home to Kandahar City, considered to be the birthplace and spiritual home of the Taliban. The province is bordered by the Registan desert stretching south to Pakistan's lawless Baluchistan Province, and by a range of mountains to the north dividing Kandahar from Orzugan Province. The Coalition had set up a base at the airport 22km south of Kandahar City which was home to 14,000 personnel.

Between Nimruz and Kandahar lay Helmand Province, the responsibility of the British battlegroup, with its headquarters in the provincial capital of Lashkar Gar. The Helmand River snakes its way south from the mountains of Orzugan Province, through the hydroelectric dam at Kajaki, down through the Sangin Valley and to the south at Garmsir, before reaching the Registan desert, twisting west in a fishhook and flowing into Nimruz. A fertile area extended for several kilometres from the river, irrigated by canals and ditches and providing a stark green contrast to the brown desert in the remainder of the province.

To the north, the Netherlands had set up a base at Tarin Kowt in Oruzgan Province, where they were supported by Australian Special Forces in a high mountainous area with valley floors largely given over to opium production.

North of Orzugan was Daykondi Province, a mountainous area dotted with US Special Forces bases in the few populated centres. To the east lay Zabul Province and the porous border with Pakistan.

Pashto is the lingua franca in both southern Afghanistan and the Pakistan provinces across the border, and in many respects the inhabitants of the two areas consider themselves one people; they view the border as scarcely more than an arbitrary line on a map, drawn a long time ago by foreigners and not really applicable to them. As the Taliban were recruited, trained and supplied from Pakistan, this meant a lot of border activity, with several routes into Afghanistan through Zabul, Kandahar and Helmand Provinces.

Added to all of this was the issue of opium. It was the opium trade that funded the Taliban movement, and the control of poppy farmers and the harvesting and refining of opium into heroin were of huge importance to them. The bulk of this activity was centred on a small town on the Helmand River called Sangin, where the opium had traditionally been traded and distributed. The British operation in Helmand, and the basing of a garrison in Sangin in particular, was a very unwelcome development for the Taliban.

I left operations and made my way back to the accommodation, just in time to meet Stuart and some of the others who were about to go to dinner. I dropped off a few things on my bed and joined them for the short drive to the American-led dining facility near the boardwalk.

I was amazed when I entered the dining facility. Apart from the huge scale of the place, with seating for several hundred people, a huge selection of high quality meals was available and every taste was catered for. I marvelled at the steak and chips on my plate as I wandered over to a well-stocked salad bar and helped myself, conscious that all I had eaten that day was a toasted bagel.

After dinner we stopped off at Tim Hortons for an obligatory coffee, watching the Canadians thrash a puck around on the floodlit hockey pitch and military personnel of varying nationalities wandering the boardwalk buying foot-long subs or bartering with an Afghan over the price of a rug depicting AK47s and RPGs.

As I walked back to the accommodation in the dark I considered how much Afghanistan had changed since I had been there last. The military deployment had grown exponentially in size and scope, but so had the fighting. The Taliban had used the distraction of Iraq to regroup and rearm and were now operating across numerous areas of the country, employing a wide range of tactics and showing themselves absolutely willing to stand and fight, even to a martyr's death if need be.

It had been a long day, and after a hot shower I set the alarm for 5.00 am and climbed into bed determined to beat Ned to sleep and miss the loud snoring.

The following morning, I woke to my alarm. It was still dark, and I had a quick shower and shave before dressing as quietly as possible in a dark room of sleeping bodies, before meeting the crew out in the car park. I would be flying for the next few weeks with John, a mature, laid-back pilot who had come to the Chinook after tours on the Sea King flying Search and Rescue missions around the UK and the Falklands. The co-pilot was Brett, a tall thin guy with very youthful looks and a strong Bristol accent, already building a good reputation on the flight. Vinnie would be the other crewman, and Dougal would be watching me for the day whilst I did my TQ.

The dining facility was still quiet as we ate breakfast and stocked up on caffeine to get us through the early start, and it was just after 5.30 when we arrived at operations to brief.

We would be flying across the Registan desert to Camp Bastion as a pair, roughly 90 miles to the west. From there we would shut down and get our tasking for the day from the battlegroup headquarters. At that time, infrastructure was still limited at Bastion, so the bulk of the Chinook detachment were based in Kandahar with a small (Forward) detachment of two aircraft and support to run a casualty evacuation standby, and an additional aircraft, known as the Helmand Reaction Flight (HRF), operating for any short-notice tasking that was required. The Apache gunships were already established at Bastion in order to be closer to the troops to whom they gave close air support. The Chinooks would deploy to Bastion early in the morning and work through their tasking before returning to Kandahar in the evening.

With the briefing complete, we collected weapons from the armoury and made our way out. By now, the aircraft were fitted with thick Kevlar matting on the cabin floor and up the side walls to the height of the windows. The Kevlar would stop the 7.62mm calibre rounds of an AK47 but offered limited protection against larger calibres or other weapons. There weren't enough M134 miniguns for such a large deployment (by now there were six aircraft, with a further two supporting Special Forces operations), so we had three M60s, two at the front and one fitted to the ramp.

We started up as the sun rose and took off to the west, arming up as we crossed the fence, and flew across the partially cultivated area of the Panjwai before zoom-climbing to 4,000ft to transit the Registan desert, a majestic red glow emanating from its surface in the dawn light.

As we crossed, Dougal pointed out key features, his commentary picking up pace as we crossed into Helmand and the green arc of the Helmand River sliced through the desert. Once west of the Helmand, we dropped into low level and skimmed the open desert towards Camp Bastion, arming down as we crossed the fence and came to the hover over the HALS, a short runway for helicopters to make running take-offs when heavy, mainly used by Apaches with a full load of ordnance.

The Chinook landing spots had been built by the Royal Engineers and consisted of a neat row of metalled squares surrounded by gravel and separated by concrete blast walls. We landed and shut down, watching the second aircraft do likewise a couple of spots down, as a Land Rover, kicking up dust, bumped its way across to us. Further down, a line of Apache gunships sat parked in a similar line of landing spots.

We climbed into the Land Rover and drove through the partially constructed base, before pulling up at a row of Hesco Bastions, with neat rows of tents beyond. The Hesco was a recent innovation, and Camp Bastion was built on it. A flat-pack wire frame, it folds out to form a cuboid of about a metre and a half into which a canvas sack, similar to standard garden refuse sacks, is then placed and filled with sand or rocks. When built into rows they form a wall that gives some protection from blasts, and apart from the lightweight and easily constructed frame, is mainly built from materials sourced locally.

On the other side of the Hesco wall, the tents each had a sun cover to trap a layer of air and keep the heat out, and an air conditioning unit feeding in cool air though a wide hose. The area around the tents was gravelled, each entrance connected to a heavy duty plastic walkway.

The wooden door of the nearest tent was painted bright red, and a cluster of folding chairs were arranged around a table consisting of a wooden cable reel placed on its side. As I inspected the area, a couple of members of the IRT crew emerged holding cups of coffee.

These guys had been up at Bastion for a few days, and I hadn't seen them since arriving. We traded some good-natured banter, but the reunion was short-lived as Dougal and John were steering me further down the dusty road to the Joint Helicopter Force operations tent so we could get a brief on the day's tasking.

Operations consisted of a similar arrangement to the accommodation, but on a larger scale, with several tents joined together to provide sufficient space to manage all the helicopter support for the battlegroup. To the left was a row of folding tables covered in radio equipment and manned by signallers from 21 Signals Regiment. In the centre was a high wooden table covered in a map of Helmand Province; known as the 'bird table', this was where we would brief our missions, together with the Apache crews who would ride shotgun in case of threat.

Beyond the bird table lay rows of tables which crews used for mission planning, and at the rear was a table with a kettle, coffee and tea bags and a row of refrigerators containing water bottles.

I saw John talking with the Chief of Staff as Dougal explained the set-up in the operations tent, and he motioned us over with one hand, holding in the other a copy of our tasking sheet. We had a few minutes before the brief, so Dougal and I looked through the task sheet, cross-comparing the landing sites with the map.

I'd be doing a lot of the flying with John as captain, which I was pretty happy with. Tall and lean, he was very well spoken but didn't take any shit and could go from 0–60 pretty quickly, expressing his displeasure clearly and very eloquently. He always reminded me of the 'Raffles the gentleman thug' character from the comic *Viz*, and we got on well.

The Apache crews filed into operations and we held the brief. We would be re-supplying the base at Gereshk, before stopping off at Lashkar Gar to pick up passengers and then returning to Bastion to pick up passengers and freight for Kajaki. On return from Kajaki, we'd have a break for a few hours before doing another run to Lashkar Gar, then re-supplying troops near Garmsir in the south. Once complete, we'd head back to Kandahar via the 'Texas Helo' range so I could re-qualify on the M60.

We briefed all aspects of the mission, including coordinating with the Apaches, who would invariably stay high to provide overwatch as we dropped to low level for our run-in to the sites. The airspace at each site was controlled by a Joint Terminal Attack Controller (JTAC), who saw aircraft in and out and called in air support from the Apaches or fast jets if required, and we ran through the frequency changes required to coordinate with the JTAC as we crossed through different airspace.

Thirty minutes later, we were sat on the landing pad with the blades turning, watching a pair of Apaches line up on the HALS ahead of us. Laden with 30mm ammunition and Hellfire missiles, they were heavy and required a running take-off to get airborne. As both crossed ahead of us, climbing slowly into the sky like a pair of angry wasps, we lifted to the hover and transitioned to follow them, checking that our No. 2 was following. We armed up as we cleared the fence and climbed as a package towards the east.

It was a short transit to Gereshk, and after five or six minutes we dropped into low level as a pair and sped across the Helmand River towards a dusty collection of blast walls, tents and shipping containers.

'Visual with the site.'

I gripped the handles of the M60 as we flashed over the few buildings outside the base. In seconds we approached the perimeter wall and John flared to bleed off speed.

'Lionel's on finals,' I called, as a cue to arm down the flares.

'Armed down,' responded Brett.

'Forward 40 descending, 30, 20, 10, 5. Height is good, 4, 3, 2, 1. Steady,' I called, as John positioned the aircraft over the gravel landing area.

'Tail clear right,' I called as John swung the tail around so the ramp was closest to the waiting troops.

'Clear below.'

John descended, and there was a firm bump as we touched down on the gravel.

John and Brett ran through a quick set of checks before informing us we were 'clear ramp', then Vinnie dropped the ramp and gave the troops on board a thumbs-up. They stood up and gathered their equipment before filing off to the rear. Once they'd gone, Vinnie gave the JTAC the thumbs-up, and the troops stood at the blast wall started walking towards the ramp.

'OK, we'll lift and depart north before turning west and stay at low level for the run to Lash,' briefed John.

As I looked out to the left I saw the last of the troops climbing up the ramp on to aircraft 2, and shortly afterwards their ramp lifted, whilst Vinnie had the last of the troops onboard and was raising our ramp. He gave me a thumbs-up, as I looked above to check the whereabouts of the Apaches.

'Apaches in the 5 o'clock, high. Clear above and behind,' I called.

John keyed the transmit twice to let the Apaches know we were lifting, then brought us into the hover. It took Brett a second to confirm we had sufficient power available, then the nose dropped and we accelerated out of the base.

'Armed up,' called Brett.

By now we were at 140 knots and 50ft above the ground, weaving between areas of habitation towards Lashkar Gar. The desert gave way to lush green vegetation as we approached the river, but it was only a few minutes before we were over a fairly large town of brown adobe buildings, with kids and people everywhere; it was distinctly reminiscent of 'Blackhawk Down'.

'Visual Lash,' called John, as I made out a blast wall with a large gravelled area beyond which served as the landing site. There were scores of shipping containers and tents beyond a further blast wall, with high watchtowers at the corners.

We crossed compounds, buildings and narrow shadow-filled alleys, people on the ground running out to see the helicopters flying overhead. I could make out kids loading slingshots down a lane. Although in the years to come I would never experience a single incident in Lashkar Gar, it always remained an uncomfortable approach over the town.

We armed down and landed; as both aircraft sat on the gravel, a few troops got off, and a larger number got on and took the seats not already occupied by the passengers we'd already picked up at Gereshk.

After a few minutes both ramps were up and we lifted to the hover, with John pitching the aircraft into a tight right turn 'over the shoulder' and running out of Lashkar Gar in a completely different direction, with No. 2 following. As we cleared the town I updated John on the position of the Apaches and both aircraft climbed rapidly up to 4,000ft and out of AK47 and RPG range for the transit back to Camp Bastion. By now it had warmed up to the low twenties and I was beginning to feel hot in my windproof smock and Shemagh scarf.

We landed at Bastion and the troops disembarked as we topped up the fuel to two tons for the trip to Kajaki and back. The refuel complete, I climbed back aboard to find a dozen or so troops, and Vinnie loading some mail atop a neat stack of boxes.

Kajaki was strategically important to both the Coalition and the Taliban, since the hydroelectric dam provided power for much of southern Afghanistan, despite two of the four turbines being out of action due to either the fighting or incompetent management. There was a small team of Americans now living there doing their best to keep the power flowing, but the dam was subject to regular attacks by the Taliban, keen to deny the Coalition any claim of success in their efforts to rebuild. There was also a high threat from mines; the previous summer at Kajaki, Corporal Mark Wright had been killed and several other members of 3 Para injured by landmines left over from the Soviet invasion.

We flew though the brown peaks, and a beautiful blue lake opened up ahead of us, a narrow valley leading off from its north-east corner. Descending over the lake as the Apaches remained at height, we started an unusual approach down over the dam and dropping into a valley that snaked to the left. It was a beautiful spot, dotted with pine trees, but I didn't have time to appreciate its aesthetic appeal as I scanned the riverbed for the landing site. Suddenly a plume of thick purple smoke erupted from a flat gravel area to the left, and I made out a cluster of quad bikes and trucks on a narrow road under the shade of the pine trees.

We approached the site and swung the tail to face back up the valley, leaving space for the other aircraft behind us. It was a tight squeeze for two aircraft, but we were soon on the ground and Vinnie was helping the troops offload the freight. With the cabin empty, we picked up just a couple of troops, probably heading off on R&R, and with ramps raised we lifted and weaved our way back up the valley and across the dam, accelerating over the lake before climbing up and following the Apaches south towards Bastion.

We had a few hours on the ground at Bastion and could grab lunch and relax with the other crews before the afternoon run to Garmsir. The Land Rover collected us again and took us to the dining facility, a very different value proposition to that at Kandahar.

Run by British Army chefs, it served good honest food but with a very narrow range compared to its American equivalent. A small salad bar held only a pair of metal tongs, having obviously been emptied in the first few minutes and never replenished. There were three or four choices, well cooked but invariably consisting of curry and rice, a roast and something and chips. However, on a long tasking day, something and chips was a welcome distraction, and at the back of your mind you knew it would represent luxury to troops in Kajaki or elsewhere heating up Menu H over a stove.

After lunch we drank coffee outside the IRT tent, catching up on events in Helmand. The tent itself was quite comfortable, with eight beds at one end and some chairs and a TV at the other. In the narrow porch was a fridge and a table equipped with a kettle and a microwave. Bergens filled the space between the beds, and stacks of magazines and DVDs littered the TV area.

As we sat in the sun sipping coffee, a field telephone rang twice and the IRT crew ran to the Land Rover before speeding off towards the flight line. They had had a shout, and somewhere in Helmand someone was in trouble. A few minutes later, the aircraft lifted into the sky beyond the shipping containers and was joined by a pair of Apaches.

With the Land Rover up at the flight line, we walked the 500m back to the aircraft and had a short brief for the afternoon mission. We'd do the run to Lashkar Gar, then return to Bastion to pick up an underslung load as we'd be re-supplying elements of 42 Commando at a grid in the desert west of Garmsir.

We departed Bastion in the early afternoon and ran into Lashkar Gar, picking up and dropping off troops, before scooting back to Bastion across the desert. With the troops offloaded, we opened a hatch in the cabin floor and dropped the large hydraulic hook out and under the aircraft. In the distance, a team from JHSU stood next to a large netted stack of ammo boxes, holding a stirrup.

We ran through the hook checks, arming the hydraulics and checking the pressure, before running in towards the load.

'Forward 10, descending.'

'8, 6, height is good, 5, 4, 2 and right, 1, steady,' I directed, talking John over a load that was some 20ft behind and below where he sat in the cockpit.

Underneath, the JHSU team reached up with a static discharge cable to earth the hook and dissipate the static charge that occasionally builds up.

'Working with the load.'

The JHSU hooker reached up with the heavy stirrup and clipped it through the gate and on to the hook with a heavy clunk.

'Load attached, up gently.'

John began to climb slowly, taking up the slack as I directed him to the overhead of the load to prevent a swing as it came clear.

'Up gently and left, up gently and left, up gently only, taking the strain, load clear of the ground.'

With 10ft under the load, I checked the rigging from top to bottom to ensure there were no tangles or snags that might work themselves free at 4,000ft.

'Good load,' I called, letting John know we were good to go, and with Brett guarding the emergency release switch, speed came on and we trickled forward before climbing. In the cabin, I guarded the manual release lever until we were at safe speed. In the event of an engine failure or power loss in the transition to forward flight, both Brett and I would have jettisoned the load to stop its weight dragging us to the ground.

We climbed and headed south towards Garmsir, with the other aircraft following, a similar load hanging from its underside. It was a transit of thirty minutes or so before we dropped into low level for the run-in to the grid 42 Commando had provided.

We were over open desert and would kick up a huge dust cloud as we approached. There would be no opportunity for a precise drop-off, and in the heavy swirl of re-circulating dust I would look for the rigging to go slack as an indication that the load was on the ground, before manually releasing it and allowing John to climb away out of the dust cloud. John, robbed of visual references in the dust cloud, would be working from instruments, and it wasn't an occasion for error or fumbling; the drop-off needed to be quick and accurate, with all the crew working together.

In the area ahead of the aircraft I saw several vehicles arranged in a box, providing security for the landing site as we re-supplied the marines. Atop the vehicles, troops manned heavy machine guns and scanned the horizon for unwelcome guests.

As Dougal wanted to watch me do the load drop-off, I was at the hatch above the hook, and Vinnie had moved up to the front door.

'Clear forward and down,' called Vinnie

'Dust cloud building. Down 40.'

'30 Ramp, 20 Centre, 10 Door,' called Vinnie, giving John updates on the load's height above the ground as the dust cloud enveloped the aircraft. Even wearing ski goggles, my face was blasted by rough sand as it funnelled past the hook and through the hatch.

'Cockpit,' called Vinnie as the cloud caught up with the aircraft, obscuring the cockpit.

I saw the stirrup slacken on the hook and released the load, seeing the rigging drop away.

'Load gone,' I called, and with an audible sigh of relief John pulled power and we climbed vertically out of the dusty maelstrom into blue skies.

Behind us, the second aircraft was also emerging from the dust.

'Good work, guys,' called John.

The drop-off had been short and sweet, and 42 Commando were now restocked with fuel, food and ammunition.

We climbed away to 4,000ft and turned to the east. There had been nothing to pick up from the marines, so with tasking complete we were going direct to Kandahar via the range. Vinnie and I swapped places so I was operating from the front door, and we continued our transit across the Registan desert.

To the south of the Kandahar area was Tarnak Farm; for several years this had been the home of Osama bin Laden, until he had fled shortly before the 9/11 attacks. It was now used by ground troops as a training area. Further south was a single large ridge rising up out of the flat desert, and it was this prominent feature, known as 'Texas Helo', that served as the air-to-ground gunnery range for helicopter crews.

We approached and did a couple of flybys to check the range, making sure it was clear of any troops, vehicles or livestock that might have wandered into the area unaware of its new zoning purpose. Once clear, Dougal gave me the briefing and we flew a variation of profiles, with me opening fire on targets nominated by Dougal. After expending a couple of belts, Dougal declared himself happy and we headed back to Kandahar, landing in late afternoon as the sun was beginning to sink.

After a crew debrief I had a short debrief with Dougal; we were both experienced QHCIs, Dougal said he hadn't been expecting any major issues and sure enough, I hadn't given him any. I was TQ day, and my night TQ was scheduled for the following evening, but by now it had been a long day and we were all ready for something to eat and a quiet evening.

* * *

On 15 January we departed Kandahar as a pair for Bastion, where we would spend the night before a dawn re-supply into the besieged base at Sangin. With sleeping bags, pillows and a change of clothes rammed into already packed rucksacks, we would load up the aircraft that night and launch at 4.30 am, aiming to take the Taliban by surprise at their dawn prayers.

I was crewed with Keith, who had given me a lift to Kabul a few years earlier. The captain was an experienced pilot called Aaron, who I hadn't flown with before but knew by reputation; he was a good hand by all accounts.

We landed at Bastion and shut down on the spot. There was an hour or so of daylight left, but with the mission involving Apaches and close air support it would be a long brief, and we were faced with either loading the aircraft in daylight or attending the brief. Eventually, we agreed that Aaron and Brett would attend the brief and Keith and I would use the remaining daylight to load the aircraft, ensuring that our time on the ground was minimized. The guys would catch us up on the brief over dinner.

In the other aircraft they made a different decision, and we watched all four disappear off to operations for the brief. There was no wrong or right decision here, just different perspectives, so Keith and I began re-rolling the cabin.

We would be using the HICS (helicopter internal loading system) for the mission. A set of rollers fastened to the floor and running the length of the cabin, the HICS system had not been used in many years by the Chinook Force, but with the threat too high to come to a hover in Sangin and drop an underslung load, it was now back in fashion.

Behind the aircraft, several wooden pallets fitted with flat wooden baseboards sat next to a bobcat forklift and a JHSU team. With the HICS fitted, I gave the team a thumbs-up; the Bobcat started up with a growl and was soon approaching the ramp with the first pallet.

Keith marshalled the pallet into position, whilst I monitored the clearances, one of the key reasons we had wanted to get the loading done in the fading daylight. With the pallet onboard, we pushed it up to the front across the fitted rollers. We repeated this five times until the cabin was full, each time checking the pallet was central and wasn't going to snag as it left the aircraft.

As the JHSU team drove off towards the other aircraft we ran a double strand of high-strength Para cord across the pallets, securing it to a floor point near the front. We then locked the pallets in place, using ratchet strops to secure them against any movement.

Due to the threat at Sangin, Keith would remove the ratchet strops as we approached Sangin, and we would land with a slight nose-up profile. As Aaron slowly taxied forward on the rear wheels, Keith would drop the ramp and I would slice through the Para cord with a 'J' knife. We would then push the pallets off the ramp. Keith had secured the Para cord so the weight of the first pallet grounding on the landing site would drag the others one by one off the ramp until they had all gone, at which point we would lift the ramp and get the hell out of Dodge.

Satisfied that the load was good to go, Keith and I prepared our kit in the last of the daylight before walking over to meet the rest of the crew, who were just finishing the brief. Over dinner they caught us up on the plan, which was pretty much unchanged from the outline we had received before leaving Kandahar. As we headed for the surge tent to climb into our sleeping bags, we saw Company Man and Liz heading out in the dark to start loading their aircraft.

The next morning, we were up at 3.30 am and had a quick caffeine infusion before heading out to the aircraft, and by 4.25 am both aircraft were turning and burning on the spots, waiting for the Apaches to taxi out.

At 4.30 am the Apaches, using their call sign 'Ugly', lifted into the darkness ahead of us. On NVG I saw them pass ahead of us, and as I cleared us above and behind, we lifted to the hover and fell into formation behind them.

The transit to the western side of the Sangin valley was about 20 minutes, and we would drop to 50ft out of sight of Sangin before running in at full speed and skimming across the Helmand River for the limited protection of the base landing site.

It was just getting light as Aaron descended to low level over a brown moonscape of low mounds and shadow-filled reentrants, almost like a dusty mogul field. I looked up and saw the Apaches remain high to provide overwatch as we ran in and to advise us on any threats, as well as providing fire support.

Aaron was expertly following the contours of the ground as we descended into the Sangin Valley at 150 knots, my hands tight on the loaded M60. I looked back at Keith, who gave me a nod; he was ready to go, and as we crossed the river, tracer started to erupt from Wombat Wood.

'They're awake,' called Aaron, referring to the Taliban, who by now would be scrambling to weapons and taking aim at the two large helicopters crossing right to left across their sights.

I heard a distant rumble like thunder as the Apaches put some 30mm fire into the visible Taliban firing points.

As we approached the wall, I reached for the 'J' Knife I had positioned on a seat back next to the door.

'Arming down,' I heard from the front.

'Tail clear.'

'Down 40, 30, 20, 10, 5, 4, 3, 2, 1,' then a bump, as the wheels hit the dirt.

'Working in the cabin,' I informed Aaron, as he started slowly trickling forward.

Keith already had the ratchet strops off and the ramp down as I sliced through the para cord with the 'J' knife. Keith pushed the rearmost pallet towards the ramp and it slid easily off on to the dirt. As it did so, the remaining pallets started to roll out one at a time, and in seconds the cabin was empty, with a neat row of pallets laid out across the landing site.

'Loads gone, clear above and behind,' I called, and Aaron immediately pulled power and we screamed into the air, lighter now we had left six tons of ammunition and water behind.

'Armed up.'

I scanned the vegetation for enemy activity, but as we banked hard to the south and accelerated out towards the safety of empty desert, the Taliban had their hands full with the Apaches. The other Chinook was on the ground.

'One from two, we have a pallet stuck in the cabin, we're a sitting duck here, so we're going to go around.'

Rather than sit on the ground awaiting the first mortar round, the other crew were going to lift and fly a circuit back to the landing site to give the guys in the cabin time to free the stuck pallet. It was a lose/lose situation for the captain, Jace, and a ballsy call.

We were now out of the main threat zone over open desert, and we orbited whilst waiting for Jace to catch up; the best thing we could do was not add to the difficulty of the situation, so we stayed out the way. As we orbited we heard a contact report from Jace's aircraft; the Taliban had realized they had been pulled into a fight by the Apaches, but now saw an easy target as Jace set up for his approach back into Sangin, the element of surprise gone.

A few minutes later, we hear Jace key the transmit switch twice as he left Sangin. The guys had freed the stuck pallet and were now heading out to join us, and it was a relief when, a minute or two later, we saw them flash across the river and climb up to join us. As we all took a breath, I looked at my watch; it was just after 5.00 am.

The Apaches remained at Sangin providing support to the garrison, who were now taking fire from the angry Taliban in Wombat Wood. We picked up the speed and the height and headed back to Bastion for breakfast.

We were sat in the dining facility putting away the bacon and eggs, when Jace and his crew joined us, all looking a little pale. After breakfast, Keith and I joked with the other crew about loading pallets in the dark, but we didn't push it too far; the lesson had been well and truly learnt that morning.

Throughout that morning we continued with tasking around Helmand Province, including a mission to Garmsir, which seemed to be unusually active. Later on, the radio net became very busy as a 45 Commando operation in the area of Jugroom Fort began to go off the rails.

The fort was a well-known location for Taliban activity, and 45 Commando, supported by artillery and Viking armoured vehicles, had launched an assault. An incident had occurred and they had been forced to withdraw, not realizing they had left the injured Lance Corporal Matthew Ford behind. Now the place was a hive of enemy activity, but the marines had strapped themselves to the wings of the Apache and recovered Ford in a daring rescue mission, carried out by both Royal Marines and Apache crews with a high degree of audacity. Sadly, Lance Corporal Ford later died of his wounds.

A few days later, I was back with John and Brett for another dawn re-supply into Sangin. In the cabin I was crewed with Curly, a very capable crewman I knew from my time as a trainer; he had a mischievous sense of humour and a laid-back attitude. John, Brett and Curly had been into Sangin a couple of days earlier and had taken a lot of fire; none was in the mood to repeat the experience. John took me aside and told me how the Taliban had opened up with AK47s from a section of missing wall at the edge of the landing site. It would be on the left as we landed, and he wanted me to keep a good eye, by which he meant gunsight, on the area whilst we were on the ground.

John glided over the low mounds, the Helmand River glistening like a silver ribbon in the first light of dawn as we dropped into the valley. We flashed over the river and crossed the wall, and Curly had the ramp down and the pallets moving as John slowly trundled across the grassy landing zone.

As Curly helped the pallets over the ramp, I aimed the gun at the missing section of wall and sure enough, a figure appeared and pointed an AK47 directly at us. I eased off the safety and took aim, taking up the tension on the trigger.

BANG! BANG! BANG! BANG! BANG!

The figure dropped, and I stood confused for a second as I hadn't actually fired. But 2,000ft above us, the Apache had seen the danger on the aircraft's infra-red sensors and directed a stream of 30mm cannon fire at the figure.

By now, Curly had the ramp up. I let John know he was good to go, and we lifted quickly and broke harshly left and right as we weaved over the poppy fields and back out to the river. We had been on the ground for eight seconds and had dropped off six tons of badly-needed ammunition.

Our departure had alerted the Taliban, and as our playmate followed us out, streams of tracer erupted from numerous locations and the other aircraft took a few rounds. We headed back to Bastion to check for damage, as the Apaches continued to ping away at enemy targets around the Sangin base.

'Nice work, mate,' John said as we cruised back to Bastion.

'Wasn't me, mate. Apache got him,' I replied.

'Nice work anyway,' said John with a chuckle; he'd got the result he wanted; next time, hopefully, there would be one fewer ten-dollar Taliban with an AK at the wall taking pot shots at him.

The sun was rising, and there was a feeling of both relief and elation as John skilfully guided the aircraft across the undulating desert, the other one following us. To someone who has never been in the military, trundling through a firefight and rolling off pallets as gunships engage Taliban in a nearby treeline may sound like a frightening proposition, but in all honesty you are so busy just following drills and trying to stay alive that it's only afterwards that it hits you. There was lots of chatter and nervous laughter as we headed back to Bastion, symptomatic of adrenalin subsiding and elation at still being in one piece.

Back at Bastion, the engineers found scoring on our aircraft where rounds had ricocheted off the airframe, and several more on the other aircraft, including a round embedded in one of the rotor blades. As the guys set to work patching holes and replacing a blade, we left them to it and headed for breakfast.

The following night, we had a task to support 45 Commando in the south near Garmsir. The Marines had developed a Mobile Outreach Group or 'MOG', a great concept consisting of a force of heavily armed vehicles patrolling the desert between Garmsir and the Pakistan border. Much of their work was interdicting the Taliban supply chain up from the Baluchistan border, thus reducing the number of weapons and fighters reaching their main battle group. It was classic desert warfare, and 45 Commando were having a lot of success hitting and running in the night, without getting into static battles or becoming pinned down as in the Platoon Houses.

We would be flying as a pair, on NVG, to re-supply the MOG in the open desert at a nominated grid, where the vehicles would have secured an area and laid out a 'desert box', a 20m x 10m rectangle with a weighted infra-red cyalume (lightstick) at each corner. As well as marking the landing area, the desert box gave a reference for pilots to visually judge their approach relative to the shape of the box.

We'd be landing simultaneously as a pair, on NVG, at a sparsely lit area in a dusty desert in enemy territory – about as high-end as you could get for our pilots. The landings had to be completely simultaneous or the dust cloud from one aircraft could 'brown out' the other at a critical moment in the approach. It required intense focus and concentration from the handling pilot, and complete support from the rest of the crew, each of us playing a crucial part in the sequence to feed data or cues John needed to get us safely on the ground.

Loaded up with stores, we got airborne from Bastion and headed south at height. We transited over the open desert, with the green zone surrounding the Helmand River on our left. It was a low moon period and dark, even with the NVG, but there was just enough light for us to get in and re-supply the MOG before the dark of the moon. Curly was down the back behind several marines and a stack of boxes and equipment, sat on the ramp giving updates on the position of the other aircraft.

A few miles out, we identified our IP or Initial Point, a known navigational feature which confirmed our position and from which we'd track in on a prescribed heading. Approaching the IP, we dropped down to 150ft, heading south-east, the lights of Garmsir just visible on the horizon through the NVG.

Brett called out the pre-landing checks, and I confirmed we were good in the cabin. As I looked back I saw Curly shaking the marines awake and giving them the two-minute sign. They gathered up weapons and got their game faces on.

'OK, guys. I'm visual with some vehicles on the nose,' called John.

'Arming down,' Brett chipped in.

Although we weren't within the confines of a base, 45 Commando would not appreciate us pumping out magnesium teflon flares into their vehicles.

'Playmates still right 4 o'clock, similar level,' added Curly, letting John know the position of our playmate.

'OK, got the boxes visual, in that case I'll take the left hand box.'

By now John was easing back the speed as the other aircraft drew level, both aircraft setting up for a gate approach. The 'gate' was a set of parameters in terms of speed and height that would signal the start of the approach to the box.

With the other aircraft now out to our right, Brett counted down heights and speeds until we were set up for the approach.

'In the gate,' called Brett, and John started a steady descent towards the box. Seeing John lift the nose to flare, the other aircraft did likewise, and both descended towards the vehicles.

'Clear forward and down, down 40,' I began.

'Dust cloud building,' added Curly

'30.'

'Dust cloud at the ramp.'

'20, 10, door.' I took over the commentary as the rear of the cabin filled with dust.

'8, 6, 5, cockpit.' By now I was almost completely browned out in the door, with only the vaguest of references on the desert floor.

'4, 3, 2 … wheels on.' There was a thud as the back wheels touched down.

John ran on a metre or so, placing the front wheels on and lowering the collective. As the dust cloud blew outwards and began to dissipate slightly in the reduced downwash, I saw the other aircraft on the ground 40m or 50m away.

'Clear ramp,' called John, and Curly was already on it.

With the ramp down, Curly flashed his torch through the dusty cabin and the marines climbed slowly out of their seats, struggling under the weight of their heavy packs, and started towards the ramp. Several figures appeared out of the darkness and helped offload the boxes and equipment, the marines we'd flown in forming a huddle over the top to weigh the boxes down. A handful of troops climbed on and took a seat as Curly lifted the ramp.

'Ramp's up, clear above and behind,' I called, and even as I was speaking, the other aircraft had keyed twice; they were also ready.

As John pulled power, the dust cloud returned and we were quickly enveloped by a swirling cyclone. Relying on instruments, John continued pulling power and we climbed until, after a couple of hundred feet, we were clear of the cloud and he tipped the nose forward.

'Playmate 5 o'clock,' called Curly, as the second aircraft cleared the cloud.

We headed back to Bastion with the task complete. The approach and departure had taken only a few minutes but had required complete focus from all.

'Well done, guys,' said John, with a hint of relief in his voice. 'Let's go home.'

Chapter 7

A Funny Thing Happened on the Way to the Hindu Kush

As the years pass, events blur into each other, but occasionally there are days you never forget, and for me one of those was our 'Brown Ring' tasking day. Each year, at the Chinook reunion, someone will laugh and say, 'Do you remember that day tasking on the Brown Ring?'

Although deployed in support of the UK battlegroup now known as 'Taskforce Helmand', the aircraft were also a Coalition asset, and occasionally we operated in support of other Coalition partners; the Brown Ring referred to a necklace of isolated patrol bases in Daykondi and Orzugan Provinces to the north of Kandahar, mainly manned by US Special Forces, or 'Green Berets'.

Small SF teams were embedded with Afghan National Army (ANA) units and manned these small outposts in the little mountain settlements, mixing patrolling with hearts-and-minds activities to maintain a presence in otherwise feral mountain communities.

We would deploy to the Dutch/Australian base at Tarin Kowt and spend the day running a hub-and-spoke service out to several of these bases. I was crewed with John and Brett again, but this time I was with Gary in the cabin. Gary was A Flights QHCI, and it was unusual to have two instructors crewed together, but that was how the chips had fallen that day.

We departed Kandahar and headed north, climbing through the mountains on a very similar track to the one we had taken on our way to Bagram in 2002. It was even more stunning in January, with the snowcapped peaks looking especially impressive against a dull winter sky.

We dropped into the valley floor and set up for an approach into Tarin Kowt, refuelling with rotors running before positioning on to a large gravelled area and shutting down. Long lines of pallets and an ancient

Dutch forklift sat along a blast wall. Judging by their number, we were in for a long day.

We teamed up with the crewmen on the other aircraft, and with the help of a handy Dutch forklift driver each aircraft was loaded with four pallets of freight for FOB Cobra, which would be our first drop of the day.

As the details of the plan emerged, it appeared that we'd be doing a run to three sites, then sweeping up with a second run at the end of the day, before heading back to Kandahar; a fairly easy day, it seemed.

In addition to the pallets, we had a slack handful of troops onboard, all heading out to Cobra, either returning or just visiting for meetings. They boarded and took their seats, placing their M4 assault rifles behind them.

We started up and headed to Cobra, a short run taking us north-west through low desert valleys at the base of towering mountains. After 20 minutes a bowl-shaped valley opened up ahead of us, and to the side of a settlement of mud-brick buildings stood an obvious fort, surrounded with concrete blast walls and with a small, tented camp dotted with temporary buildings and the obligatory shipping containers. To one side, within the blast wall, was a large, gravelled area that acted as a helicopter landing site, and we set up for a straight-in approach, arming down as we crossed the wall and landing short to give space to roll forward.

In the cabin, Gary and I released the pallets and, with John keeping the nose of the aircraft raised, Gary levelled the ramp and we trickled forward, dropping pallets as we went; to our left, the other aircraft was doing the same. With the pallets offloaded, John dropped on to four wheels and lowered the collective.

'Clear ramp,' he called, and Gary and I gave the Americans the thumbs-up to disembark.

They picked up their bags and trooped off, leaving their weapons onboard. As we sat on the gravel, a couple of troops came up and got onboard as we readied for departure. With the re-supply complete, we lifted to the hover and, ensuring the other aircraft was also airborne, transitioned away from Cobra and retraced our track back to Tarin Kowt.

As I refuelled the aircraft at Tarin Kowt, John and Brett ran through the task sheet; our next run was to Deh Rawood, a patrol base in a valley settlement in the mountains north-east of Kajaki, an irrigated area fed by the Helmand river as it snaked through the high ground before reaching the dam. It was a notorious Taliban stronghold.

We'd be taking in troops, so as I refuelled, Gary folded down the rearmost seats in the cabin that we had stowed away earlier in order to load the pallets. With the tanks full, we lifted and repositioned back to the main parking area to load the troops, who all climbed onboard and piled their heavy rucksacks in a pyramid arrangement near the front.

Gary and I exchanged glances; the Chinook seats were designed for troops to sit in whilst wearing their rucksack and were fitted with a longer seat belt for that very reason. Sure, it's more comfortable to take your rucksack off for a long trip, but we were only flying 25 minutes up the valley. We shrugged, threw a couple of ratchet strops over the pyramid as best we could and got going.

Despite Deh Rawood's reputation as a Taliban holdout, we arrived and departed without incident, dropping the troops on the landing site. As we headed back to Tarin Kowt, I noticed there were now even more M4 rifles spread across the cabin. Gary and I shoved them behind the seats to stop them moving about or falling over in the vibrating aircraft (all helicopters shake).

Back at Tarin Kowt we topped up the fuel and then landed to pick up a caged dog; this was a fairly substantial animal with a fearsome set of teeth, and it was somewhat unhappy about being put in a cage and driven out to a noisy helicopter. I'm a huge dog-lover, but as this thing tried to chew through the metal cage, I had to admit to some relief it had come in a container. With some trepidation I approached the moving cage and threw a ratchet strop over it to hold it in place, while the beast from hell barked loudly and tried its best to eat its way out to me.

We'd also be taking an underslung load into our next port of call, FOB Anaconda, so Gary lifted the hatch and prepared the hook, as John lifted to the hover and I talked him towards the overhead of a large pile of ammo boxes and jerry cans encased in a heavy net. As we approached the load, Gary took over the directions, and we were soon climbing out of Tarin Kowt with the netted load swinging gently in the airflow.

Again, Anaconda was just a short hop through the valleys, and as the sun shone brightly we made our way up to a patch of high ground to a soundtrack of angry barks. As the ground flattened out, the FOB opened up ahead of us, looking very much like all the other bases in the area. As we approached, a spiral of purple smoke began climbing from a large gravelled area which had several patches of snow lying on it.

A Funny Thing Happened on the Way to the Hindu Kush 85

'OK, the wind looks fairly light so we'll approach from this direction. We'll drop the load short, and once it's gone, move forward and down to land,' briefed John

'Copied,' I replied.

'Hook master live,' called Brett, letting Gary know the emergency jettison system for the hook was now armed.

'Um, there's some kind of parade going on at the edge of the site,' called John.

I looked down the approach and saw a loose group of soldiers lined up at the edge of the gravel. It was a bit weird, but they'd already popped smoke for our landing, and by now our speed was slowing and we were trailing a 4-ton load beneath us.

'Continuing,' called John

'Clear forward and down,' I called.

'Down 40, crossing the wall, 30, tail clear, 20, 10.'

'Down 8 for the load,' called Gary, taking over from the hatch as I checked the clearances.

'6, 5, 4, 3, 2, 1, load on the ground, down 5 and right, 4, 3, 2, 1, height is good. Release, release,' he continued.

In the cockpit Brett pressed the release button, and the rigging dropped away from the hook.

'Load gone,' called Gary.

John moved forward clear of the load and landed. As he lowered the collective, I glanced out right and saw the line of ANA soldiers now bent double in the downwash, their arms over their heads to protect them from flying gravel. Many had lost their berets in the downwash.

'What the fuck is going on over there?' asked John in astonishment, as Gary dropped the ramp.

Out to the side sat our playmate, no doubt also wondering what the hell was going on. As they saw the ramp drop, a second group of ANA soldiers appeared from the side of a building carrying a coffin.

'Shit!' said John. 'It's an Afghan ramp ceremony. Why didn't they tell us?'

Ramp ceremonies were held when a fallen comrade was being repatriated for burial. The British and Americans held them at Kandahar and Bastion, but usually they were well organized, and everyone was aware and minimized activity. Nobody had thought to inform us that we would be picking up a coffin, or that there would be ramp ceremony; this was more than a little annoying.

Before anyone could say anything, the Afghans marched out to the aircraft, up the ramp and placed the coffin on the cabin floor behind the angry mutt. The dog erupted in fury at the sight of the bearded soldiers, who quickly took flight.

I now had to get the animal, who was still trying to eat through metal, off past this unexpected coffin. I looked for Gary, but there was no sign of him.

I managed to get the strop off the cage, and I edged one corner on to the roller, thinking I could roll the cage to the ramp. That's when I noticed the ANA had placed the coffin on the roller and it was slowly shuffling back and forth. I leapt forward and managed to hook a foot around the end of the coffin to stop it rolling backwards towards the ramp. Still alone, I released my grip on the cage and moved down to get hold of the coffin and gently ease it off the rollers on to the main floor, whilst the rabid dog, which didn't seem to have a waiting owner at Anaconda, went crazy. Then, unaware of my predicament in the cabin, John spoke up:

'Please tell me that isn't Gary throwing snowballs at the other aircraft.'

In the midst of the ramp ceremony and the utter chaos in the cabin, Gary had got off and was scooping up balls of snow from the ground and launching them at the other aircraft. After a minute or so, he climbed back on and plugged back into the intercom.

'Haha, just launched a few snowballs at the other cab,' he chuckled in his strong London accent.

'Gary, we're in the middle of a ramp ceremony,' replied John through clenched teeth.

All of a sudden I saw it dawn on Gary, and he frowned. It still hadn't registered on him that I was lying on the cabin floor at full stretch trying to keep a coffin and a killer dog apart.

'Any chance you can give me a hand, mate?' I enquired.

Gary helped me get the last corner of the coffin on to the main floor, while the cage moved towards us a few inches at a time as the dog threw himself at the mesh. Very carefully, we eased the cage on to the rollers and, acutely aware of where we were putting our fingers, we pushed it to the ramp and motioned some Americans towards us to come and collect the animal.

It was with some relief that we lifted out of Anaconda and headed back to Tarin Kowt. I was exhausted, and Gary was quiet. We refuelled at Tarin Kowt and radioed operations to confirm the tasking for the second half of the day.

There was a second load of pallets for Cobra, but otherwise it was just pick-ups of small numbers of troops at each site. We should be able to drop the pallets at Cobra and route direct to De Rawood and Anaconda, only returning to Tarin Kowt at the end. I was also relieved, because the number of weapons that had been left onboard had started to concern me; there were now twenty or so assault rifles, and I had no idea which belonged to whom, or at what site.

The afternoon was a lot more straightforward, and with the pallets delivered at Cobra, we collected a handful of troops who, to my relief, claimed some of the M4s and took their seats. At De Rawood the remaining weapons were claimed, and at Anaconda, mercifully cleared of parading ANA, we picked up a last couple of Americans before making best speed through the tight valleys back to Tarin Kowt.

Refuelled, we departed south to Kandahar and a hearty dinner, our first meal of the day. As we sat and ate, Stuart was laughing.

'What are you laughing at?' I asked.

'Gary at Anaconda, mate,' he replied, and I started laughing too. When I explained about the dog and the coffin, he laughed even harder.

* * *

By February it was clear something would have to be done about Sangin. The base there had been under siege for nine months, and re-supplying the garrison entailed steadily more and more risk to the precious helicopter assets in Helmand.

As plans for a ground assault were being developed within the various headquarters, we received a rather strange task as part of the shaping work for the assault: we would be conducting a leaflet drop over Sangin in the middle of the night.

As Curly and I arrived at the aircraft, a white pick-up was already parked next to the ramp, its flatbed stacked with what looked like boxes of photocopier refill paper. Two camouflaged figures were loitering next to the cab in the setting sun.

'G'day mate, what's the go with these?' I asked, patting the boxes.

The young officer from the psychological warfare wing dropped the tailgate and pulled out on the boxes. Para cord held the box loosely together, and a long lanyard was threaded through a hole in the lid.

'See, they've been specially rigged,' he answered. 'All you have to do is tie them to a hard point and kick them out. When they reach the end of the lanyard, the jerk will release the rigging and the box will collapse, releasing the leaflets.'

Simple enough. There were about fifteen boxes, which we carefully manhandled on to the aircraft and stacked near the ramp.

'Anywhere specific we need to drop them?' I asked.

'Just over Sangin District Centre. From 4,000ft they'll disperse across a wide area.'

'OK, I am sure we can manage that,' I replied.

Curly and I did a walk round and checked the weapons, and our captain for the evening, Zippy, arrived. We gave him the brief, and he seemed happy enough, heading up to the cockpit and strapping in.

It was dark as we sat, rotors turning, awaiting clearance to take off from Bastion. As it came through, we lifted with our Apache escort and headed north towards Sangin, climbing into the night sky. Down the back, I steadily moved the boxes on to the ramp and tied off the lanyards securely on to floor points, even positioning a 'J' knife near the ramp in case we needed to cut any boxes clear.

With the cabin prepared, we positioned to be above Sangin and conduct the drop as we ran north to south over the turbulent settlement. At 4,000ft we were above the threat band for small arms or RPG, but occasionally we would see tracer fire; either an exchange of fire on the ground, or inaccurate firing at the noise of the Chinook which was deceptive to the ears.

We turned south and I dropped the ramp to slightly below the horizontal. Curly had taken up a position in mid-cabin in case I required any help.

'OK, guys, just coming up to the northern edge of Sangin. You are clear to drop,' Zippy informed us.

I kicked the first box off the ramp sill and it dropped away, jerking the lanyard taut at about eight feet out, at which point the box blew apart releasing hundreds of leaflets into our downwash.

'Sweet,' I said to myself and helped a second, third and fourth box off the ramp, each reaching the limit of the lanyard and blossoming into a shower of paper. This was cool, so off went more and more boxes, until there was just one left.

'Last box,' I called, and gave it a firm push off the ramp with my foot.

It travelled to the lanyard and stopped; there was a firm jerk but nothing else. We were trailing a photocopier box behind the aircraft on a piece of string.

I was a bit torn as I reached for the knife. For all I knew, these leaflets said what nice guys we were, and I didn't want to undermine that message by putting a boxful of them through someone's roof, so I gave the lanyard a hefty pull to try and activate the rigging.

As I did so, I fell backwards and the box flew up towards the ramp, hovering in the airflow for a split second before the rigging did indeed work and the box gave way, filling the cabin with leaflets.

Leaflets had wedged themselves between me and the NVGs, and I was completely blind as I stood on the ramp in the dark, 4,000ft over Sangin. The cabin was a swirling mass of leaflets and Curly was doubled up with laughter.

'Guys, there's leaflets in the cockpit,' called Zippy with a trace of alarm.

That just cracked Curly up even more. By now the cabin was plastered in leaflets, and more danced in the airflow from the ramp all the way to the cockpit.

'Yeah, mate, we had a box burst in the cabin,' I told him. 'Can you cock off a bit?'

Cocking off heading a few degrees drives more airflow in through the front cabin door and is normally used to clear smoke and fumes. Luckily, Zippy knew exactly what I needed, and within seconds the cabin was like a wind tunnel as we trailed paper through the night sky.

As the cabin cleared, we resumed heading and made for Bastion, Curly still chuckling to himself at the image of a cabin full of leaflets and me on the ramp with a face full of paper.

We landed and shut down, and as Zippy climbed out of the cockpit, Curly and I were in the cabin on hands and knees gathering as many as the remaining leaflets as we could find. We saved a few as souvenirs of the evening. One side was green, with a picture of an ISAF soldier and some Pashto script which I assumed translated as 'ISAF good'; the reverse was red, with an outlined of a turbaned Taliban fighter and more Pashto, probably 'Taliban bad', if I had to guess.

That evening was a fitting close to my return to Afghanistan and introduction to Operation Herrick. No two days were the same; the environment was harsh, the enemy determined and it didn't particularly seem like the Coalition was winning.

The following day, the familiar faces of B Flight arrived to replace A Flight. It was time for me to head back to the UK and start working up C Flight for our own deployment across the heat of the summer.

Chapter 8

Fighting Season

RAF Odiham
Hampshire
February 2007

As I returned from Afghanistan I learnt Dave Winters had been moved to 2i/c of the squadron, a job I knew he would detest but a sadly necessary step on the ladder of promotion. He had been replaced by the former 2i/c, an experienced Squadron Leader, JP.

JP had followed a strange career path for an RAF officer; selected for an exchange to the Army Air Corps as his first tour, he had gone through the Army helicopter pilot system as an RAF pilot and converted to the Lynx as his first operational type. A gifted leader, he had a humorous streak and an acerbic wit that endeared him to the crews.

By now, one of our female pilots, Hannah, had been made 2i/c. This was a mixed blessing for her; it was a good tick in the box for promotion to Squadron Leader, but since JP wasn't big on paperwork and tended to emit a 'phew' when faced with staff admin, he would toss it to the long-suffering Hannah, who was equally uninterested in data-gathering or ethnicity-monitoring surveys.

As a new flight, the ragtag collection of crews given over by the other flights on formation had shaken together well during their deployment the previous winter. However, we were still 'light' on manpower, and the training system, racing to catch up with the demands placed on it by Afghanistan, was busy churning out fresh pilots and crewmen. This meant we had a high dilution rate in experience, and it gave both myself and Dave, the flight QHI, a heavy training workload leading into a summer deployment to Afghanistan, the height of the fighting season.

Fortunately, I had inherited some very capable trainers who could mentor some of the new guys whilst I concentrated on their progression, and focus on those with a higher learning curve. I was also helped by having a very experienced QHCI as crewman leader in the Ruffler; slowly but surely we chipped away at the work-up and began to absorb the new arrivals and gel as a flight.

Amongst the new arrivals I had an experienced Flight Sergeant who had crossed over from the Nimrod fleet. Galvo was mature, capable and a natural fit for the Chinook Force. I also had one of my former students from Shawbury, 'Trigger', who was generally competent but also had the occasional moment of madness. I would concentrate my efforts on these two newest arrivals and fly with them for the first week in Afghanistan, before pairing them separately with a trainer.

In March I had been in Scotland on exercise when my mobile rang at 8.00 am. Having been flying until 2.00 am I was a bit groggy as I answered, but soon woke up as I heard Dave Winters on the other end.

'Morning Mick, I have some good news, mate. The results of the promotion board were released this morning and you've been promoted,' he informed me.

'Oh, wow. OK, thanks, Dave,' I replied.

'No worries. I'll let you get back to sleep, mate,' he laughed.

Good news as it was, within minutes I was back in a deep sleep.

It was May when Ralph, the squadron standards officer, reminded me I was due a Combat Ready check in the near future. Although I'd previously held Combat Ready status on the Chinook, and was the flight QHCI, I hadn't re-qualified as Combat Ready since returning from Shawbury.

'Shit, mate, I'd forgotten about that,' I told him. 'I'm maxed with the pre-deployment work up right now.'

'It's OK, mate, I have a plan. It will be as painless as possible,' he hinted as he left.

A week later, with Ralph watching my every move and scribbling notes, we departed Odiham for a two-day airshow in Belgium. Ralph threw in a series of practice emergencies and made sure I followed the SOPs as we coasted out over the Channel. As we landed at a small Belgian airbase near Liège we shut down, and Ralph summoned me over for a debrief. From behind his back he produced a can of Stella Artois and handed it to me.

'No points, mate. Congratulations on becoming CR again,' he smiled.

Back at Odiham the training continued, culminating in a few days at the FIBUA area at Longmoor Camp practising downed aircraft drills.

That night, over a beer, I sat with JP, the Ruffler and Hazz as we talked through how we, as a flight, should handle events like losing an aircraft. It was a necessary but sobering conversation and a reminder we were about to head back to Afghanistan in the middle of the Taliban fighting season. Generally, though, we'd come a long way in a short time and were as prepared as we were going to be in the time available.

In the two weeks remaining we continued to push the flight hard, cramming in as much training as we could, eventually working the new crews up to pairs-landing at night in the driver training area on Salisbury plain, the dustiest place available to us.

By early July we were tying up the last administrative ends and sitting in on the latest intelligence briefs. A few weeks earlier, a US Army Chinook, call sign 'Flipper 75', had been shot down in Helmand near Kajaki, reportedly by a rocket-propelled grenade, with the loss of seven personnel, including Corporal Mike Gilyeat of the Royal Military Police. However, as we listened to the intelligence summary, it was clear there were some discrepancies in the story. It would only be in 2010 that the full details were released, revealing a cover-up of the loss of 'Flipper 75' to a US-manufactured Stinger missile, a weapon supplied to the Mujahedeen during the Soviet occupation. Although we knew they were out there, they were thought to be unusable due to degraded battery packs.

Kandahar/Camp Bastion
Operation Herrick
July 2007

The Tristar banged down on to the runway in the dark, and as it taxied to a halt many of the passengers ignored the pleading air steward, got up and started getting their kit together. For some there would still be a C130 flight to Bastion and a helicopter ride out to an FOB.

As I stepped out of the door on to the steps, the temperature was still in the high thirties despite it being late at night. We filled out the obligatory admin forms, most of which were the same forms we'd filled out before leaving Odiham, and headed out to collect our kit. In the car park the guys from 18 Squadron had a couple of 4-ton trucks, and we slung our baggage into one and climbed on to the other for the ride to our accommodation block.

Since I'd been there in February, 12 Mechanised Brigade had replaced the marines of 3 Commando Brigade, and the British had constructed a camp known as 'Cambridge Lines' at Kandahar. It was to one of the accommodation blocks within the new camp that 18 Squadron took us, their own guys having moved out that day into temporary accommodation. We'd already decided to bunk by crew, so together with Cuthy, Pete and Galvo I found a room and we dumped our stuff. The room was large enough for two bunk beds, with some lockers and a large table and chairs in the centre. Clean bedding lay on each of the bunks, and we quickly made our beds, undressed and climbed in.

The following morning, we had breakfast in the new dining facility across the road, then headed up to operations for a briefing by the outgoing 18 Squadron crews. Most of the talking was done by Major Mark Hammond, a Royal Marine on exchange, who was, as ever, blunt and accurate in describing the picture across the area of operations.

In March, B Flight from 27 Squadron had supported the US Marine Corp in Operation Silver, pushing through the Sangin area, moving the Taliban out and finally providing some respite for the garrison there. Although a high threat remained in the Sangin Valley, the operation had cleared out many of the Taliban, and B1 bombers had levelled Wombat Wood.

The poppy season had ended some weeks earlier, and enemy activity had slowly risen over previous weeks as sickles were exchanged for AK47s. Added to this, the US were going ahead with a drug-eradication programme, running bulldozers through poppy fields or spraying defoliants from helicopters. This was a dangerous strategy; many of the poppy farmers grew opium because it was the only crop they could sell to feed their families, and destroying it would only turn them to the Taliban. Moreover, dispersing defoliants from helicopters made all of us legitimate targets. It was going to be an interesting few months.

After Mark Hammond had finished, the commander of the Joint Helicopter Force updated us on the latest strategy, known as 'ink spot'. The UK would capture ground and build small patrol bases which, like ink spots, would slowly join up to provide a secure environment. It sounded fine, but I did wonder how it would be accomplished with the relatively small force deployed to Helmand. Then I remembered that wasn't my job and focused back on moving shit from A to B.

We had a couple of hours free after the briefings, so we went shopping at the US forces exchange, where we picked up a coffee machine for the room and some essentials.

Cuthy and I left Pete and Galvo the next morning and headed off to complete our TQ. With Mark Hammond onboard, along with a QHI from 18 Squadron, we departed Kandahar and headed initially to Bastion, before heading into a *wadi* nearby to practise some dust landings. We'd got the technique down pat on Salisbury Plain, but it was great to get back in the saddle with a dense dust cloud engulfing the aircraft each time.

During the afternoon we carried out some tasking across Helmand and I saw the 'ink spot' strategy in action; small forts had sprung up across the province, most notably around Sangin, where they would keep much of the Taliban activity outside the District Centre. It seemed strange landing at Sangin in broad daylight and without a major eruption of fire from either the Taliban or the Apaches. By evening we were back at Kandahar and joined Pete and Galvo for dinner.

The following day, we would have an early start at 5.00 am, and there was a discussion over who should wake up early to put the coffee machine on. Cuthy argued that as captain it shouldn't be him, and I argued it should be someone not yet combat-ready. That left Galvo and Pete, and with his almost twenty years in the Air Force, Galvo made the decision for poor Pete. It was all good-natured, and we never really expected Pete to set his alarm that early; but we hadn't reckoned on the co-pilot from heaven, and the next morning we all woke to the smell of freshly brewed coffee and a smiling Pete.

We were very lucky in our crew. Cuthy was a great captain; a laid-back guy from the North-East, he had a good set of hands, a great sense of humour and always remained calm. Pete was fairly new; a pale, fair-haired guy, he was well spoken, if a little awkward socially, and would eventually become known as 'C3PO', which fitted him to a T. Although new to the Chinook, Galvo had been around the block a few times on the Nimrod fleet and fitted in perfectly, despite his weird predilection for early 90s dance classics.

We would be heading up to Bastion that day to relieve the 18 Squadron guys on 'HRF', a standby duty to carry out short-notice tasking for the battlegroup, such as urgent ammo re-supplies. Also travelling to Bastion were the 'Eurotrash' crew. One of our pilots, Alex Duncan, was of mixed French and Scottish parentage and known imaginatively as 'Frenchie'. His fellow pilot was actually from Essex, but with blond hair and square jaw he looked rather Teutonic and had been known for some time as 'German'. Only JP would have the twisted humour to crew Frenchie and German together and refer to them as 'Eurotrash', after the 1980s cult TV show.

Eurotrash would take over the Incident Response Team aircraft, call sign Tricky 73, which contained a full surgical team and was on permanent standby for casualty evacuations. We would share the tent and hold HRF standby whilst Cuthy and I got Pete, Galvo and Trigger through their TQ. A few days later, we would relieve Eurotrash on IRT, and so we'd eventually cycle through back to Kandahar for daily tasking.

We hitched a lift on the tasking aircraft, which was positioning to Bastion for the day, and as we arrived at Bastion and shut down, the 18 Squadron guys drove out to meet us and make sure we got to the tent. We'd hand over with them during the day, and they would depart on the tasking aircraft that evening to Kandahar and then take the Tristar back to the UK.

Eurotrash moved into one side of the tent, and we into the other. The tent was unchanged, apart from the addition of a deck area outside built of wooden pallets topped with plastic matting. It was a great facility, but every now and again a chair leg would break through the plastic between the slats in the pallets and the unwary occupant would be unexpectedly pitched backwards.

Pete and Galvo got the coffee machine going as Cuthy, Frenchie, German and I got an update from the 18 Squadron guys. They were averaging one or two IRT shouts a day, but HRF was generally quiet. We arranged a time in the early afternoon for the handover and, with a fresh coffee in hand, I showed Pete, Galvo and Trigger around the camp so they could get their bearings.

At 2.00 pm we took our weapons and equipment out to the aircraft along with the outgoing crews and took over the aircraft. The 18 Squadron guys removed their kit, and we placed ours, each crew position prepared for a quick start-up. With that complete, the outgoing crews handed over the radio and headed off to wait for the tasking aircraft.

I took Galvo and Trigger through the aircraft fit and talked them through the sequence of events if we were called out. Our helmets sat on our seats, and in late afternoon the squippers would go out and fit our NVG for the night.

We drove back to the tent and parked the Land Rover, walking the last few yards across the dusty road to operations. I explained the bird table and briefing process to the guys. For HRF it was quite straightforward, but on an IRT shout the captain would go directly to operations for the brief, with the No. 2 crewman driving the co-pilot and No. 1 crewman out to start the aircraft, returning to collect the captain. By the time the captain and No. 2 crewman arrived, the APU would be running and the rotors ready to turn.

The 18 Squadron guys had been true to their word, and our time on HRF had passed without much activity, but it allowed us to do some training with Pete, Galvo and Trigger. Within a few days I was happy with the performance as we rolled on to IRT.

We had handed over and spent the morning drinking coffee and exchanging banter, and it was early afternoon when we heard the two rings on the field telephone that signalled a shout. Cuthy ran over to operations as I drove Pete, Galvo and Trigger out to the aircraft, before returning to pick up Cuthy. As I pulled up, he ran out and climbed in and we sped out to the aircraft.

Pete and Galvo had already got the start underway as Cuthy and I ran up the ramp. Trigger was in the front cabin door jotting down the details as I pulled on the Mark 60 jacket and strapped my pistol to my leg before pulling on my helmet. Within minutes the MERT team had joined us and we were lifting to the hover and transitioning east towards Gereshk, with the Apache sat on our right-hand side.

Gereshk was only ten minutes flying from Bastion, and as we'd stayed low-level all the way we headed straight in from the west, Cuthy flaring as we crossed the blast wall and coming to a hover over the pad.

As we landed, Galvo had the ramp down, and the MERT paramedic ran off to speak with the medics on the ground, returning with the first of several stretchers. Somehow an Afghan Army soldier and a civilian had been involved in a blast. We picked up three stretchers, the third case having serious head trauma.

The MERT seemed very worried about the third guy, and as Trigger and Galvo worked with Cuthy, I had spare capacity. The army nurse, Liz, pointed to the front stretcher, a civilian Afghan male in his forties, and asked if I'd check him over.

As I crouched over him, I felt the aircraft lurch into the hover. The guy was conscious and breathing and although he wasn't screaming he was clearly in a lot of pain. He had no obvious injury, and as I checked him over I couldn't find any bleeding. I ran my hands over him trying to find any bleeding or deformation and when I got to his pelvis he cried out in pain. I lifted his robe and saw that his pelvis was deformed and heavily bruised.

'Broken pelvis,' I mouthed at Liz, who nodded and tossed me a morphine injector, before turning her attention back to the second stretcher.

'OK, I guess it's up to me,' I thought, as I placed the injector against his thigh and pressed it home.

As he relaxed and went 'night', I scrawled a letter 'M' and the time on his forehead.

'Tower, Tricky 73 inbound from the east, for Nightingale,' Cuthy called.

'Tricky 73, clear direct Nightingale,' replied the controller, holding all the other aircraft clear of our route.

By now we were approaching Bastion then screaming across the camp, with Cuthy positioning the aircraft over the Nightingale landing site. A line of ambulances stood at the edge of the pad, along with a fire engine, and as we landed and Galvo dropped the ramp, the firefighters helped the MERT transfer the stretchers to the waiting ambulances.

With a quick refuel, we positioned back to the parking bay and shut down. The guys had done well, and apart from a few minor points we'd have a very positive debrief back at the tent over coffee. Later that afternoon, we'd be back out with the MERT for a CASEVAC from Kajaki.

The following day followed in a similar fashion, hours of boredom punctuated by short periods of intense activity, and we were ready to hand over to another crew and head back to Kandahar for a day off before picking up the daily tasking lines. By now I had seen enough of Trigger to satisfy me that he was fine to operate with Craig, one of the trainers, and he left our crew. I remained with Galvo and continued working on each new aspect as it arose.

Returning to Kandahar, even after a few days up country, was a bit of a culture shock. We went from the front-line where people were dying, to a huge base where some had too little to worry about. We also had a constant battle with the 'hat police'.

Our accommodation was about ten yards from the dining facility, and we would walk the short distance for meals, often forgetting the standing order about wearing hats within Cambridge Lines. To halt any such egregious decline in standards, someone had formed a group of junior NCOs to picket the area outside the dining facility and take the names of those not wearing a hat. Thus the 'hat police', our arch nemesis, entered the war.

Remembering to wear a hat was no great burden, but this was symptomatic of a mindset in which petty rules burned resources and energy which should have been directed towards supporting the guys living and dying in very harsh conditions in the FOBs. It was a contradiction I struggled with every time I deployed and found a new raft of rules designed to normalize a situation that shouldn't be normalized. I was not the only one who struggled with the constant transition from life and death to the trivial.

Chapter 9

Send Fat Cow, Over

A few days later, we were back up at Bastion on HRF. It had been a fairly quiet day, but in the early evening Cuthy was called over to operations. To be honest, we were so busy watching a DVD that it was an hour or so before I noticed he still wasn't back and wandered across the road to see what was up. As I walked in and saw a Special Forces signaller sat at a radio I knew something was up.

It appeared that 7 Squadron had flown in a Special Forces team to a location an hour or so north of Bastion, and as they dropped the guys, a heavy firefight had kicked off. One of them had been hit, and the Chinooks had remained on the target supporting the team with the aircraft miniguns and making the decision to drop below fuel minima. When they'd recovered the team and come off target they didn't have the fuel to make it to Bastion and so had landed in the desert 40 minutes away.

'They're requesting Fat Cow,' the signaller relayed.

'What's a Fat Cow?' asked the operations officer, without really knowing who to address his question to.

'It's a Forward Air Refuelling Kit that we fit to the Chinook so it can land, run out hoses and refuel other aircraft,' I answered, as he fixed his gaze on me.

'Ah, OK. So how long will it take to fit it?'

'Quite a fucking while. It's in Kandahar.'

'Oh. Don't we have one here?'

'Not usually. We would have positioned one here if we'd known we might need it,' I retorted with some frustration; this discussion was not solving the problem.

The Sergeant from TSW now piped up:

'We've got a pump and filters rigged in a trailer. We could take it out with a fuel bladder and refuel them in the desert.'

That would work, I thought to myself, but putting an underslung load into the open desert at night wasn't the easiest of propositions.

'We have it set up as we did with the Merlins in Iraq,' he added.

We could empty the trailer into a net and undersling it in as two loads. Putting a tandem load into the desert would, however, place a lot of pressure on Galvo, who had only just completed his TQ earlier that day.

'It's not Iraq where they are,' I said, 'and I don't want to be putting a tandem load into a dustbowl on NVG. It's bad enough putting in one load. We'll undersling the fuel bladder on the centre hook, and load the trailer internally.'

With a plan agreed, Galvo and I left operations to prepare the aircraft. We lifted the seats to make space for the trailer and set up the internal cargo winch so that, once it turned on, we could winch it onboard and get going, conscious that the 7 Squadron crews were sat in a desert after a pretty eventful evening. After 40 minutes there was still no sign of a trailer or any other activity.

'I'm going to see what's happening,' I called to Galvo as I climbed into the Land Rover. I drove around to the area JHSU used for rigging loads and saw an empty trailer and a JCB forklift positioning a pump on a cargo net laid out on the ground.

'What are you doing?' I asked the nearest hooker. 'We are taking the trailer internally.'

'Yep, that's what we thought, but he insisted we put it in a net,' he replied motioning at the TSW guy.

'OK,' I muttered as I walked over to the guy.

'What's going on? I thought we agreed we'd take the trailer internally?' I asked, frustrated.

'This is how we did it in Iraq ...'

'We're not in fucking Iraq,' I shouted. 'We've been dicking around for 40 minutes, with guys sat in a desert, and now there isn't time to switch it back. Now I have to position a tandem load into a dust cloud on NVG, you fucking muppet.'

Furious, I climbed back into the Land Rover and drove back to the spot, stopping to pick up Cuthy and C3PO on the way. When I told Cuthy what had happened, he looked as pissed-off as I did.

'Did he mention Iraq?' he asked, and we all laughed, releasing some steam.

We started up and lifted to the hover, Cuthy positioning us back from the load.

'Load will be the net direct to the front hook, and the fuel bladder on a 3-metre strop to the centre hook. We're well within C of G,' I briefed.

'Forward 10, height is good,' and Cuthy eased the aircraft forward.

'8,' cut in Galvo as he became visual with the load from the hatch.

'6, 5, 4, 3, 2, 1, steady.'

'Down 5, 4, 3, 2, 1. Height is good, working with the front load.'

'Front load attached, up gently and left, up gently, taking the strain on the front load.'

From the front door I saw the net clear the ground and the hooker run to the next load.

'Front load clear of the ground. Up gently and back for the centre load.'

'Working with the centre load, centre load attached, continue up gently and back,' Galvo instructed calmly, with Cuthy following through on the controls.

'Centre load clear of the ground. Two good loads,' he said finally.

'Pulling 85 per cent in the hover,' C3PO added.

A second underslung load added complexity, but the key issue was that in the dust cloud Galvo would be completely blind on the front load at the drop-off. We needed to descend so we didn't drop it from 6ft and wreck the pump, but we had to check the descent before we hit the load and damaged the aircraft. At night, working on the limited view from NVG and in heavy re-circulating dust, it would be a tough call for Galvo.

We headed out with our Apache escort, climbing to medium level as we tracked north-west. It was approaching midnight and we'd been up since 7.00 am and had already flown twice that day, but the transit was fairly quiet. With Galvo monitoring the load, Cuthy and I scanned the desert for the 7 Squadron aircraft as we set up an orbit at the grid we'd been given.

'Low 2 o'clock, middle distance,' I called as I saw the distinct shape of one Chinook, then a second, appear as dark green shadows against the lighter desert.

'Seen. I'll set up from the south and approach to put us parallel with the furthest aircraft,' Cuthy briefed.

'You going to be OK?' I asked.

I heard Cuthy exhale.

'Yeah, should be OK, but I'll be doing it on the hover meter, mate.'

Using the hover meter meant Cuthy prolonging our time in a heavy dust cloud near the ground as Galvo delivered the two loads. It was a difficult task and he would be heads in the cabin, scanning instruments and trying to keep us in a set of cross hairs on the instrument panel. This was the kind of additional workload at a critical phase of flight I'd hoped to avoid by taking the trailer internally.

As Cuthy approached the hover a dust cloud of epic proportions engulfed the aircraft, and there were several uncomfortable seconds before Galvo called that the loads were gone. Needing no second invitation, Cuthy pulled power and we accelerated out of the cloud.

It took two orbits of the site before the dust had dissipated enough for us to make an approach, but without the loads hanging from the aircraft, we could make a standard dust landing approach, which was far easier than coming to a hover.

We landed, and as the dust cloud settled, I saw the other Chinooks out to our left, with the pumps and fuel bladders between us. Galvo dropped the ramp, and the two TSW guys ran off to set up the pumps.

'Mick, notice anything odd about the loads?' asked Galvo with a smile.

I strained my eyes through the NVG, and it took several seconds before I noticed. The loads had swapped position, and the fuel bladder was now at the front.

'I reckon the fuel bladder must have hit the ground and bounced over the net,' he said.

Considering a full bladder weighs two tons, this showed what we were dealing with in the dust cloud.

We were going to be there for some time, so I told Cuthy I was going off the back and stepped off the ramp and walked towards two figures standing fifty or so yards back from the aircraft. Still using my NVG to see, I walked up to them unheard under the noise of the downwash.

'All right, fellas?' I called, making them jump.

As they turned, I saw it was two of the crewmen from the nearest aircraft.

'Heard you needed some fuel', I said.

They laughed as we shook hands, but they were pretty quiet, and I could tell they'd had a long night, one which was far from over.

By the time I walked back on to the aircraft, the TSW guys had set up the pump and the fuel bladder was slowly deflating as its contents transferred to the aircraft fuel system. As they disconnected, the guys on the ground gave them a hand to carry the heavy pumps up the ramp and into the cabin. As we finished loading, the two 7 Squadron aircraft lifted into the hover and departed.

'Let's fuck off,' said Cuthy, aware that our defensive perimeter was now at 500ft and heading south.

The only thing left was the fuel bladder. Weighing a couple of hundred pounds even when empty, there was no way we'd be able to recover it with the two TSW guys. I asked them what they wanted to do, and they just shrugged.

'Deny it,' said Cuthy, keen not to leave behind anything that could be useful to the Taliban.

And so, as we lifted and departed, Cuthy did a lazy orbit of the landing site and I put a hundred rounds from the minigun through the bladder.

'I think we'll call that your night TQ,' I called to Galvo as we sped back towards Bastion. Considering I'd only signed him up for day TQ that afternoon, his performance this evening had been spot-on.

Two days later, we were tasked with delivering five pallets of razor wire to a new FOB that was being set up in the desert near Ghorak. Galvo and I loaded the pallets on the roller system, with help from the JHSU team, and secured them as best as we could without cutting ourselves.

We landed in one of the heaviest dust clouds I'd ever experienced and, even as Galvo dropped the ramp and we started pushing the pallets, the cabin remained full of re-circulating dust. Wearing a scarf and ski goggles over our flying helmets, we pushed the pallets out, but dust still made it into our eyes, and literally everything on the pallets was designed to cut and tear skin. It was a relief for both of us when the last pallet rolled off the ramp; I looked at Galvo, and he seemed as happy with his lot as I did that morning.

'How's it going back there?' asked Cuthy.

'I've had better mornings,' I replied

'Almost spilt my coffee on some of those ruts,' he joked.

By now, several troops had walked on and taken seats, which Galvo had hastily folded down. The cabin was still full of dust.

'Clear above and behind.'

Cuthy lifted, we departed and the day continued. We'd do several more runs into Ghorak that day, but fortunately there was no more razor wire.

* * *

As July drew to a close we were back at Bastion, pre-positioning for a deliberate operation. The battlegroup had identified a forward operating base, and we would be flying several waves of an air assault as part of a larger operation led by ground forces to clear an area of the Upper Sangin Valley between Hyderabad and Mirmandab. Operation Hammer would begin under the cover of darkness, early on 24 July. Operating as a pair, we would fly in troops to assault a village and link up with a ground party that was moving in from the south.

The insertion was fairly straightforward, and we managed to get the troops in, returning to Bastion to load up with a second wave. As we dropped in the second wave there was some sporadic tracer fire, but it was fairly inaccurate and seemed to be just 'spray and pray' from a small number of Taliban diehards.

By now the Apache fleet had been burning through airframe hours at quite a rate, and efforts were being made to conserve hours to balance deep maintenance. This meant that we were operating with Dutch Apaches, call signs Stab 41 and 42.

As we departed the landing zone, we informed Stab 41/42 that we would be returning in thirty minutes with an underslung load.

'For sure, no problem,' replied the lead Dutch pilot.

At Bastion, the JHSS team hooked up a netted load of ammo, water and fuel, and we departed as a pair back towards the Op Hammer area. As we entered the AO, I called the Apaches on the radio.

'Stab 41, this is Splinter 21 entering the area from the south. Estimate landing site in figures 5,' I called, as Galvo started preparing for the load drop-off in the cabin.

'Splinter 21, this is Stab 41,' came the reply. 'We see Taliban north of your landing site armed with RPG. They seem to be waiting for your next drop-off.'

There was a collective pause, as each of us absorbed both that an RPG gunner was waiting for us in the darkness, and that the Dutch Apache seemed to be a spectator rather than a participant. The silence was broken by a further message.

'Splinter 21, this is Stab 41. We are RTB Tarin Kowt now. Bye.'

The Apache, having pointed out the imminent enemy threat at our destination, was now heading home for the night. Nice work if you can get it.

'Hello Zero, confirm you copied the last from Stab 41?' I enquired.

There was a long pause; it seemed operations at Bastion were as surprised as us by Stab 41/42's unscheduled departure. Eventually, I recognized the voice of the Force 2i/c.

'Roger that. Bring the load back to Bastion. I guess you're done for the night.'

Cuthy banked the aircraft to the right in a lazy turn towards Bastion and we headed back, trailing the ammo, water, and fuel below us. Hopefully, the troops on the ground would be OK with getting it later in the morning.

* * *

One morning we were sitting in the sun drinking coffee and chatting about life in general, when we heard the two rings on the field telephone in the tent that signalled a shout. Tricky 73 was required to evacuate two Afghan civilians from the area to the east of Gereshk, and with Cuthy, Pete and Galvo we were quickly airborne, the MERT preparing equipment in the cabin.

'What's the status of the casualties?' I asked, as the MERT often had a bit more detail above and beyond what was on the nine-liner, the formal request for casualty evacuation.

'Not much detail, Mick. We believe one has burns,' the paramedic replied.

Time was of the essence, and Cuthy kept the speed up at 150 knots as we remained low-level, with the Apache behind and slightly above us. Both the MERT and IRT aircraft normally collected injured troops, but we picked up quite a few Afghan civilians, and it wasn't unknown for us to evacuate and treat Taliban fighters.

We approached a flat area next to a compound at the grid operations had provided, Cuthy bleeding off speed as we approached and landing in a thick cloud of dust. As the cloud dissipated, Galvo dropped the ramp and the MERT got off, with the force protection guys keeping a careful eye on the small crowd that had gathered.

Two stretchers appeared and were placed on the cabin floor as the MERT sprang into action. With the force protection back on board, the ramp lifted and Cuthy pulled power as we raced back to Bastion, heading for Nightingale, the hospital landing site.

'Hello Zero, this is Zulu One Alpha, inbound Nightingale figures five with two casualties. Request two ambulances on arrival,' I transmitted to Bastion operations.

'Zulu One Alpha, all copied,' the signaller responded.

'All copied, Zulu One Alpha. Out.'

In the cabin the MERT were working hard, kneeling between the two stretchers, monitoring equipment and doing their thing. The casualties were a father and daughter who had been injured when a propane cylinder used for cooking had caught fire and exploded in the small adobe building they called home. A fragment of the cylinder had sliced through the father's throat, and the MERT were now fighting to maintain his airway and stem the blood loss. The daughter had received quite severe and very painful burns from the explosion, and the team were battling to treat her. Over the noise of the speeding aircraft I could make out occasional screams.

'How's it going back there?' asked Pete.

'The MERT are working on them. Keep the speed on,' I replied.

'150 knots. I'll see if I can knock the speed up a few knots,' said Cuthy, and the vibration increased in the cabin as we approached maximum speed of 160 knots.

We flashed over the perimeter fence and straight-lined across the top of the camp at 150 knots, Cuthy flaring hard as he turned towards Nightingale, where a fire tender and two ambulances sat waiting for us.

Cuthy positioned us over the metalled landing pad, with ramp towards the ambulances, and descended slowly, landing on remarkably gently, given the speed we'd been doing just seconds earlier. As the ramp went down, the firefighters came on and helped carry the stretchers to the ambulances. The paramedic went with them to the hospital.

Our job done, we lifted and returned to the parking area, where the engineers were waiting to refuel the aircraft and check it over. They'd obviously been alerted to our imminent arrival when Cuthy blasted over the camp a few minutes earlier.

We shut down and drove back to the IRT tent, Cuthy and Pete asking questions about the casualties; to be honest, neither Galvo nor I had many answers other than they didn't look to be in a good way. That afternoon, the MERT came up to the IRT tent for coffee, and we learned that the daughter was in a lot of pain but would survive, albeit with significant scarring. The father had died shortly arriving at the hospital.

I felt quite sad and remember thinking it might have been kinder if they had both died that day; in the chaos that was Helmand Province in 2007, the outlook for a scarred teenage girl with no father to provide for or protect her wasn't exceptionally good.

Chapter 10

Black Cats Aren't Always Lucky

Camp Bastion
Helmand Province
Operation Herrick
May 2008

The spring of 2008 was unnervingly quiet in Helmand Province; there had been some intense fighting during the winter, when the Taliban traditionally took a break and regrouped, but as the snow melted and the rivers flowed, their focus was on the upcoming poppy harvest.

Laid out across the fertile plains irrigated by the Helmand River was a blanket of red opium poppies. A stunningly beautiful sight, the smell was pungent at low level and clawed at our nostrils as we skimmed overhead, the farmers looking up from their scythes with obvious hostility.

The RIP or 'Relief in Place' had recently finished, with a battlegroup from 16 Air Assault Brigade replacing 52 Infantry Brigade. The paratroopers of the 2nd and 3rd Battalion, the Parachute Regiment were back in Helmand and they weren't there to watch an agricultural display.

3 Para quickly identified a target they wanted to clear in an area known as the Panjwai, to the west of Kandahar. The district of Maywand wasn't completely unknown to the British Army; in 1880 a British and Indian force was routed by an Afghan army led by Ayub Khan in a rare defeat for the British Empire.

Maywand lay within the Panjwai and, more importantly, on Route 1, the circular road that connected most of Afghanistan and was a major supply route for NATO forces. In recent months, travelling through the area had become a hazardous pastime due to roadside bombs, but 3 Para were targeting the bomb-makers and keen to clear the Taliban out of the area and make it safe for both military and civilian traffic.

The insertion would be by air assault, with Chinooks dropping 3 Para just short of their objectives, while Apache gunships provided close air support, particularly during the critical approach phase when, heavily loaded with troops, the helicopters would be magnets for Taliban AK47 fire and RPGs.

With a plan in place, we spent a few hours running through drills with the guys of 3 Para. Loaded up with their kit for assaulting Maywand, we repeatedly practised getting forty troops at a time on and off the aircraft, each time a little quicker. This level of detail and their repetitive drills set the Paras apart from other units; they realize that whilst it may be laborious and a bit 'noddy', those couple of seconds shaved off the disembarkation can mean the difference between life and death on the battlefield.

Once the troops had left, we went over the aircraft checking equipment and weapons for the mission the following morning. We would hit Maywand at dawn, which meant a 'dark o'clock' departure from Kandahar.

With the aircraft prepared and our kit in place, we headed off to grab dinner at the DFAC and get some sleep ahead of the 3.00 am alarm call. Whilst an air assault into Taliban territory might seem an ominous task to some, it is perhaps testament to the training that crews undergo that we were too busy with checklists, drills and preparations to really think too deeply about what we were doing. Despite the risks we would face, 3.00 am was 3.00 am, and sleep would come easily, as it so often did in Afghanistan.

The next morning, we carried out the final checks on the aircraft and crewed in, just in time for 3 Para to emerge from the gloom of the early morning and dump their kit at the back of the aircraft. The silence of the night was punctured first by auxiliary power units whining into life, then by engines and finally by the beat of rotor blades.

With everything up and running, the paratroopers traipsed up the ramp and took their places on the aircraft, filling up from the front. The lucky ones got seats, while those at the back sat on the floor cradling ladders, dogs, mortars and heavy weapons, their alert faces smeared in cam cream and resigned to an uncomfortable morning.

One after the other, we taxied out to the main runway, until all three Chinooks sat turning and burning, flanked by two Apaches making up the complete package.

'Ultimate, Tower,' came over the radio.

'Tower.'
'Ultimate, request departure runway 23.'
'Ultimate, clear take-off runway 23.'
'Ultimate.'

As the clearance was issued, the six aircraft lifted to the hover and, one by one, their noses dipped and they accelerated to the west.

The green glow of Kandahar disappeared under the NVG as the base gave way to open desert. At 50ft the Chinooks sped towards the Panjwai, the Apaches sitting higher up so they could spot targets. In all, the transit was probably 15 to 20 minutes, and dawn was breaking as we reached the IP; lifting the goggles and adjusting to the first light was a challenging moment to be running into the chaos of an air assault.

As we passed the IP we ran through the pre-landing checks and closed up on the other two aircraft as we identified the landing zone on the horizon, a smudge of shadow under the rising sun. As we got closer we could make out revetments carved into the landing area, with deep channels filled with some form of vines.

'Going for the area next to the target,' called the lead, nominating a more suitable flat area immediately next to a group of adobe buildings.

There was a cloud of dust as we settled on the ground, the miniguns from each aircraft trained on the compound as the Apaches watched from above through their infra-red gun cameras. In the cabin the ramps were down and the paratroopers were off, running forwards and taking up assault positions.

Ahead of us, the dust swirled as the lead aircraft lifted. As the ramp came up, we too lifted, as did the third aircraft. With a lot of radio chatter as the Paras began their assault, all three aircraft emerged from the dust cloud and headed back towards Kandahar. Despite the unsuitability of the landing site, we had adapted and overcome, and the troops were in as planned.

With the first company on the ground in Maywand, the race was now on to get the remaining two companies in to join them. As we arrived back at Kandahar we stopped at the FARP and took on some fuel before repositioning and picking up the next chalk of troops.

The sun was well up by the time we passed the IP for the second time, and again I gripped the minigun tightly as we headed in; the Taliban would be awake and alert this time. Purple smoke suddenly rose from an area that the troops had identified as an alternate LZ. There was some sporadic and ineffective fire from the Taliban as we approached, but we got in safely, and the company disembarked to link up with the others.

Again we took some fuel at Kandahar and picked up the remaining company before retracing our route back to the LZ, where purple smoke billowed up again to mark the spot. With the third and final company on the ground and in the fight, we headed back to Kandahar; it was 7.00 am and time for breakfast.

* * *

With a fresh influx of pilots from the training system, JP decided to shuffle some of the crew pairings in early May, mainly to give some of the more junior pilots some captaincy experience in theatre, and I found myself bidding farewell to Frenchie and Lurch and moving my kit over to join Piggy and FLURP.

A few days later, Frenchie's crew, call sign Black Cat 22, was on routine tasking picking up the Governor of Helmand Province, Gulab Mangal, from Musa Qala, when they were hit by an RPG as they crossed a ridgeline on the way out of the besieged town. Fortunately, due to the short range at which it was launched, the warhead didn't have time to arm, but the unexploded projectile passed through the aft pylon, tearing through the thin aluminum and missing the vertical synchronized transmission shaft by inches, before passing out through the other side and smashing a couple of feet off the end of one of the rear rotor blades.

With heavy vibration from the damaged blade shaking the aircraft, and with multiple systems inoperative, Frenchie managed to steer Black Cat 22 away from the Taliban and towards the safety of FOB Edinburgh, where he made an emergency landing and shut the aircraft down safely, much to the relief of everyone onboard. There is no doubt that his quick thinking and skilled flying saved everyone that day, including Governor Mangal, and he would subsequently be awarded the Distinguished Flying Cross for his actions.

It was not lost on any of the crew or engineers that if the Taliban shooter had pulled the trigger a split second earlier, there would have been a very different result. The poppy harvest was over and the fighting season had commenced.

As close a call as the attack on Black Cat 22 was, Frenchie and the crew lived to fight another day, but the incident reminded us all how real the threat was. Drills became slicker, routes varied, flight profiles became unpredictable and time on the ground was minimized.

As the poppies disappeared into baskets and headed for the drug labs, spring came to an end and temperatures rose. Silently, many of us had wondered how the aircraft would fare after a direct hit from an RPG, and now we wondered no more. It would bloody hurt, and we wouldn't be as lucky next time.

A few days later, we were called out on IRT to an area near Lashkar Gah. A firefight had broken out in an irrigated field near the Helmand River, a network of flooded paddy fields, and several civilians had taken cover and been pinned down by Taliban fire. One of them had been a young Afghan woman, and her baby had fallen into the water during the chaos. The child, about six months old, had been face down in the water for almost forty minutes when we arrived.

As soon as we were on the ground, the ramp dropped and the paramedic was off the back to assess the child. As he made his way back onboard holding the baby I shot him a look, and he shook his head. The baby had a faint pulse but was otherwise unresponsive, and as soon as they were onboard we lifted and departed for Bastion at low level and high speed, racing towards the hospital and aware of the small life hanging in the balance.

We racked the aircraft around the turn off the main runway at Bastion and set up the approach to the hospital landing site at Nightingale. The ambulance was waiting, and as soon as we touched down, the paramedic was off and into the ambulance with the child. Hoping for the best but fearing the worst, we repositioned the aircraft and shut down.

The incident was not discussed for the rest of the day, and as we watched TV or read, nobody dared mention the baby in case the result was as we all feared; to delay the inevitable, we just ignored it. After a sleepless night for all, we headed for breakfast to the DFAC, where we bumped into the paramedic.

'Hey, mate, how's it going?' I asked.

'Yeah, all good, mate,' he responded as he sliced some toast.

'What was the score with the baby?' I enquired, aware that the rest of the crew had gathered next to me to hear his response.

'Shit, mate, you wouldn't believe it. We released the kid back to his mother this morning. Not a single thing wrong with him.'

Collectively, we all exhaled with relief.

'But all that time face down in the water?' asked Piggy.

'Right as rain. Seems like the thing about drunks and little kids is true.'

With a little more spring in our step, we grabbed some breakfast and headed back to the tent to await the next shout.

* * *

A week or so later, we were called to a meeting at operations at Kandahar; there was an operation brewing in Kandahar Province, down towards the border with Pakistan. As we entered we saw a ragtag bunch of heavily tattooed muscle with beards, clearly Special Forces operators.

'Gents, these gentlemen are from TF49 and require your assistance,' said the operations officer. 'I'll leave you guys to it,' he added as he walked off.

'Hi, I'm JP, this is Morris, Hannah and Mick. What can we do for you?' asked JP, leaning forward to shake hands.

'I am Dan. We are from GROM, or TF49, and this is a colleague from the Lithuanian Special Forces,' the Polish leader of the group said, motioning to a figure behind him who raised his hand as Dan opened a map on the bird table.

'We need to clear a village in the Bolan valley, currently a centre for Taliban activity and a staging post for fighters coming over the border,' he began, in flawless English.

'We'll be deploying in squadron strength, 120 men. We need a direct air assault on to the valley floor at dawn, and sniper teams putting in on overwatch across these areas of high ground.'

He pointed out several features on the map.

'When?' asked JP

'Two days from now; dawn insertion and an extraction late afternoon,' Dan explained. 'We asked both the US and 7 Squadron for assistance, but they are all tied up with other operations. We hoped you could help?'

'Three aircraft, forty troops per cab. We'll need Apache escorts,' stated JP.

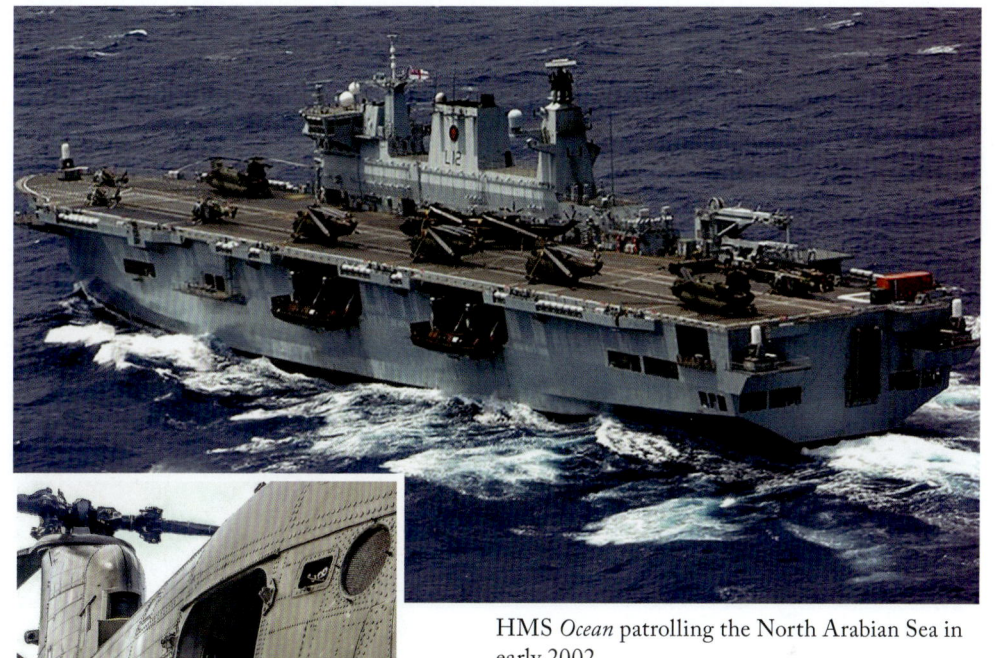

HMS *Ocean* patrolling the North Arabian Sea in early 2002.

Capable of firing 4,000 rounds per minute, the M134 minigun was our primary form of defence.

Night Vision Goggles (NVG) provided a night capability, but the additional weight was hard on the neck. (*MoD*)

Setting up amongst the rubble and abandoned Russian hardware at Bagram, 2002.

The spectacular scenery at Bagram, April 2002.

Offloading aid in Nahrin following the earthquake in 2002.

A Chinook departs from the Landing Site at Basra Palace, 2003.

Our initial home at Basra Airport, the abandoned Airport Administration Building, 2003.

The Black Watch version of remodelling on the ground floor of the Administration Building, 2003.

The new tented camp we moved into in the late summer of 2003.

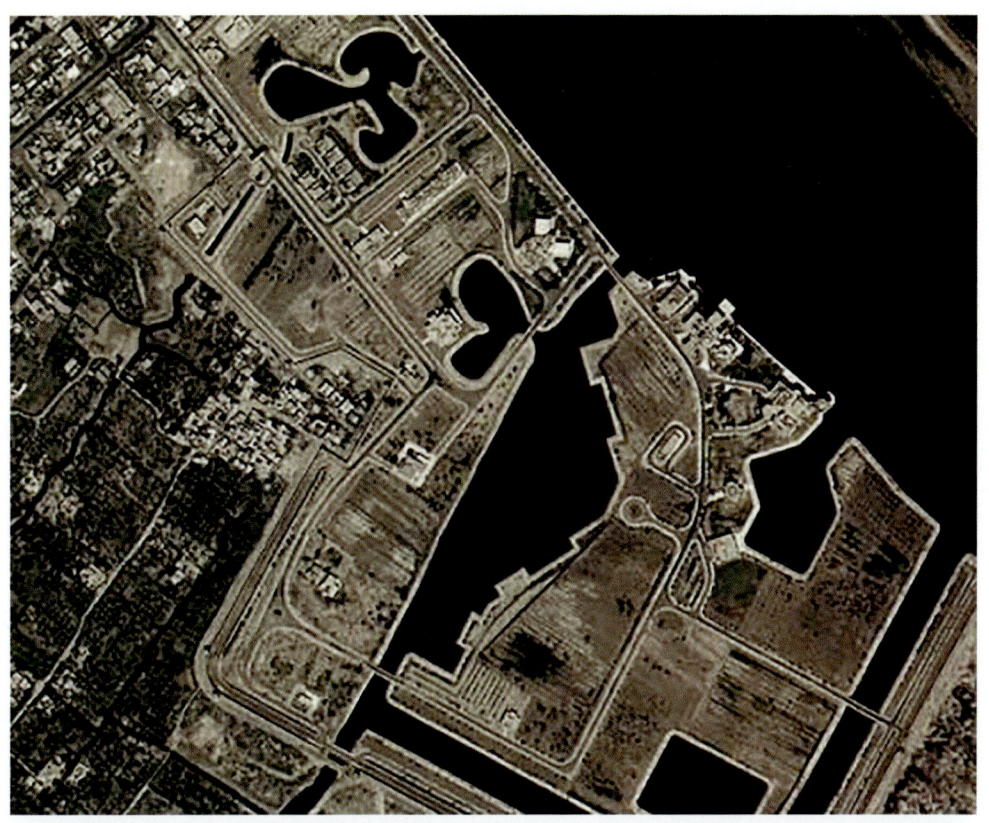

Satellite image of Basra Palace, Saddam Hussein's retreat on the Shatt al-Arab waterway. (*CNN*)

Quick Reaction Force troops board a Chinook on the Landing Site at Al Amarah, 2003.

The sun sets over the Helmand River, with Lashkar Gar bottom left.

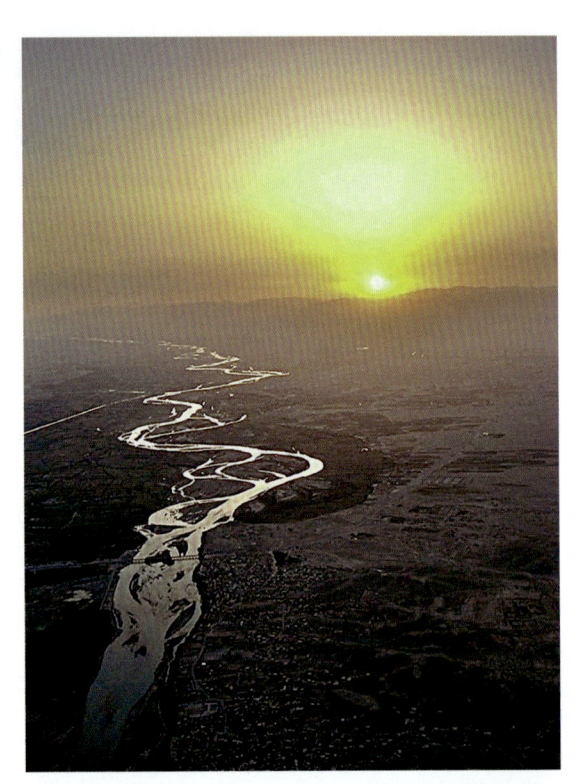

Taxiing along the helicopter flight line at Kandahar as Ultimate 21 taxis in.

The IRT tent was such a home from home we renamed it Odiham High Street.

Army Air Corps WAH-64 Apache, our constant companion in Helmand.

Cabin layout for the IRT aircraft. Note the ballistic matting and yellow medical waste bags.

A sight familiar to all Chinook crews: a casualty is loaded for extraction to the hospital at Bastion. (*Di Lauro*)

Crossing the Helmand River and Green Zone.

A Chinook flares as it approaches the Landing Site at Lashkar Gar.

Loading HICHS pallets prior to a re-supply drop, 2007.

Crew photo a week or so prior to the shootdown of Blackcat 22. The author is centre, Flight Lieutenant Alex Duncan DFC, AFC is at far right.

Despatching pallets using the HICHS system at a Forward Operating Base.

Blackcat 22 with damage from the RPG visible on the rotor blade, 2008.

Apache guntape footage of the GROM insertion into the Bolan Valley, 2008. (*MoD*)

Troops of 3 Para look on as a Chinook approaches to re-supply them during sweep operations, 2008. (*Wroth*)

Splinter 21 and 22 passing overhead 3 Para Mortar Troop, 2008. (*Wroth*)

The IRT tent door with artwork from 1310 flight crews. The door was saved for posterity by the RAF Museum.

The workhorse of Helmand, leaking several types of fluid and covered in fine dust, 2007. (*Author*)

Offloading at Kajaki Dam Landing Site.

JHSU hookers ready to hook up a slingload as the crewman marshals the aircraft into position.

JHSU helping us pick up a load destined for 3 Para, 2008.

Troops await pick-up in a field of opium poppies. (*MoD*)

A four-ship Air Assault package departs Bastion. (*MoD*)

Troops arriving by Chinook in Nad Ali, 2010. (*MoD*)

At Buckingham Palace with Frenchie to collect his Air Force Cross, 2012. (*Duncan*)

Flight Lieutenant Roly Roberts, tragically killed in Kabul, 2015.

'Not an issue, already approved,' the operations officer confirmed, as he re-entered with two Royal Navy pilots. 'You will also have two Sea Kings.'

'How many troops can you carry?' Dan asked the Navy pilots.

'Not many, to be honest, not at that elevation and this time of year,' one replied.

'OK. Can you pick up detainees if we have any?'

The pilots looked at each other for a second. 'Yes. Will they have escorts?'

'Of course. Two escorts per detainee. How many can you take?' asked Dan.

'Um, one.'

Dan raised a quizzical eyebrow as he turned towards his 2i/c, but it wasn't the Navy's fault. The Sea King just didn't have the power to operate in a hot and high environment during the summer months.

'OK, so you remain at Kandahar on call, in case we have detainees,' said Dan dismissively.

Over the next hour we put together the bare bones of the insertion and extraction, but as the GROM guys left, Morris's brow was furrowed to a degree I hadn't seen since we planned the weights to leave the carrier in 2002.

'The insertion's OK, but we don't have the payload for the extraction. We're about a ton short,' he said, as he ran a ruler across a performance graph, double-checking his figures.

In the cooler air of dawn we would just about have the performance to carry the forty troops and a quad bike, but as the sun rose and temperatures climbed, we would be overweight. Although Bolan to Kandahar was a short hop, we couldn't split the runs, as that would leave a small remainder of troops exposed for between forty and sixty minutes.

We ran through the figures, racking our brains about how to find the extra performance, and it was fifteen minutes before the penny dropped.

'I've got it!' I exclaimed, and Morris lifted his gaze from the performance graphs.

'The ballistic protection weighs 1.5 tons. If we are going to take rounds it's going to be on the way in, and we know we have the power then anyway. But for the extraction, the GROM guys should have the area secure. How about we remove the ballistic fit whilst we are on the ground between the insert and extraction?'

'That would work ...' began Morris, then added, 'But it's a risk, and we'd need to get the crews to buy in.'

A short while later, Morris closed the data manual and we went to meet JP for a coffee and update him on the planning. We'd be getting together with the GROM guys and the Apache and Sea King crews for a more in-depth brief the following morning.

JP recognized the problem straight away and agreed that removing the ballistic fit was probably the only option. The Ruffler, who had joined us, also agreed, and we assembled the crews that evening and talked them through the plan. To be fair, the operation was a break from the usual routine, and none of the pilots or aircrew had any issues with it at all.

As we headed to dinner, JP went off to speak to the Helicopter Force Commander to outline the risks and seek approval for the plan, which was granted. We were good to go.

The following morning, we assembled for a briefing, with JP and Dan running through the insertion and extraction phases, and the Apache guys asking questions and taking notes. We would be vulnerable during the insertion and would rely on their sensors to identify threats on the ground.

We would load up at 4.30 am the next morning and, with the Apaches riding shotgun as usual, a package of three Chinooks would fly low-level to the valley and air-assault the village, all three aircraft landing just short of the settlement. Thirty-two of the troops and a quad bike would disembark from each aircraft and begin the assault. With the Apaches in overwatch, we'd then drop off the sniper teams on the craggy peaks that towered several hundred feet above the valley. None of the peaks was suitable for landing; we'd be positioning the back wheels on the rocks whilst the snipers climbed off the ramp and took up fire positions.

With the insertion complete, we'd return to Kandahar and refuel, before shutting down as the engineers removed the heavy Kevlar matting to reduce our weight. Then, in late afternoon, we'd return to collect the guys and take them back to Kandahar.

Morris was still worried about the weights; we'd used a planning figure, and the GROM guys didn't look like they travelled light. The crewmen and I would be running them through some safety drills that afternoon, and Ruffler suggested we get some scales and weigh each of the troops.

Dan and his 2i/c, whom we'd nicknamed General Zod for his resemblance to the villain in an early Superman film, remained behind after the brief, and the Ruffler and I went over to explain our concerns.

'It's important the guys are carrying everything they will have tomorrow,' said the Ruffler.

'OK, they carry everything,' replied Dan.

'Everything,' confirmed General Zod, smiling.

'Jesus, these guys are going to be a nightmare,' I said to the Ruffler as we walked down to meet them on the flight line that afternoon.

'Hmmm,' he replied.

A crowd of bearded troops, weighed down by equipment and with dogs, ladders and all manner of other kit, loitered at the back of a parked Chinook. To one side were two of the biggest quad bikes I'd ever seen, as well as a trio of previously unmentioned motorbikes.

'Fuck me,' said Craig, surveying the mountain of kit. 'Morris will have a fucking heart attack.'

We separated the mass of troops into their three groups, and I motioned the first forty Poles on to the aircraft, where they sat either on the fold-down seats or along the cabin floor. Dogs sat on laps and ladders were stowed under seats, but they were on, and the ramp was free for the quad.

It was clear that many of the troops didn't speak much English, so I ran them through a safety brief mainly by pointing at stuff. I only knew one word in Polish, and I added '*dobra*' (good) at the end of each section.

'*Dobra*,' they would all reply in unison.

Whenever there was any confusion, Dan would translate into Polish, and we muddled through the drills somehow.

'*Dobra*,' I said, giving two thumbs-up to signal the briefing was complete.

'Fucking *dobra*,' they all said, smiling and sticking up two thumbs.

I liked these guys already!

As they made their way off the ramp, Craig directed them to the guys who had a set of scales and would weigh each troop.

I repeated the brief with the second bunch of Poles, and got the same 'Fucking *dobra*' as I finished. The Lithuanians were a different breed;

quieter, they showed little response or emotion but sat in silence as I ran through the brief, their commander nodding from time to time.

'Right, where did the motorbikes come from? Nobody told us about them when we did the planning,' I asked.

Shrugs all round, but there were fewer of them than the Poles, and somehow we made it work with the motorbikes stacked upright near the ramp. There was no *'Dobra'* or thumbs-up; they just filed off quietly to get weighed.

'How did it go with the Lithuanians?' the Ruffler asked as I walked over to the weighing scales.

'Bit quiet to be honest. If there is a problem in the morning, it'll be them,' I offered.

Slowly but surely the 120 troops moved through the scales and were weighed, Craig making a note of the weights. Once each group was weighed, they moved off towards the hangar and their waiting vehicles.

'How's it going?' the Ruffler asked Craig as he tallied up the weights.

Craig pulled a face, and double-checked the figures.

'Heavy. We should be OK, but the issue is the quads. They are fucking monsters and weigh half a ton.'

'Hmm,' we replied in unison.

Tomorrow would be an interesting day.

The following morning was an early start, and we updated the brief and gathered at 3.30 am, checking over the aircraft as three chalks walked out and gathered at the ramp.

'Fucking *dobra*!' they cheered when they saw me.

'Fucking *dobra*,' I replied. 'Now get your arses on board!'

I laughed as they filed up the ramp and crammed into the cabin. With some help, we reversed the quad up the ramp and, once in position, secured it with a ratchet strop. The cabin was full, and I felt for the guys carrying the Lithuanians and the motorbikes; they would be packed to the gunwales.

Morris clicked on the intercom, and we ran through the start. We would be the second of the three aircraft, with JP as lead. With the rotors turning, we sat on the parking slot as we pumped the waypoints into the GPS, confirming each point. In the front cabin door I checked over the minigun, ensuring the test light illuminated to confirm power to the system.

'All good,' I told Morris.

'GMASS going safe,' he replied.

We'd power up the system as we cleared Kandahar.

We saw JP pull forward out of the parking slot, and as he passed ahead of us, Morris slipped off the brakes and we taxied out behind him, the third aircraft following on as we turned on to the runway and took up a position behind the Apaches and JP. The two Apaches lifted to the hover, with JP lifting behind them.

'Clear above and behind,' I called, as Morris pulled in power and we got airborne. Behind us, the third aircraft got airborne too; the package was ready, and the Bolan valley was about to receive a visit. In the cabin the Poles sat quietly checking their equipment.

One by one, each aircraft dropped its nose and transitioned forward, accelerating down the runway as the package departed the airfield and settled at a height of 150ft in the last of the darkness. We armed up and settled in en route for the first turning point.

As dawn broke we lifted our NVG and dropped down to 50ft, running in fast. We reached the IP, and the Apaches climbed up rapidly to get a better view of the valley, sweeping ahead with their FLIR.

'Two minutes,' advised Morris.

I shook the nearest of the Poles and held up two fingers. He was instantly alert, then the message was passed down the cabin and the game faces appeared, each of the troops checking weapons and mentally running through drills.

We ran in fast as first light crept across the valley. With the village ahead we continued behind JP holding 140 knots. By now the Taliban would have heard the rotors, and the village would be scrambling out of their adobe compounds to see what the noise was. We slid to the left of JP as the village appeared ahead of us.

'Clear forward and down,' I said, sweeping the area with the minigun.

'Down 40, 30, dust cloud building, 20, ramp, 10, centre, 8, 6, door, 5, 4, cockpit, 3, 2, 1,' I pattered as we were enveloped by a dust cloud.

'Wheels on.'

'Clear ramp,' confirmed Morris.

By now Gammo had dropped the ramp and released the strop securing the quad bike, which roared off the ramp, followed by the main assault force; only the sniper teams remained onboard. To our right the Poles were clearing JP's ramp, and behind us the Lithuanians were roaring towards the village on their motorbikes as their assault party followed, making their way towards their objective.

Ahead, JP was already pulling power and lifting.

'Clear above and behind.'

Morris pulled power and we lurched into the sky, with a cloud erupting around the last aircraft as it too pulled in the power. With the Apaches high overhead, the three Chinooks climbed away from the valley floor, each setting up for an approach to the jagged peaks.

As Morris positioned the aircraft's rear over a narrow ridge, Gammo talked on the back wheels and dropped the ramp for the remaining sniper teams.

Leaning out of the front door, I was monitoring clearance under the aircraft, well aware that although the back wheels were on terra firma, below me was a drop of 600–700ft down to the valley floor; not a great position to be in if you suffer from vertigo.

Then I noticed a figure on the valley floor below us lifting a tube on to his shoulder. We were horribly exposed, with the sniper team half on and half off the ramp.

'Shit, RPG!' I thought as I felt for the intercom.

Suddenly the figure on the valley floor jerked back and fell to the ground. I looked around to see where the shot had come from and saw General Zod with his sniper rifle coming out of the aim. Cradling the weapon, he gave me the thumbs-up.

'Fucking *dobra*!' I thought.

With the sniper team in position, we lifted off the ridge and dropped sharply into the valley, picking up speed before accelerating to join JP. Behind us the last aircraft had dropped off their sniper team and lifted to join on. Back in formation, JP dropped the height and notched up the speed as we raced back towards Kandahar at 50ft.

'Did you see …?' Gammo started.

'Yep,' I replied, cutting him off as he sat down the back chuckling to himself.

'These GROM guys are awesome dudes,' he continued.

Morris in the cockpit guided us back to Kandahar, completely unaware of how close he'd come to getting an RPG up his trouser leg. So far so good; we'd got GROM on the ground safely, but now it was up to us to get them back later in the day.

We landed back at Kandahar behind JP, all three aircraft taxiing into their parking spots and shutting down. Behind the parking slots the engineers waited with vehicles, and as the APU wound down they were onboard and lifting seats to remove the ballistic fit. As they removed a panel, we would replace the seats ready for the extraction, and within an hour each set of Kevlar matting was neatly stacked on a flatbed. Now on standby for the day, we found some coffee and gathered on the aircraft to chat; everyone was buzzing after the insertion, coffee and adrenalin countering the early start as the day wore on.

We saw the Sea Kings depart and head south-east; the GROM guys had obviously found some persons of interest and had called them in to recover detainees. In mid-afternoon we got an update from operations: we would be required back on target at 3.00 pm for the extraction. We had agreed that there was too much risk in sitting on the ground as we reversed the quads on to each ramp. Our aircraft would take all the vehicles onboard, and the sniper teams who had made their way down to the valley to join the assault team.

We started up and departed Kandahar, JP again leading the formation down in the weeds at 50ft and high speed to the IP. We tracked in and landed in the same point as in the morning, and as Gammo dropped the ramp, the two quads and the motorcycles sped up it and braked hard into position in the cabin. The guys filed up and filled up the remaining space, as the last troops fell back to the third aircraft in a collapsing box.

With all of them onboard, we lifted and departed back to Kandahar to a chorus of 'Fucking *dobra*' from the cabin. We'd put the GROM guys in and bought them all back, and as the shadows lengthened in the late afternoon, we flew back in silence. We were tired, but it had been a successful operation, and as a flight we'd adapted and performed well.

Back at Kandahar, there were plenty of handshakes and 'fucking *dobra*' as the GROM guys gathered their kit and headed off. As they vacated the aircraft, the engineers were already pulling up to replace the Kevlar. The war machine rolled on.

A few days later, we would be watching Sky News when the operation hit the headlines, and to our delight the UK was treated to FLIR images from the Apache of the aircraft positioned on the ridgeline with its back wheels on, as shadowy figures climbed off the ramp.

A week or so later, we joined the GROM guys for a BBQ at their compound and experienced Polish hospitality at first hand, catching up with General Zod and thanking him for his intervention as we sat on the ridge. For several weeks it was not uncommon to hear a loud 'fucking *dobra*' as we walked into the dining facility.

Chapter 11

Boom, Boom, Shake the Room

Kandahar
Operation Herrick
November 2008

The relief in place had taken place the previous month, a battlegroup led by 42 Commando Royal Marines replacing 16 Air Assault Brigade. I arrived back in Kandahar late at night, after a long day of military waiting time and an eight-hour flight. I was with Justin, an instructor who was just returning from Shawbury to the Chinook and needed to familiarize himself with Afghanistan.

We stretched our legs as we walked from the Tristar to the makeshift air terminal, and we spotted the guys from B Flight almost immediately.

'All right, fellas?' I said, shaking hands.

'All right, Mick. As soon as you've snotted through the admin and got your shit, we'll run you over to the accommodation.'

After several next-of-kin forms and the 'identify the identical bags by torchlight' routine, we had our gear together. As Justin watched the bags, I reclaimed the weapon bundle and threw it in the back of a battered Land Rover, followed by our bags and finally ourselves.

Having dropped the weapons off at the armoury, the guys drove us to the accommodation at Cambridge Lines, where we did the normal late-night arrival thing of dropping bags, undressing in the dark and sliding into bed.

The following morning, I was up early and found Justin already dressed and busy unpacking his bags.

'Breakfast?' I enquired.

He nodded, and I motioned towards the door and guided him out into the bright morning light.

'You'll need a hat, mate,' I informed him. 'Apparently it's really important.'

We crossed the road and entered the DFAC, washing our hands as we did so. Inside, the room was busy with men and women in different uniforms but all sucking down coffee like their life depended on it. Justin joined me at a table, setting down a plate of bacon and eggs, and a bread roll.

'Wow, this is way better than I expected,' he said as he slid into a plastic chair.

I nodded. 'But don't get too excited, Bastion is more in line with your expectations.'

We settled into some serious bacon eradication and slurped coffee for ten minutes as we chatted through the forthcoming day. Justin would be in for Helmand 101 today, so I walked him through the lie of the land, which was unique to say the least.

As we walked up to the Joint Helicopter Force (Afghanistan) headquarters I indicated points of interest and local landmarks such as the boardwalk, a large wooden recreation area encircled by fast food places and local shops selling carpets and other stuff. Eventually, we crunched across gravel and entered a series of pre-fabricated buildings.

I led Justin down a corridor to a locker room, where we dumped our go kits and other equipment. For the uninitiated, a go kit is the bag containing whatever you're taking on the run after a forced landing. Its contents are mainly a matter of personal choice, and they vary according to environment and terrain. In Helmand I'd gone heavy on ammo and water. Lighting a fire and boiling up a curry were going to be a long way down my to-do list, behind running like fuck and shooting backwards over my shoulder.

Next up were the safety equipment fitters, the 'squippers'. We dropped off our flying helmets and they fitted us with LCJs, or load-carrying jerkins. These vests contain Kevlar plates and have a number of pouches for radios and survival equipment, the mandatory items that you carried alongside your go kit. The LCJs were fairly new and only issued in Afghanistan, so it took a while for the squippers to talk Justin through the fitting and contents.

Once Justin was kitted out, I took him down to flight planning. As we entered, Nutty, one of the B Flight pilots, came over to say hello. Within a few minutes the intelligence officer had joined us and gave us a quick rundown on enemy activity, upcoming operations and where aircraft were taking the most fire. I was surprised to learn that the area around Lashkar Gah had become quite volatile.

As the IntO left us, I talked through individual patrol bases and forward operating bases on the map, explaining why each one was important and pointing out any features or procedures that were worthy of note. Finally, we read through and signed for the theatre orders.

'All good?' I asked, once Justin had finished.

'Yeah, all good. Actually, it's a lot like Northern Ireland,' he replied, forcing a smile as I recalled the 'South Armagh with teeth' simile from a few years earlier.

'Hmm, this place can go from 0 to 60 pretty fucking quick, mate,' I told him. 'Whilst it's not dissimilar to Ireland, you need to expect the unexpected.'

We left ops to go to lunch, and Justin brought up Northern Ireland a lot in conversation, which worried me a little. If he was drawing a parallel between Belfast and Helmand he was going to experience a steep learning curve.

We took the rest of the day to settle in and for Justin to find his feet, whilst I mainly drank coffee and caught up with the B Flight guys. Most of them were up at Bastion, with just a small number back in Kandahar. We would be flying the next day on tasking, so Justin would get to see much of the AO as we went about the day's work.

We had a fairly reasonable start the next day, up at 6.00 am for an 8.00 am departure from Kandahar across the red desert and into Bastion, where we would shut down and brief for the day's tasking along with the Apache crews. As we crossed the desert I pointed out features to Justin, starting with the Panjwai and Maywand. As we entered Helmand at 4,000ft I pointed out the green zone snaking through the brown desert, and the Helmand River shimmering amid the vegetation. It is an incredibly beautiful sight, however deadly the reality may be.

At Bastion we briefed and had an hour or so spare before we lifted for the first task, so I showed Justin around as much as I could, although we'd be heading up there in a few days anyway. With the other crew we started up and did several hours' tasking, re-supplying various FOBs and changing over troops: fresh-faced boys going in, tired, dusty men coming back.

By late afternoon we were heading back over the red desert to Kandahar, landing in the last of the sunshine as the chill of evening began to set in. It had been the quietest tasking day I had ever had in Afghanistan; the tasking had run to plan, the weather was good and the Taliban had seemingly taken the day off.

As we walked back in from the aircraft carrying our go kits and weapons, Justin started on again about the similarities between Helmand and Armagh. I sighed and handed my rifle and sidearm back to the armourer as Justin returned the aircraft tool kit to the engineering line.

Suddenly I heard the familiar whistling of a rocket, and it sounded close in. I hit the deck and rolled sideways into a storm drain as an ear-splitting explosion rocked the nearby hangar. As I looked up I saw Justin appear from the hangar at a great rate of knots with a mental look on his face. In my storm drain I laughed as I motioned him over, and he jumped in next to me.

Rockets normally come in pairs, and after a few seconds it seemed like we might just be getting one that day, so I grabbed Justin and we ran the twenty metres to a concrete shelter.

'You OK?' I asked as we joined a huddled group of figures in the shelter.

'I think so,' he sighed, before adding, 'I haven't been mortared since I was in Northern Ireland.'

'Technically speaking that was a Chinese-made 107mm rocket, so you still haven't been mortared since Northern Ireland,' said Griz, one of the crewmen who had come across from the Army.

After a while we heard the 'all clear' and headed for dinner. As we walked, Griz caught my eye and winked; I wasn't the only one who had picked up on the constant Northern Ireland comparisons.

* * *

A few days later, we were planning an operation with the Commandos; they wanted to clear a section of the Panjwai near Maywand, and as I looked at the imagery of the landing site I felt a sense of déjà vu.

'Has anyone taken a good look at the LS?' I asked.

'Only from the imagery,' came the reply.

I explained about the operation we'd conducted with 16 Air Assault Brigade earlier in the year, and the ops staff took notes as I explained about the revetments and how we'd had to land on the target compound.

'Can you get a recce aircraft over the top?' I asked.

'I'll go and enquire,' replied the ops officer as he walked off.

The following day, an RAF Harrier GR9 passed over the Panjwai clicking away with a high-powered camera as it went. Lo and behold, deep shadows were found on the proposed landing site, very similar in pattern to those we'd seen earlier in the year. A suitable landing site was identified nearby, but this incident illustrated how the rotational nature of operations in Afghanistan meant that critical lessons often had to be re-learned several times.

Justin and I took part in the air assault, which was very similar in execution to 16 Air Assault Brigade's earlier operation, and with comparable results. Bomb factories were found and 'repurposed', and the guys from 42 Commando made a significant find in the form of an extremely ugly Chinese motorized bike packed with explosives and with a trigger mechanism hanging from the handlebars.

With a sense of relief we extracted 42 Commando and flew them back to Kandahar at the end of the operation, dark rings of fatigue visible around the eyes of the guys as they fell asleep on the short transit.

The following evening, we were night-tasking in Helmand and crossing the green zone north of Lashkar Gah, when the sky lit up with what looked like a stream of bright green cannonballs. Under the NVG we could see that this was triple A fire, the Taliban shooting at the noise of our rotors. Fortunately, the sound of a Chinook is deceptive and the flak was well clear of us, but it was unnerving to know they had access to weapons of that size and to have seen its effect so clearly under NVG.

When we landed at Bastion we reported the triple A, and the intelligence officer whisked us to one side to take detailed notes and plot the general area on a map. It confirmed information he had received through reporting and other sources.

Whilst Lashkar Gah was pretty much as ever, the nearby districts in the green zone were becoming more and more hazardous, none more so than Nad e Ali.

In late 2008 the Royal Marines had set up 'Patrol Base Argyll' in the district of Nad e Ali, deep in the green zone and 12km west of Lashkar Gah. It was surrounded by Taliban and constantly under attack; during our time there it had come close to being overrun several times, and flights in were classed as a deliberate operation, with two Apaches as top cover.

We had been into PB Argyll several times, and these trips weren't for the faint-hearted. There were limited routes in, and Taliban positions would ping you with ground fire on the way in and out, including from the village of Shinkalay, which seemed to be some kind of AK47 testing site. It was what is commonly referred to as 'a shithole'.

It would be on a trip into PB Argyll in the early hours of a December morning that I would encounter the bravest person I think I'll ever meet.

Scheduled for a 2.00 am re-supply into Nad e Ali, Justin and I had prepared the aircraft and headed to dinner at the Bastion DFAC, when this strange-looking guy appeared at our table.

'Evening, Padre,' I nodded, noticing his rank and the cross.

'Evening, guys. Would you be heading into Nad e Ali tonight? he enquired.

I looked at him. 'Possibly. What can we do for you?'

'I need dropping off at PB Argyll,' he replied as he slid into a seat and joined us for dinner.

'I'm Padre Tudor,' he added, shaking hands with both of us.

Justin and I exchanged glances; just how mental do you have to be to volunteer for a stay at Argyll?

'Well, if you're crazy enough to go to Nad e Ali, Padre, we can drop you off,' I informed him.

He sighed with relief. 'Thank you.'

'We've lost a few of our flock there this week, and I want to support the guys,' he explained.

I had heard there had been a few KIA in Nad e Ali that week, and now it all fell into place. I am sure that whether they were religious or not the inmates of PB Argyll would be glad of any support.

'OK,' I told him. 'You'll need to be at JHF(A) operations at 11.30 pm, Padre.'

He nodded, got up and disappeared into the throng of camouflaged diners, as Justin and I continued with our dinner. Very little surprised us by that point, and being accosted by a Padre with a death wish during dinner was all in a day's work.

We headed back to the IRT tent to watch DVDs for a few hours and get the caffeine levels to a suitable level for the evening outing to the green zone. At 11.00 pm or so we grabbed our gear and walked over to operations. The Padre was already there clutching a small rucksack, and that's when it hit me; we weren't just dropping him off in Nad e Ali alone and in the middle of the night, but also completely unarmed.

We got him a brew and drove him out to the aircraft, flicking on the battery and bathing the cabin in blue light. Inside the aircraft on the roller floor were five pallets of ammunition and water for the besieged fort, each restrained with a cutaway for quick removal. I would be up the front, and Justin would be down the back.

'You're up the front with me, Padre,' I called, and motioned to him from the side of the pallets.

He squeezed down with his rucksack in hand, and I pointed to a couple of seats that hadn't been folded up to accommodate freight. Whilst we waited for the pilots to do pilot stuff, I ran the Padre through a safety brief and showed him where various bits of equipment were. Eventually, I explained what was going to happen when we got to PB Argyll.

'Padre, the landing site is outside the wire,' I began. 'We'll land and taxi forward as Justin releases the restraint. It will be dark, so put your hand on this pallet, and when I tap you on the shoulder start walking and follow the pallet towards the ramp and off the aircraft. When you're off, you get down next to the pallet and do not move. We'll lift, and the guys will come and get you. OK?'

'OK, yes, thank you,' he said, but I could see in his eyes that he was summoning up every atom of courage he possessed, and I didn't blame him.

The pilots had joined us, and we were now slipping into our LCJs and slapping magazines on to weapons as Padre Tudor sat quietly in his seat.

'Sorry, Mick,' he said. 'Can we just run through it again?'

'Sure, Padre,' I smiled, and ran through the plan again.

Then, just as the pilots were about to climb into the cockpit, he stood up and said, 'Gents, I am so grateful for you taking me with you tonight, and I want to give you this.'

He handed me a thin metal disc.

'I only have the one, but it's a combat cross, and I want you guys to have the Lord watching over you in your work.'

We all felt completely humbled; here was a man overcoming fear and about to do a very courageous thing to provide comfort to his men, yet his first thoughts were for our safety.

'Thanks, Padre, but I think you should have it this evening. Your need might be greater than ours,' I joked, relieving the tension. We all laughed, the Padre included.

We started up and sat on the spot waiting for the two Apaches to call that they were ready, before moving out on to the HALS. Under the NVG I saw the gunships taxi out and pause behind us, just as the radio call came through that they were ready.

'Clear above and behind,' I called.

'Lifting.'

The aircraft lifted into the hover, where it settled, before the nose dropped and we accelerated forward as a three-ship package. It would be a short ride to Argyll, which was only 25km away, and as we headed low across the dark desert we ran through checks before we hit Taliban country. As we approached the vegetation of the green zone, the Apaches went high and lit up their sensors to pick out the bad guys.

We passed roughly 1km or so south of Shinkalay, and right on schedule an Apache informed us we were taking fire from the edge of the village. I gripped the minigun as we flashed across trees, paddy fields and dirt tracks, until we were visual with the district centre and a wisp of smoke.

We flared, bleeding off speed, and approached to bang the back wheels into the dirt, lowering the nose and gently taxiing forward. In the cabin, Justin was furiously slashing the cutaways with a J knife and rolling each pallet off the ramp. As they settled on the ground, I motioned to the Padre and put his hand on the pallet.

'Good luck, Padre. I hope we meet again,' I shouted, and he nodded nervously.

Justin and I gave the pallet a push and it started trundling slowly down the cabin with Padre Tudor following it. Eventually, it tipped off the ramp and landed on the dirt in a small cloud of dust. In the darkness, the Padre of 3 Commando Brigade stepped down off the aircraft and crouched next to the pallet, exactly as we had briefed him.

As we raised the ramp and lifted to the hover, transitioning into forward flight almost immediately, I glanced back at the figure huddled next to a pallet of ammunition, in the dark, alone and completely unarmed in probably the shittiest part of Afghanistan. This was an act of exceptional courage, but I didn't have to long to dwell on it as we were now providing a second viewing for the Shinkalay chapter of the AK47 appreciation society.

It was with some relief that we emerged from the green zone at 150 knots over the relative safety of the open desert, closing the short distance between ourselves and Camp Bastion. Behind us, the Apaches had stayed on station, providing support to the troops on the ground.

'I tell you what, I reckon I'll sleep well tonight,' I said over the intercom.

Three 'Ayes' told me I wasn't alone.

By now, B Flight's tour was coming to an end, and as was the convention, any visitors from other flights would be thinned out first. As the 18 Squadron guys arrived, I gave B Flight a hand with the checks to get the newcomers through quicker and our guys home sooner.

Within a few days we had handed back our kit and were on the Tristar to the UK and Christmas. That was a pretty good feeling.

Chapter 12

Groundhog Month

Camp Bastion
Afghanistan
February 2009

Having left Afghanistan at the end of December with B Flight, I was back at Brize Norton with C Flight in late January for my own deployment. Tired and bored, we sat in the air terminal drinking what passed for coffee and willing the tortuous journey to be over, when a bolt from the blue hit me.

From the troops milling around the vending machines emerged a strange-looking Padre heading straight for me. It was Tudor, whom I had last seen crouched next to a pallet in the dark.

'Mick, I thought it was you,' he announced as he bowled over and grabbed my hand, shaking it vigorously.

'Hey, Padre, good to see you,' I said, meaning every word.

He then filled me in on what had happened. The troops had apparently got to him very quickly after we left and escorted him safely to the Patrol Base, while others gathered up every ounce of much needed ammunition and water. It seems the guys at PB Argyll had been through the wringer, and I have no doubt that a fruitcake Padre arriving will have lifted their spirits.

Having been back to the UK for a week on R&R, he was now heading back to Helmand to see out the remainder of his tour. After a minute or so he spotted one of his flock he needed to speak to, and with another vigorous handshake he disappeared into the camouflaged throng.

It's always easy in war to measure success in terms of rounds sent and rounds received, hoping to keep the latter at zero, but sometimes it is the intangible things that bring you the most satisfaction; and getting the padre into Nad e Ali and bumping into him months later was one of those things.

Eight or so hours later, the Tristar landed at Kandahar. Disembarking, we gathered our kit and met up with the 18 Squadron reception party, who helped load our kit into vehicles and ferried us to the accommodation.

The next morning, we were up and running through the usual arrival routine, broken by the arrival of COMJAG. Commander Joint Air Group was a tri-service appointment, and the current incumbent was the Station Commander from RAF Odiham. Ambitious and capable, the boss was a dyed-in-the-wool helicopter pilot, and it was good to have one of our own at the helm. However, although he would watch our backs and make sure we had what we needed, he set high expectations and would work us hard. It was going to be a busy few months, and we knew it.

Before long, the first crews were heading up to Bastion to start taking over from 18 Squadron and get read into the upcoming missions, of which there were many.

As we filtered up to Bastion we commenced the planning cycle for Operation Diesel, an air assault into the Sangin Valley planned for early February. The operation was intended to seize Taliban weapons caches and drug production facilities, cutting off funding for their fighting season. Four Chinooks and elements of the Commando Helicopter Force would carry in over 500 troops from 3 Commando Brigade over two waves.

In the early hours of 7 February we lifted off from Bastion and, with Apache and Lynx escorts, headed north to the Upper Sangin Valley. In the blacked-out cabin sat forty Commandos, quietly cradling weapons and getting their heads into the game.

The assault involved a large number of aircraft spread across different landing sites, so avoiding other aircraft in the dark was just as critical as avoiding the enemy. Our nominated landing site was less than ideal and involved flying up a valley until it ended in steeply rising ground. As a four-ship we'd turn 180° and descend steeply into the desert landing site, heavy and in the dark.

JP was in the lead aircraft, and before long we entered the valley. As expected, it was a bit of a challenge turning at the far end and descending, but at just after midnight all four aircraft were sitting on the desert floor as the Commandos disembarked.

With the first wave on the ground we returned to Bastion to load up, before heading back for a second time. Again, we negotiated the end of the valley and landed safely, disgorging another 160 or so troops.

With the air assault complete, we lifted and flew back to Bastion. When we taxied in and shut down, there was a rush for the limited vehicles we had, as all four crews headed off to bed. Some were flying again eight hours later.

Operation Diesel had gone far more smoothly than many expected. Over the next day or so 3 Commando Brigade would destroy £50m worth of unrefined heroin and kill twenty Taliban fighters. An unexpected gift was the discovery of a motorbike rigged with explosive that was obviously destined for some upcoming attack.

Later, 1310 Flight were heavily involved in extracting the guys from the Upper Sangin Valley, but we were not; we had rolled on to a period of IRT standby.

The year 2009 would see some particularly harrowing IRT call-outs, which took their toll on both the MERT and the crews. The transition from drinking coffee and watching TV to dealing with enemy fire, death and life-changing injuries, then back to the TV, could happen very quickly and began to have an impact on our mental health, particularly that of the rear crew.

Shortly after taking over, we were sat watching 'Oz Aerobics' one day, when the phone went and we all stopped. It was a shout, and we were soon running out to the aircraft and starting up.

We lifted and departed from Bastion, heading east at maximum speed with an Apache escort going balls-out to keep up. According to the information we had, a Danish patrol had hit a mine on Route 1 near Gereshk and they weren't in a good way. In the cabin, the MERT prepared their kit, ready to deal with whatever casualties Helmand would throw at them. As we slowed down to identify the grid we'd been given as part of the nine-liner, the Apache climbed and settled into an orbit above us, keeping a watchful eye on the area.

Finding the grid wasn't hard; a deep crater in the road surrounded the badly mangled wreck of a vehicle, with a couple of British WMIK vehicles blocking traffic and securing the site. It looked pretty grim. We set up for an approach and landed in a slight dust cloud south of the road and adjacent to the vehicle.

As the dust settled, I glanced across and saw it was actually a British vehicle; almost simultaneously, radio updates began to filter slowly through the secure comms. The patrol was British, not Danish; that made no difference to how we approached the task, but it perhaps hit us all closer to home.

Corporal Tom Gaden, Lance Corporal Paul Upton and Rifleman Jamie Gunn, all of the 1st Battalion, The Rifles, had been killed when their vehicle hit a roadside bomb.

We sat at the edge of the highway as the MERT and the Force Protection guys carried on three black body bags and placed them down the centre of the aircraft. Everyone stopped for a moment, aware that, though we'd never met, these men were brothers.

'Hello, Zero, this is Tricky 73.'

'Zero, send. Over,' came the response

'Tricky 73, returning your location figures 5 with three KIA. Request ambulances at Nightingale. Over.'

'Zero, copied. Out,' with an obvious tone of sadness.

We lifted and headed back to Bastion, the first leg of the journey home for the three young soldiers. Very little was said as we flew west, and within minutes we were on the ground at Nightingale as the medics offloaded the guys.

As we taxied into the refuel spot we all did a buddy check. There had been very little said since we had arrived on scene, and it was good just to check on how we all felt, which was universally 'a bit shit'. We shut down and walked over to ops to debrief. As we walked in, a few heads turned to look at us, which I put down to the grim task we'd just completed.

'You guys should buy lottery tickets,' said the ops officer.

We looked at him, confused; we weren't feeling exceptionally lucky, and his comment seemed highly inappropriate.

'Shit, you guys don't know, do you?' he offered, reading our faces.

'Know what?' we quizzed.

'The IED guys found a massive secondary device at the side of the road which for some reason didn't go off.'

'Which side?' I asked

'South. You guys landed right on top of it,' he added, shaking his head.

We looked at each other for a few seconds.

'Coffee?' I asked

'Coffee,' everyone responded in unison, and we headed over to the IRT tent.

As we walked we'd already begun the mental healing process and were arguing over whose turn it was to get the brews on and what DVD we were going to watch. It sounds callous, but that's the only way to deal with stuff of that intensity; otherwise you'd just curl up in a ball and stop coping altogether.

A couple of weeks later, we would be called to a similar incident, this time to the south near Garmsir, where a Jackal vehicle had detonated an explosive device. In addition to the MERT we also picked up a small extraction team of firefighters with specialist equipment.

It was late afternoon on a Sunday as we flew south towards the grid reference we'd been passed. The sun was low in the sky by the time we arrived on scene and made an approach to a flat patch of desert at the base of a gentle slope. The Jackal lay on its side near the top of the slope, and a further vehicle was parked on the high ground providing overwatch of the site.

As we landed, the firemen followed the paramedic off the ramp and up towards the stricken vehicle. We sat with the rotors turning as they did what they needed to do. After a short while one of the firemen came running back to the aircraft; they needed body bags. As I looked through the onboard medical equipment I could only locate one and I handed it over. The expression on the fireman's face told me that more than one was needed.

I went to my go kit and retrieved one of my prized possessions, an Australian Army-issue poncho, which I had held on to for years.

'Here, use this,' I said, handing it to the fireman, who took it and headed back up the hill.

As we would later learn, Corporal Dean John and Corporal Graeme Stiff had been killed instantly when their Jackal detonated an explosive device.

I sat in the door watching progress and after a few minutes saw a group approaching the aircraft carrying the first of the casualties in my old poncho. They brought him on to the aircraft and placed him on the floor next to me, before turning and heading back to the crash site.

We sat there for some time, and then I began talking to the body next to me. I told him it was OK, he was going home now – not in a weird way, but talking seemed more appropriate than sitting there trying to ignore the fact there was a dead soldier lying next to me wrapped in my poncho.

And then, as the sun sank into the desert and the team made their way back towards me with the second casualty, I had a thought which would take months to get out of my head.

It was by now early evening in Helmand, mid-afternoon on Sunday in the UK, and I had an image in my head of a family eating their Sunday dinner as someone crunched up the gravel to break the saddest of news. I instantly felt deflated and sad, and for months afterwards, even when I got home, the sight or thought of a family dinner would instantly transport me back to that patch of desert near Garmsir.

The mind is a strange thing, and having gone through some fairly fucked-up shit in Afghanistan over the years, I am always surprised at the things that do affect you and the stuff that you can manage OK; they are often not what most people would expect.

With the team back onboard, it was now dark and we lifted and headed back towards Bastion in a sombre mood. I fitted my NVG, flipping them down as I radioed ops to let them know we had two KIA onboard and to arrange ambulances to collect them from Nightingale. More coffee and DVDs would be required.

* * *

It would be early March when I reached 'peak Helmand' and experienced a day that will stay with me forever.

We had spent the morning on IRT standby, chatting with Piggy about how he felt about becoming a father when he got home, and taking the piss out of Mark, with whom I was crewed. Mark was a great guy, completely bald, and from a certain angle looked a lot like a Bond villain, the kind that should be stroking a white cat.

Boeing had sent a press team to Afghanistan to speak to crews who were operating Boeing aircraft in-theatre, and they had joined us for coffee at the IRT tent. One of the journos was interviewing me when the phone went. We all turned round, and instantly knew it was a shout as the Apache crew ran past towards ops.

Within minutes we were airborne and heading north as I punched in the grid reference from the nine-liner into the GPS. Cross-checking with the map showed an area in the green zone near Sangin. The radio was busy with chatter, the casualty had a gunshot wound to the head and it appeared there was a TIC ongoing.

Cuthy set up for the approach and we descended into a clearing surrounded by dense vegetation; as we approached I could see tracer slicing through the air around us. An RPG detonated at the far end of the clearing just as we settled into the ground. We were in the middle of some pretty intensive fighting, and it was only going to be a matter of time before we got pinged.

By now the paramedic was near the ramp as troops carried the casualty towards us. As they carried him on, the MERT set to work in the cabin. The Apache overhead had a bird's eye view, and as we often did, I asked the pilot over the secure radio which was our best escape heading on our way out.

'Pick one. You're pretty much surrounded, mate,' he replied, confirming our worst fears.

I glanced at the map. Heading west was the shortest distance over the green zone before we hit open desert, so that was the route I advised Cuthy to take. As we lifted, the fire increased; tracer criss-crossed the clearing, and several bangs, presumably RPGs, could be heard.

Cuthy pulled as much power as he dared, and we shot across the green zone and out to open desert, all of us scanning instruments and systems, convinced that something must have hit us as we fled the maelstrom of fire.

Instantly I was on the radio to confirm we would be going to Kandahar, the usual destination for head trauma. Ops confirmed, and we climbed to medium level and headed east.

We had left the Apache on target, and with the hammer down it was not long before we snotted over the fence and down the main runway at Kandahar, keeping the speed on before turning off for the hospital, where a team were waiting for the casualty.

Flaring to drop the speed, we landed on the spot and trickled forward before stopping. Mark had the ramp down, and the paramedic gave the Kandahar team a handover as the casualty was rushed to the trauma unit. With the paramedic back onboard, we lifted the ramp and headed over to refuel.

Having gassed up, we departed Kandahar and climbed to 4,000ft, heading back across the red desert to Bastion. We chatted en route, mainly about how we never wanted to see that clearing near Sangin again, and we were high over the Helmand River when we felt the aircraft rock.

'What the fuck?' said Cuthy. 'Did you feel that?'

'Yep. Stand by.'

I leaned out over the minigun, looked below the aircraft as best as I could and saw a greyish cloud dissipating a couple of hundred feet below us.

'Some kind of cloud, mate, a few hundred feet below,' I said.

'Yeah, pretty sure someone fired something at us, but we're up at 4,000ft so I'm not sure what. We'll speak to the IntO when we get back,' Cuthy replied.

The rest of the mission was unremarkable, and we landed and refuelled before repositioning and shutting down. As the APU wound down and I removed my helmet, I heard a strange siren and saw people rushing around.

'What's going on?' I asked

'No idea, but that's the mass casualty alarm,' the paramedic chimed in.

Almost immediately someone appeared and told us to start up. Next to us we saw Hannah turning the blades on the HRF aircraft.

We started the APU, and the secure radio sprang into life. In seconds, the nine-liner was coming through and I was relaying the details to Cuthy. There were an estimated twenty children and adolescents with frag and blast injuries. I began reading out the grid reference and stopped. Cuthy immediately realized what I had.

'That's the same clearing we went to earlier,' he said.

'It is,' I confirmed, as everyone on the aircraft sighed. 'Ops reckon the TIC is closed, so it shouldn't be as bad.'

'Some of the casualties have started turning up at Sangin DC, so Hannah will take the District Centre and we'll take the grid,' Cuthy added.

'Roger.'

The Apaches were ready, so we lifted and departed, racing north with Hannah tucked in behind us. As we approached the IP, Hannah continued north with the second Apache as we set up for a second approach into the clearing of doom.

As the Apache climbed, we passed over a group of people and settled into the long grass of the clearing. This time there was no tracer or RPGs. As soon as we were on the ground, the ramp was down and the paramedic was off, talking to the ground forces.

A few minutes later, an unconscious Afghan girl in her teens was deposited next to me on a stretcher, the MERT instantly beginning to work on her. I would find out later what had happened: after the explosion the local doctor had administered ketamine, but in the confusion, she had been overdosed her with 100mg instead of 10mg, and the MERT were now trying flat-out to save her.

A line of stretchers was now queuing up at the ramp, some with two or three kids on, and the next hour or so would be like a scene from Hell. In the cabin, I had no option but to face the unfolding horror in front of me, but in the cockpit there was no reason for an excited and expectant father to see what was going on.

'It's, er, a bit dusty back here. I am just going to close the curtain,' I said, drawing a heavy dust blanket across the jump seat and separating the cockpit from the cabin.

'Roger,' replied Cuthy.

By now the cabin floor was covered in Afghan children on stretchers, some bandaged and some with visible cuts and abrasions. The MERT continued to work on the overdosed teenager as Mark raised the ramp and took a seat; in his arms was a toddler.

I took a long look down the aircraft and hoped that nothing I would ever see again would be as sad or harrowing as an aircraft full of injured kids.

'Clear above and behind,' I called, and Cuthy pulled in the power and we lifted.

He dropped the nose and headed south.

'Bastion?' he enquired.

'Standby,' I replied as I flicked to radio.

'Hello Zero, this is Tricky 73. Over.'

'Zero, send.'

'Tricky 73, sixteen casualties on board. Confirm RTB Bastion. Over.'

'Zero, negative. The hospital here is full, your destination is Kandahar. Over.'

'Tricky 73, I copy Kandahar. Out.'

'Coming left,' called Cuthy as the aircraft banked and we raced for Kandahar.

In the cabin, Mark was still sat down the back holding the toddler, probably because of the lack of stretchers.

'You OK, mate?' I asked

'I've had better days, Mick, if I'm honest,' he replied

I nodded. As bad as it was up the front, Mark had borne the brunt of it, surrounded by injured kids with the force protection administering some first aid and applying bandages. The MERT were still busy with the overdosed kid next to my feet.

Cuthy got us to Kandahar as quick as he could, and as Piggy armed down, we flared and touched down outside the hospital. A team of medics began offloading the kids and taking them in, as the MERT continued to work on the girl until a crash team were on hand to take her.

As the last of the kids were taken into medical care and the paramedic came back onboard, we lifted and departed for Bastion. Other than radio calls, nobody spoke, and after 40 minutes we landed at Bastion and shut down.

When we reached the tent, the others walked inside and I sat outside and lit a cigarette. I know smoking is bad for you, but I maintain it's the reason I am still sane. After every IRT shout I would take five minutes alone to have a cigarette and run through events. I'd ask myself if there was anything I could have done better, and if the answer was no I'd file the event as closed. Maybe more people needed to smoke.

I was just finishing my cigarette when the anesthetist from the MERT sat down next to me.

'Give me one of those.'

'I didn't have you down as a smoker,' I joked

'I'm not normally. But today hasn't been exactly normal,' he said with an arched eyebrow as I handed him the pack and a lighter.

We sat in silence for a few minutes before he turned to look at me.

'How are you doing?' he asked.

'Probably the same as you,' I replied.

He nodded, said, 'Thanks for the smoke, Mick,' and walked off towards ops.

As he left, the journalist we had spoken to four hours previously emerged from the tent and walked over to where I was sitting.

'Hey, Mick, what just happened?' she asked. 'The others look like they've seen a ghost.'

'Bad day. Can we finish the interview up tomorrow?'

'Sure.'

They took the hint and walked off. We were clearly different people to the ones they had been talking to earlier.

I walked into the tent and poured a cup of coffee. Hannah's crew were already back in, sitting with Cuthy and Mark. Nobody really spoke. Then Piggy appeared next to me.

'Thanks, mate,' he said.

I was genuinely lost for a minute. 'What for?'

'The curtain. I know why you closed it, and thanks.'

I nodded. ''s OK mate. No point you seeing stuff you don't need to.'

It would take a long time to tape over that day's events. Of all the IRT call-outs I was involved in I would rate that day as the worst. I am surprised that now it actually crosses my mind very infrequently, a fact I am grateful for.

It was with some surprise that I found myself in the doctor's office at Bastion a few days later. After a busy few days flying I had woken up one morning with my legs very stiff. After a few days the stiffness remained and I found stepping up and down quite painful on the knees. Some anti-inflammatories did help a bit, but the stiffness remained for the remainder of the deployment.

* * *

About halfway through the tour we had an early morning re-supply run into Garmsir and had climbed out of our sleeping bags at 3.00 am to brief. Compared with 2006, the Garmsir area was much safer, but the FOB we'd be re-supplying was in a fairly contested area and so we were keen to make it in before too many Taliban were up and about.

The first light of dawn was just cutting across the Helmand River in silver shafts as we emerged from the desert at 150 knots and 50ft. Cuthy was weaving between compounds as we crossed the river and flared to slow down for a landing inside the compound at FOB Delhi; but as we slowed we heard the Lynx escort call that we were taking fire.

As we sat on the ground at Delhi, with the re-supply complete, we made a quick visual inspection of the aircraft and found some scoring from AK fire that had hit us. Content that nothing critical had been damaged, and that all systems were behaving themselves, we lifted and departed back to Bastion, FLURP arming up as Cuthy accelerated quickly, manoeuvring to throw the aim of any Taliban gunners.

As we crossed the river and entered empty desert, Cuthy traded speed for height and we climbed rapidly up to 4,000ft for the transit back to Bastion. We would route over the open desert a few kilometres west of the green zone, and the transit would take us roughly 30 minutes.

By this point in the deployment, fatigue was a constant companion, and 3.00 am starts didn't help. As we cruised over the desert, my mind began to wander as I sat in the doorway looking out towards the green zone.

As we passed abeam the area of Marjah there was stretch of green zone a kilometre or so in length that juts out into the desert and was known as 'the Schlong', and it was as we passed over the tip of the Schlong at 4,000ft that my mind was slowly brought back to the present by an old military adage about straight lines and patterns not occurring in nature.

About 50m to the right of the aircraft was a perfectly round grey cloud, with another further back and then another, all evenly spaced. As I watched, yet another perfectly round grey cloud appeared behind the others and I realized we were being targeted by triple A; the clouds were the ammo burning out at the limit of its range.

'Come left,' I instructed, and Cuthy banked to the left, increasing the distance between aircraft and flak.

'What's up?' asked FLURP

'We've got flak off to our right. Probably coming from the Schlong,' I replied

As I finished explaining to FLURP, I went heads into radio ops and passed on a contact report and grid for the Apaches to investigate. I couldn't see our Lynx escort. As I went heads in, the aircraft banked hard to the left.

'Flak should be a break left, Mick,' said FLURP, as I tried to right myself.

'We were beyond effective range and I didn't want anyone doing something too erratic, as I'm not sure where the Lynx is,' I replied.

'7 o'clock high,' replied Mark. 'Miles back.'

To be fair to FLURP, he was correct, although I didn't feel we were in any danger. However, when I look back now, without the fatigue and with the power of hindsight, I suspect I was just becoming a little too comfortable with people firing weapons at us.

As humans we adapt to our surroundings pretty quickly, and if the surroundings involve fast-moving shit coming past you, you get used to fast-moving shit coming past you. It goes back to the arrogance of 'it will never happen to me'. I've argued with FLURP about all sorts of things over the years, but he was probably right; it should have been a 'break left' not a 'come left', but we're all still here, so all good.

We descended across the desert and hopped over the perimeter fence at Bastion and landed, shutting down and asking the engineers to take a good look at the aircraft. There was, unsurprisingly, no damage from the flak, but there was a fair amount of scoring and a 7.62mm round in one of the blades from our run into Delhi.

Cuthy signed the aircraft back in and we headed to breakfast. Undercooked bacon and overcooked eggs were washed down with coffee as a FLURP soundtrack played in the background.

The triple A was the 23mm gun I'd seen with Justin a few months earlier. It had moved about in the green zone until settling in Marjah. However, as most aircraft avoided Marjah, they'd moved it into the Schlong to target traffic just like us. The Apaches eventually hunted it down and destroyed it. One of our female Apache pilots flew up and down to draw the Taliban's fire until they couldn't resist and opened up, at which point the other Apache zapped them.

The funniest thing about this incident was that I'd have no issues calling a break a few days later as a surface-to-air missile passed us on our way to work.

We'd crewed in early in the morning at Kandahar. We would depart as a pair and meet up with our Apache escorts overhead the Ghorak pass, after which the other aircraft would land at the small FOB at Ghorak to drop off some equipment, whilst we remained airborne. Once they were complete, we would drop into an FOB near Lashkar Gah, whilst they remained airborne, before all three aircraft headed to Bastion for breakfast and new tasking.

By this point in the deployment our Force Commander was obviously keen to get out of the office and would be coming with us. He would be doing the flying from the right-hand seat, with Cuthy as captain in the left. I'd flown with the boss before, and he was good value; a decent set of hands and very much one of the crew for the day. He would also explain stuff to us as we flew, and had much more to give than the IntO.

It was a beautiful dawn as we headed across the red desert, and we chatted quietly during the transit, with a flask of coffee making an appearance; steaming brown liquid was always guaranteed to lift morale, and we'd quite often let the aroma waft through to the cockpit until one of the pilots asked, 'Is that coffee I can smell?'

We approached the RV point and made comms with the Apache, who was still a few minutes away; this didn't worry us unduly, as Ghorak was a fairly quiet area by Helmand standards. A dusty valley just under 20 miles east of Sangi, Ghorak had played an understated yet invaluable role in the NATO efforts in Afghanistan during Operation Oqab Tsuka a year earlier, when British forces had rolled through the Ghorak pass with a new generator for the Kajaki hydroelectric plant, completely bypassing the Taliban strongholds in the Sangin valley, the expected route for the convoy.

A small FOB remained, a dusty collection of barbed wire and shipping containers that looked more like a rubbish tip than a military base, and it was into here that our playmate dropped that morning, whilst we remained airborne, flying an orbit at 4,000ft and awaiting the Apache.

As we orbited we were chatting about life when a missile streaked past the right-hand side of the aircraft at very high speed and continued high up into the sky, where we lost it.

'Break left!' I called immediately, but the boss was already ahead of me and manoeuvring away from the threat.

Once confident the threat had gone, our heart rates lowered to a mere rapid. Whatever it was had been fast and fairly close.

'Mick, did that look like a SAM to you?' asked the boss calmly, as if discussing the weather.

'Yes, Boss, it looked very much like a SAM,' I replied.

'Hmm,' he said.

I put out a contact report and follow-up, letting ops know that we'd been targeted by an unknown weapon system and passing the grid.

By now the Apache had arrived and we had two clicks on the radio signalling our playmate was lifting out of Ghorak. As they joined us at height, we headed west with the Apache riding shotgun, all of us keen to egress the area. Whatever had been fired was new to us and we didn't really like it.

Our approach into the FOB went smoothly, despite an approach across the green zone, and as we sat on the pad, Andy and I discussed the incident; we two sitting on the right-hand side were the only people to have seen it.

With the FOB re-supplied, and some troops onboard starting the trip back to the UK for R&R, we lifted and headed to Bastion in a rather uneventful transit. We landed and shut down, heading over to ops to debrief before breakfast. When I entered the ops I found the IntO hunched over a map.

'Hey, we got shot at by some sort of missile this morning near Ghorak,' I offered

'Probably an RPG,' he grunted. 'Ultimate 23?'

I nodded. 'Trust me, I know what an RPG looks like, and that wasn't it.'

'Well, possibly a GMLRS,' he suggested.

The GMLRS is a GPS-guided missile fired from a multiple rocket launch system and known as 'the 60km sniper'. However, there were no GMLRS batteries near Ghorak, and the thing is fucking huge; it would be like Saturn 5 passing you, and that wasn't what we'd seen.

'Nope, it looked like a manpad.'

I held firm, describing what we'd seen, as the IntO's brow furrowed; he just didn't want to believe there were SAMs in Helmand.

'It wasn't a SAM,' he declared firmly.

'It was definitely a SAM,' said the boss as he joined the conversation.

'You saw it as well, Sir?' asked the IntO, his tone changing.

'I did – scared the shit out of us.'

The IntO scribbled some notes as Andy and I described what had happened, but I still felt he was only making an effort because of the involvement of a Group Captain.

It wasn't just the triple A and SAMs; there were very few days when we didn't encounter some AK47 fire, or RPG if we were having an exceptional day; it was fatiguing flying long hours in challenging terrain and often under fire. However, nobody complained, because we knew the guys on the ground and in the FOBs had a far worse time on tour.

As the US Marines slowly moved into Helmand during 2009, relieving the British troops at some of the FOBs, they made the fundamental mistake of withdrawing from many of the patrol bases and concentrating around the FOBs. This reduced the visibility of enemy activity around the actual FOB, meaning more IEDs were planted and patrols incurred many more casualties when they eventually ventured out.

Before long, the number of amputees we were picking up on shouts started to rise, and as the tour stretched out these began to include double and triple amputations. It was only a matter of time before this affected the mental health of the MERT and aircrew, and ultimately it did. Called out to Gereshk, we picked up Afghan National Army casualties from a negligent discharge in a trench of an RPG. Yes, you read that correctly. One of the casualties had already died when we got there, and a couple more were carried on, one of whom had significant injuries and was obviously a priority, given that most of the MERT were knelt over him in the darkness of the cabin.

Looking through the dark green picture of NVGs, we lifted and departed for the 10-minute transit back to Bastion, with Piggy at the controls. A few minutes in and we were at 150ft as an arc of tracer crossed the nose, narrowly missing the cockpit.

'Contact right two o'clock. Next to compound,' called Piggy.

I scanned forward and right with the minigun and saw a figure crouched next to the compound from where the tracer fire had emanated, as a second burst came towards the aircraft.

'Target seen, target sighted,' I called.

'Open fire,' instructed Piggy.

I flicked up the guard on the minigun and pressed send; fire erupted from the barrels as six electrically driven rotating barrels started spewing rounds at the mind-bending rate of 66 per second. I saw the ground erupting around the gunner as I looked under the goggles, avoiding the glare from the barrels. After a few seconds I stopped firing and flicked back to NVG. The figure was no longer visible; either he had set the 100m sprint record to the compound, or he was no longer standing. Either way, the firing had stopped.

As the adrenalin subsided I glanced down the cabin to see I was now officially more interesting than the man with bits of RPG sticking out of him. Crouched in the cabin, the doctor and paramedic were both looking at me with pen torches in their mouths, bathing me in blue light as I stood in the door.

'We're all good,' I said over the intercom, and they went back to work on the casualty, plunging me back in darkness.

I put out a contact report, and within minutes we were over the fence and back in Bastion, dropping the casualties at Nightingale, then debriefing with operations. Despite what Hollywood would have you believe, war is not free of administration; having pressed send on 300 rounds of ammunition, an after-action report was required and the shooting would be investigated by the RMP if necessary. I had some significant pen-and-paper time that evening.

After an elongated stay in Bastion with some nasty shouts and a lot of unfriendly fire, we would be heading back to KAF Vegas for a few days. We were enthusiastic about the change of scene and a break from the recent intensity. How little we knew.

Chapter 13

Maps, Windows and Lightning Strike at Inopportune Moments

We were called to operations, and entering the planning area we were quite surprised to see the tall figure of the Special Forces Air Commander (SFAC), whom I knew by reputation. This, I sensed, meant a change to the normal routine.

The early US strategy of drug eradication had been a failure and had pushed many farmers from peaceful non-participation into the clutches of the Taliban. However, given that Helmand Province was the source of 30 per cent of the world's heroin and this was one of the reasons given to the British public for the operation in Afghanistan, something had to be done.

Driving bulldozers across poppy fields or spraying defoliants from helicopters had been dismal failures. In a rare moment of common sense, the decision had been made to allow the farmers to grow and sell poppies to the Taliban and then to strike at the stockpiles or laboratories where the opium was refined into heroin; in this way, the only losers would be the Taliban.

A compound had been identified as a potential drug lab in a remote settlement only a few kilometres from the border with Baluchistan, way to the south of Kandahar. We would launch early the following morning, pick up an assault force from TF333 at a lying-up point (LUP) south of Gereshk and assault the compound at dawn.

Task Force 333 were the Afghan Special Forces, the elite of the newly formed Afghan National Army, trained and mentored by UK Special Forces operators. We'd had little contact with them up to that point but were assured they were good guys and supervised by a small team of SBS. The presence of the SFAC now made sense.

We briefed the mission, then headed off to get something to eat and have an early night; our alarm would be set for 2.30 am the following morning. I'd be flying with Piggy, with FLURP as Captain/Mission Commander in the left-hand seat. The SFAC would be in the jump seat.

We rose in the middle of the night and made our way to operations. When we arrived, the SFAC was already there, and as I looked at the imagery he made his way off to grab a coffee.

'I'm just nipping out for a smoke,' I said.

'Um, Mick, I think you need to do some route study,' suggested FLURP in a mildly condescending tone.

'Inbound from the north until we reach the high ground, left-hand turn on to 090, across two *wadis* and it's the only compound for miles in any direction,' I retorted. 'Route study complete.'

I walked outside and lit up. Part of me was pissed off with FLURP; I'd been doing this for years and knew only too well how to prep for a mission. But another part of me knew he would be feeling the pressure of leading an SF assault with the SFAC sat on the jump seat looking over his shoulder, so I put my resentment to the back of my mind.

I walked back in and we ran through a quick brief, updating any overnight changes and re-briefing the rules of engagement. Complete, we gathered our kit and walked out to the aircraft, FLURP carrying the classified imagery and tasking sheets.

We departed Kandahar on NVG, as it was still a few hours before dawn. We tracked south-west, skirting Garmsir and identifying the area of the LUP in an expanse of dead ground. As we landed in the darkness and dropped the ramp, figures started to emerge from the rocks and mounds around the LUP and formed up behind the aircraft.

First up the ramp was a bearded operator, and I offered him a headset, which he took. It was clear that he and the SFAC knew each other well. As they spoke, the troops walked on and took their seats. After a few minutes I saw the other aircraft lift their ramp.

'Good to go in the cabin, clear above and behind.'

Piggy raised the collective, and the dust rose as we lifted to the hover and picked up speed, the other aircraft following and tucking in tight.

We headed south as the first light of dawn started to creep across the desert. We were only minutes out from the IP when I heard a 'Fuck! Fuck!' from FLURP and felt Piggy bank the aircraft into an orbit. FLURP had opened the cockpit and the airflow had sucked out the map, imagery and task sheet. Classified imagery of the targets was now spread over the desert like confetti.

Maps, Windows and Lightning Strike at Inopportune Moments   151

'1 from 2,' I heard over the radio as the Ruffler transmitted.

'1 – go.'

'Problem?'

'Maps and windows,' I replied.

I heard Ruffler chuckling as he replied, 'Copied.'

By now the shutters were coming down and FLURP was having a meltdown. This was going to turn into a clusterfuck if we weren't careful.

'All right, FLURP, it could happen to anyone …' I began. 'Remember the route study, mate, high ground on the nose, 090, two *wadis* and it's the only compound. Get your head back in the game, mate.'

Piggy was back on heading and we closed the distance to the IP.

'Clear left,' as we hit the IP.

Piggy banked hard and rolled out heading east. I checked the minigun was live as we flashed over the first *wadi*, giving the troops a two-minute signal.

As we crossed the second wadi, the target compound appeared ahead of us. The other aircraft was still tucked in tightly on our shoulder.

'Visual with the target,' called Piggy.

We hit the drop point at speed, flaring hard and sinking quickly to a firm landing, the ramp dropping and the troops racing out to take up assault positions. As the last man left the ramp, it lifted and we were airborne. We would clear the area and orbit 5 miles away to the north until called back in by the assault force.

As Piggy set up in a lazy racetrack pattern, the adrenalin began to fade and I relaxed my grip on the minigun.

'You cock. How could you lose all the fucking maps?' I asked.

'I thought you said it could happen to anyone,' FLURP responded defensively.

'He was getting your head back in the game,' the SFAC chipped in.

We flew patterns over the desert in silence for a few minutes, until the radio crackled into life. The compound was a dry hole; it was clear it had been used as a drug lab in the past, but it was long abandoned.

We headed back to pick up the guys as the SFAC spoke with the TF 333 liaison. They had a second target nearby which they wanted to hit. This was a compound on the edge of the village of Barum Cha, only 500m inside the Afghanistan border.

As we rolled into low level and set up for the drop, the ground commander asked us to keep an eye out for 'squirters' and contain them with warning shots if required. I raised the rules of engagement, which did not allow for warning shots, but was advised by the SFAC that dispensation had been granted.

By now we were thumping the back wheels into the desert as the dust cloud enveloped the aircraft; the ramp hit the desert floor, then the troops were out and heading for points of entry to a nearby compound about 400m from the main settlement.

Anxious to be out of the way before shit started blowing up, we lifted and departed into an orbit roughly 300ft above the guys, providing top cover with the minigun. As they made their entry, a small handful of figures emerged from the far side of the compound and ran towards the desert.

As we rolled out, I took aim a good 200m ahead of the squirters and let off a short burst on the minigun which kicked up a line of sand ahead of them, well clear but definitely visible. They got the message and stopped.

To the south, the Ruffler was doing something similar with a technical which had driven off from the compound at high speed towards the border. That had also halted, and the ground troops were approaching its occupants.

We continued to orbit for several minutes, before being called in to pick up the troops. They came onboard escorting a few detainees. Most of those who had tried to flee initially had been questioned and now watched from the ground as we lifted and headed north, with the playmate falling in to our right.

We flew north and dropped the troops back at the LUP, before climbing up to medium level and heading back to Kandahar. FLURP was understandably quiet on the route home, but to a degree we all were. By the time we had eaten and got back to the accommodation it was early evening and the curtain of darkness had fallen. I woke up at 6.00 am the following morning fully dressed; I had literally just taken off my boots and passed out into a deep sleep.

JP was also at Kandahar and more than a little worn out by PowerPoint slides and planning meetings; we were due to return to the Bolan Valley, where we had inserted the Polish SF some months earlier. This time we'd be inserting 'Easy Company', 101st Airborne, which was a unit designator many of us were familiar with from the HBO series.

The 101st Airborne had their own extensive fleet of Chinooks, and it was unclear why we were required – but we were, and that's all I needed to know. The 101st were going through a lengthy planning process, at which JP was present and which included a fire-and-brimstone blessing by the unit's padre.

What vexed JP slightly was the clear divergence in operating procedures. With a huge fleet of helicopters, US Army aviation tended to fly from A to B at 100 knots and 400ft, which was very safe from an operating standard, but very hazardous as we saw it from the point of enemy fire. Our method was to fly as low and as fast as possible, closer to 140 knots and 50ft for the run into target.

In the spirit of compromise it was agreed we'd all depart and transit as a package, but on the run-in from the IP we would have freedom of manoeuvre and would go in fast and low as the Yanks did their own thing, then come together to hit the target.

And so, in darkness, we loaded up four aircraft of US paratroopers, while several more US Army Chinooks also loaded up. Thirty minutes or so before dawn we taxied out, and all eight Chinooks lifted and departed east, a pair of US Apaches sitting off to one side.

As dawn began to cross the desert we reached the IP and broke away from the US formation to run in fast and low, weaving across the desert floor to throw the aim of any Taliban weapons and to ensure that, despite our extra speed, we arrived on target with the Yanks. As all eight aircraft settled on to the desert floor in a series of dust clouds, with the Apaches providing close air support above, it was going according to the plan that JP and the Americans had spent several days making.

As ramps came up, we lifted and headed back out across the desert, with NVGs folded up as it was now daylight, returning as quickly as we could to Kandahar to collect the second wave of troops. Those we had dropped off would be vulnerable until the full strength was on the ground.

I looked back and began to chuckle; tucked in behind us at 50ft and full speed were the US Chinooks, who had obviously taken one look at our run into the target and thought, 'That works.'

Arriving back, we refuelled and picked up the second wave; it was an impressive sight as the eight large helicopters and two gunships taxied in one after the other to lines of waiting troops. Very few people at Kandahar would have been left unaware that a major operation was ongoing.

As we took on fuel and troops, NVGs and counter-weights were unclipped from helmets and stowed. It was always a relief to remove the best part of a kilo from your head and feel the strain on your neck subside.

The second insertion went off without incident, the Yanks adopting our operating methods as we arrived on target again as a package, descending to a horseshoe of troops and a plume of green smoke. We were back at Kandahar by mid-morning, ready for a late breakfast. Easy Company would be on the ground for a few days, and another set of crews would extract them. For now, JP enjoyed the relative peace of commanding ten helicopter crews across Afghanistan.

* * *

Our time at Kandahar was cut short. Someone had decided that we couldn't afford to just ignore the Taliban occupation of Marjah, and ahead of an operation planned for later in the year, 3 Commando Brigade would be infiltrated by Chinook into the surrounding area to carry out some recce activity.

This operation would require all available aircraft, and we would need to ferry one from Kandahar to Bastion, where another crew would take it over for the assault. The aircraft was currently in maintenance and would need a successful ground run before we could ferry it to Bastion.

By mid-afternoon the maintenance had overrun and we were pestering the engineers for a time for the ground run. To be fair to the engineering flight sergeant, a no-nonsense Geordie, the answer was consistently, 'You'll get it when it's serviceable.'

It was early evening by the time Geordie handed us the tech log to sign and we loaded our kit into the aircraft. We would carry out the ground run, starting the engines and rotors whilst the HUMS gathered data, before shutting down and checking the results. If there were no issues or exceedances, we would start up again and depart for Bastion. We had briefed at 1800 local time, and ops had all left for the day or gone to dinner; there had been no weather forecast, not that weather conditions changed much at that time of year.

The ground run was successful, and we started up and taxied out towards the main runway. As we taxied, the tower advised us that an inbound C17 aircraft had reported seeing ground fire.

'Probably from the Panjwai,' I guessed, unsurprised, as I flipped down my NVG and switched them on.

'Probably,' agreed Piggy.

Maps, Windows and Lightning Strike at Inopportune Moments

Once cleared, we lifted to the hover and transitioned down the runway before climbing to 2,000ft and heading west, boxing south of the Panjwai just in case.

As we flew south of the Panjwai I could see some major flashes well to our north.

'Shit! Looks like someone's getting the good news for firing at the C17,' I said.

'You'd like to think so,' replied Mark.

Over the next few minutes the flashes got closer, and we began to get a little twitchy, until suddenly we were all pulled from whatever special awareness we had, as the world went from green to black and to brilliant white, again and again, and the goggles backed down. Without the NVG it was just as confusing, as it merely flashed from black to brilliant white.

'Guys, I don't like this,' said Piggy as, like all of us, he tried to make sense of what was happening, desperately watching the aircraft instruments.

Suddenly the aircraft lost electrical power and the instruments died for a split second, before coming back on. I heard the tone from the secure radio as it started back up again.

'What the fuck just happened?' asked FLURP.

As we worked through the problem I was aware of a strange sensation in my knee, and when I put my hand down to see what was wrong I felt heavy rain coming in through the door.

'Heavy rain outside,' I called, as the flashing started again.

'Shit! We're in a CB!' shouted Piggy.

We'd been so focused on enemy activity in the Panjwai that we'd not realized the flashes were actually lightning and we were heading into a thunderstorm.

'Turning back for Kandahar.'

'Copied. Good plan, mate,' I replied.

There had been a lot of pressure to get the aircraft to Bastion that evening, and it was reassuring for Piggy as a new Captain to let him know we were behind his decision. Our situation was going to get worse before it got better, and we headed back into black-and-white flashing mode before popping out of the clag with the runway lights on the horizon.

An obviously relieved Piggy updated the controller on the weather situation as we taxied in and shut down, the engineers emerging from the hangar as the blades slowed.

'What's up? I thought the ground run was all right?' asked Geordie as we climbed out of the aircraft.

'Yeah, that was fine,' replied Piggy

'Weather issues,' I added, possibly unnecessarily, as rain began to fall and lightning flashed in the distance.

'As long as you didn't get hit by fucking lightning,' Geordie rasped.

'Er ...' began Piggy.

'We lost all power at one point and the secure flicked off and on again,' I completed.

You could sense the wave of frustration passing behind Geordie's eyes, about to take a turn for the worse.

'Fuck me, Flight, you should see it up here; it's a right mess,' called one of his guys who was carrying out an inspection on the forward rotorhead.

As I climbed up and crouched on the inspection platform I could see the damage. The thick weatherproof shield that sat under the rotorhead assembly showed a long black scorch mark and had partially melted. Above it, one of the lag dampers at the blade root had exploded. It was obvious we'd been struck by lightning.

'That looks like you were hit by a stone,' said Geordie with a deadpan expression.

'At 2,000ft? No, it looks like we were hit by lightning,' replied Piggy, confused.

'I'll grant you it does at first glance Sir, but if you had theoretically been hit by lightning, according to the manual I'd have to inspect every fucking wire in that aircraft before it can fly again, and that'll take fucking days. Plus, you will be an aircraft down for the op tonight.'

We looked at each other for a few seconds.

'Are you sure you weren't hit by a stone, Sir?' pressed Geordie.

I nodded at Piggy.

'Now you come to mention it, Geordie, it could have been a stone.' said Piggy apprehensively.

'Very good, Sir,' replied Geordie. 'I'll get the guys to change the lag damper and do a full inspection, and then you can do a quick air test before you head to Bastion.'

As soon as the words had left Geordie's mouth, my LCJ was off and I headed to the back of the hangar for a smoke. The few minutes in that thundercloud had been more frightening than anything the Taliban had thrown at me.

Maps, Windows and Lightning Strike at Inopportune Moments

We went off to watch TV and drink coffee, and it was almost midnight by the time Geordie called to say the aircraft was ready.

'She's all good now, Sir,' smiled Geordie, as Piggy signed the F700.

We started up and checked everything carefully, but all the systems were fine. With the repair to the blade, we'd do a quick functional air test in the circuit at Kandahar before heading off to Bastion, just to make sure the aircraft was behaving itself. Geordie was right; all the systems were good as we left the circuit and headed for Bastion. On the plus side, the storm had long since passed through and the skies were now clear.

It was well after 1.00 am when we landed at Bastion, shutting down as the oncoming crew waited at the back of the spot. As soon as the rotors had stopped, they were up the ramp and dumping their kit as quickly as we could remove ours. Long as our day had been, theirs was just beginning and would involve a run into Marjah.

The following morning, I climbed out of my sleeping bag and emerged, squinting, from the surge tent. Finding my flip-flops, I walked up to join the others drinking coffee outside the IRT tent and was relieved to hear that it had actually been pretty quiet and had gone off largely without incident.

As we sat in the morning sun we all felt a little relief from the fatigue and stress of the previous months, probably due to the fact that A Flight were due to arrive a few days later and we'd be heading home.

* * *

As the second half of the detachment wore on, we were tasked into Orzugan Province to re-supply an Australian SAS Regiment who were conducting vehicle-mounted patrols in a deep valley between Tarin Kowt and Kajaki. Operating from Bastion, we had some tasking in Kajaki and would head up to Tarin Kowt from there to load up with supplies.

We dropped some stuff at Kajaki, landing next to the Helmand River in a beautiful valley just downstream of the hydroelectric dam, before heading off to the north-east along a valley near Khandak Kalay and picking up the Tirin valley heading east towards Tarin Kowt, when …

'What the fuck was that?' shouted Piggy.

I looked out of the door just in time to see a light-coloured object flash by very close to the aircraft.

'Whoa, shit! What was that?'

As I looked back I saw a drone heading away in the opposite direction; no alteration in course, and its launchers probably had no idea they had come close to taking out a helicopter. In places like Afghanistan, with intense aerial activity, airspace is split into blocks by altitude, and whoever was on the PlayStation end of the drone hadn't got it in the right block.

'Drone, right 5 o'clock, 500m going away.'

Everyone sighed with relief as Pete fixed our position for the proximity report we would file later, and Piggy started descending as the area of the Dutch base at Tarin Kowt opened up to the north of the river.

We landed and shut down whilst we loaded up some supplies, then set off for the grid we'd been supplied with by operations. After fifteen minutes or so we descended into a steep-sided river valley.

'Hello, Charlie zero one, this is Zulu one zero.'

'Zulu one zero, this is Charlie zero one, pass your message. Over.'

'Your location figures two for drop off. Over.'

'Good copy, we have you visual. Site is secure, popping purple smoke. Over.'

'Copy purple smoke. Out.'

As we continued to descend we saw a wisp of purple smoke spiral up 400m ahead of us, before billowing into a thick plume as the smoke grenade kicked into life. We flared to wash off speed and set up to a slightly sloping area of gravel right next to the river. As we approached the area I saw a number of vehicles across the valley in overwatch, gunners manning .50 cals and a small group next to a fire.

We landed, and Tarqs dropped the ramp as the group ran in and started offloading the supplies. I watched as the cabin emptied and the pile grew next to the fire. As the last items were going off, one of them gave me a 'two-minute' sign and they ran off.

'I think they have something to go back to TK,' I updated Piggy.

'Nothing on the tasking sheet,' said Pete.

'Oh, fuck me,' chimed in Tarqs, and as I looked out I saw six of the Australians carrying in a substantial gearbox, leaking oil as they went.

As they clambered over the gravel under their heavy load, I put down some plastic and paper roll as best as I could, to contain the leaking oil. They dumped the gearbox unceremoniously on the plastic, shook hands and were gone.

'Clear above and behind,' I called, as Tarqs lifted the ramp.

Lifting to the hover, we slid over the shoulder and headed back up the valley, overflying the waving Aussies and leaving them in the midst of the Taliban heartland.

Having dropped the gearbox at Tarin Kowt, there was miraculously little oil on the cabin floor, which filled me with joy as I tidied up and Tarqs did the refuel. We'd be returning to Bastion and shutting down for some dinner, before a couple of hours' tasking in the evening. That might sound like it had been scheduled so we could eat, but operations rarely factored things such as meals or fatigue into the equation; the main reason for the break was the short 'red illume' period.

NVGs require some ambient light in order to work, and in Afghanistan there is very little compared with somewhere like the UK, where the glow from cities and towns is almost ubiquitous; night flying in remote parts of Wales and Scotland is therefore highly valued because ambient light levels there are so low.

With the lack of ambient light in Afghanistan, naturally occurring light from the moon and stars was a major factor in planning and scheduling. At that point in March 2009 there was a gap of a couple of hours between the setting of the sun and the rising of the moon; a period in which NVGs struggled to provide anything other than a vague, fuzzy picture that was extremely challenging to fly on.

This was known to the crews as a 'red illumination period' or 'red illume', and tasking was avoided during it. To us on this occasion it meant there was a fair chance for once of making dinner.

We headed off back towards Helmand Province, thanking the Dutch controller for his help as we switched back on to British military frequencies. I dialled up operations at Bastion on the secure comms and radioed them with an update.

'Hello Zero, this is Zulu one zero. Over.'

'Zulu one zero, this is Zero, send. Over,' replied a Scottish voice.

'Zulu one zero is complete tasking to serial 11 and returning your location for shutdown. Over.'

'Zero, that's all copied. Do not shut down. Over.'

'Confirm remain rotors running? Over.'

'Yes, remain rotors running. Serial 12 and follow-on tasking now brought forward. Over.'

'That's red illume period,' interjected Piggy on the intercom.

'Zero, confirm you are aware of the illumination levels for that period. Over,' I relayed.

'Yes. Over.'

In the front I saw Piggy shake his head, but there was nothing further we could do.

'Zulu one zero, I copy remain rotors running and roll into serial 12. Out.'

Dinner would be reheated in a box again, and we'd be working pretty frigging hard in the dark.

We refuelled at Bastion and loaded up for the evening as the sun sank into the desert and darkness crept across the almost lunar landscape. First up it was just freight for a new FOB called Tanda, south of Nad e Ali and well inside the green zone.

As we finished loading, our Apache escort started up down the flight line. Ugly 52 was flown that night by the QHI, a very capable pilot called Marc. Fully loaded, we sat for a few moments as Marc got the sensors on the Apache online, before both aircraft taxied out on to the HALS.

Departing, we headed south-east, initially to position to the south of Tanda and run in heading north across the shortest patch of green zone. The light levels at 4,000ft were pretty poor, but we still had the slight benefit of the last rays of sun from over the horizon.

As we dropped to low level the visibility decreased further, and I could tell by the pitch of Piggy's voice that he was working hard, as was Pete, passing him navigation patter whilst struggling to make out any features.

At 150ft we tracked in towards the FOB at very low speed, literally navigating field by field as stuff became visible. Luckily, the Taliban must have been at dinner, because we were a sitting duck for much of the run into Tanda, descending as we went to pick up more detail – although an RPG would at least have provided some ambient light.

'STOP, STOP, MAST RIGHT ON THE NOSE!' screamed Tarqs on the intercom.

Sure enough, just ahead of the aircraft's nose was a whip aerial. None of us had seen it in the dark green gloop, but for some reason Tarqs was at an angle to pick it up and had stopped us before an almost certain collision.

Piggy brought the aircraft slowly clear of the mast and we continued into Tanda, landing in a cloud of dust as the troops rushed in to offload the freight.

'Fuck me, that was hard going,' muttered Piggy.

'You guys OK?' asked Marc from the Apache overhead. 'That looked like hard work from up here.'

'Just changing our pants,' I replied.

'Right, we'll exit left and climb to height as soon as we have some speed on,' briefed Piggy, and we all agreed.

Nobody wanted to be low at that moment.

Tarqs bought the ramp up and the last of the troops cleared the rotor disc. I scanned the sky above us for the Apache.

'Apache's five o'clock high. Clear above and behind.'

'Lifting,' responded Piggy.

The dust cloud built as we lifted and departed left, Piggy pulling all the power he could now we were empty to get the speed on so we could climb.

'Armed up,' called Pete.

'Apache?' enquired Piggy

'Seven o'clock high, well clear,' called Tarqs.

Piggy pulled back on the cyclic and we began to climb away from the murky darkness of the green zone, before levelling out and putting Bastion on the nose. Marc fell in behind us as we headed back to refuel and pick up our next load. Our next port of call was Patrol Base Argyll in Nad e Ali.

It was still very dark when we lifted from Bastion, but in the time it had taken to refuel and load the cabin the illumination levels had improved slightly. We flew east at low level for the short hop to Argyll, with Marc sitting high above us, scanning the green zone ahead with the Apache's FLIR.

With pre-landing checks complete we reached the IP and crossed into the green zone. Almost immediately I saw muzzle flashes in the distance.

'You're taking heavy fire from Shinkalay,' Marc updated us.

Heavy lines of tracer began to arc towards the aircraft, although by that point I was more worried about the bullets I couldn't see.

Suddenly I became aware of a bright light in the sky; Marc had switched on every external light on his Apache and was now lit up like a Christmas tree as he flew overhead drawing the enemy fire away from us. As we approached Argyll and slowed, the tracer had already switched to the selfless fool in the gunship above.

'You are one crazy, lovely man,' I muttered to myself as I scanned the area around us with the minigun and we crossed the fence and descended on to the landing site at Argyll. As soon as we touched the ground Marc went dark again, turning off every light and manoeuvring hard.

'Did you see …?' Piggy began.

'Yep. Ballsy call,' I replied.

With Argyll re-supplied, we lifted and departed the FOB like a cat with a firework up its backside, climbing quickly and joining up with Marc for the short run back to Bastion.

We never got to thank Marc that evening, since he was straight out to another task, but several years later, after both of us had left the military, we would catch up at a trade fair in Amsterdam and I'd thank him for his brave actions over a beer or three.

'It's OK. You guys looked like you were having a bit of a shit evening,' was his modest response.

* * *

As Galvo and his guys arrived, we had a clean-up and started handing back ammunition and morphine and handing over LCJs to our replacements. Piggy, C3PO, Jim and I had found ourselves back at Kandahar with three days to wait around before the Tristar.

As we sat having coffee with the engineers, one of them let slip that one of the aircraft was going back to Brize that night on a C17. We looked at each other, then climbed into a vehicle to go and talk with the movers.

'Hey, mate, you've got a Chinook flying out tonight for Brize?' I enquired.

'Yep. That's right. You travelling with it?'

'Er, not at the moment. But we are its crew; theoretically can we change from Friday's Tristar to tonight's flight?'

'Don't see why not. It's empty otherwise,' he replied sitting down at a laptop. 'What are the names?'

As I passed him the names he tapped away. 'All done, you're booked on the C17. Be at the TLS at midnight.'

'Awesome. Thanks, mate.'

'Well?' asked Piggy as Jim and I walked out of the office.

'TLS at midnight. We're going home tonight,' I beamed, a little smugly if I am honest.

'Winner!' called Piggy as we all silently pondered why it had been so easy.

We told JP what we'd wangled, and he was happy for us to go early, so we gathered our kit together and went for dinner. With full bellies we were at the TLS hours before midnight, sitting in sight of the C17 as they winched the Chinook into it, determined it was not going to leave Kandahar without us.

At midnight we were escorted up the ramp and into a floodlit cabin, where a Chinook sat resplendent, with heavy chains securing it to the floor. A blade box was secured next to it, and up front, the rear pylon sat securely on a trolley.

I recognized the loadmaster from my time at Cranwell, and he finished checking the load before coming down to brief us.

'Sorry, guys, we didn't know about the four of you until we'd left Incirlik, so we didn't cater for you, but there's a tray of sandwiches up front, and help yourself to tea and coffee in the galley. Flight time's about four hours, and there's only you guys, so once we're above 10k feel free to spread out and make yourself comfortable.'

If Carlsberg did flights back to the UK they'd look a lot like the C17 that night, and shortly after getting airborne we were stretched out in our sleeping bags and asleep, weeks of fatigue kicking in. Neither the galley nor the sandwiches saw any action from us.

The cabin filled with light and I was aware of someone shaking me. I looked up and it was the loadie.

'Hey, Mick, we're on finals for Incirlik,' he shouted, and I nodded, peeling my face from the sleeping bag and taking a seat next to Jim.

Ten minutes later, we bumped on to the ground at Incirlik in southern Turkey, taxiing in and shutting down.

'Guys, we're doing a crew change now and will be on the ground for three hours. Rather than sitting out here, we'll take you back to the crew house and the oncoming crew can bring you back. OK?'

It sounded good, and we were soon pulling up outside an apartment block on the base. Incirlik had definitely changed since I had spent the summer there in 1995. Once inside, pizzas were ordered, and the C17 guys passed out ice-cold bottles from the fridge.

'Beer?' they asked, smiling.

It was a lovely gesture by the guys, and we sat for a couple of hours drinking Budweiser, eating pizza and chatting, until the oncoming crew told us it was time to leave.

Back in the C17, after our first beers we were back in the sleeping bags pushing out z's not long after getting airborne, to be woken again with a shake as we started the descent into Brize Norton. A rain shower had just passed through as we thanked the guys from 99 Squadron and set off to wait for transport to Odiham. Carlsberg had obviously called ahead, because for the first time in living memory a minibus was waiting and we were soon on the A34 heading home.

Every time I returned from the desert I marvelled at how green the UK was, and as I sat in the minibus watching Piggy drool in his sleep, I was just happy to be home. Of all the tours I had completed in Helmand, this had been the most draining of them all.

Chapter 14

A Brief Glimmer of Normality

RAF Odiham
Hampshire
May 2009

The year 2009 would be a long and bloody one in Helmand. In August a 7 Squadron aircraft was shot down by an RPG near Kajaki; the crew were recovered safely by their playmate and the aircraft was destroyed. Ten days later, a crew from B Flight would experience a blade strike whilst landing at an FOB; the aircraft was damaged beyond repair and blown up *in situ*. The crew and passengers were recovered safely, but fatigue was cited as a major contributory factor. In two weeks the UK had lost two Chinooks in Afghanistan, although thankfully with no loss of life.

The issue with my knees remained, and they could be quite painful at times. After a number of GP appointments and an MRI scan it was discovered that I had a small tear in one knee and patella tendinosis in both. In short, the muscles in my legs were unbalanced and were gradually pulling the kneecaps out of position. Kneeling on a vibrating cabin floor wearing 30kg of body armour and ammunition will undoubtedly have changed the muscle structure.

I was booked in for an intensive physio course later in the year which would ultimately be delayed due to a posting to 18 Squadron. After almost three years back on 27 Squadron, I would be joining the OCF as an instructor in October. I was also approaching the end of my Masters degree course, and being able to spend more time at home would be particularly welcome as I finalized my dissertation. It was with mixed feelings that I emptied my locker and moved to the next hangar. I'd miss the guys on 27 Squadron, particularly C Flight; but whilst I had joined a newly created flight in the early stages of an enduring operation, I was leaving an well established unit.

The truth of the matter was that I enjoyed instructing and was pretty good at it, so the OCF was an interesting place to work, particularly since the throughput was intense as the squadrons requested more and more crews to replace those injured or just exhausted from years of deployment in Iraq and Afghanistan.

It wasn't just the students who were new; Odiham had pushed a fair number of very experienced and very deserving crewmen through CFS(H) and on to the OCF for a short respite from relentless deployments, and this meant there was a large number of B2 and newly minted B1 instructors. There was only one A2 and a small handful of experienced B1s. After a few months instructing, I was called in by Gus, the Senior Instructor and our only A2.

'Mate, I am posted,' he began.

'Cool beans, well done, mate. Who's taking over from you?'

'Ginge.'

'Awesome.'

Ginge was a great bloke and well respected on the Wing; I couldn't think of anyone better qualified.

'Yeah, but it is going to create a few issues.'

'Er, OK ...' I replied cautiously.

'You've done a good job since you got here and you have a good way with people. We could do with someone experienced to replace Ginge as training officer,' he continued.

'Sure, if that's what you need, mate, I'd be more than happy,' I told him.

When the chat had begun I wasn't sure what I was being warmed up for, but actually I liked the idea of the training officer's role.

And so, a few weeks later, we saw Gus off with a few beers and, as Ginge cleared his desk, I moved my meagre belongings in. My role was to train new instructors on type and to carry out periodic checks to make sure they were instructing to standard and within the syllabus. Of course, the OCF was still thin on manning, so I'd still be instructing the students on the courses too.

In mid-December 37 Course were almost finished. For various reasons, several of the students had not been able to complete night checks earlier in the course, and we were now pushing them through. Most had already completed the rest of the course, and the night check was the last pass-or-fail element before they joined their new flight.

On one exceptionally cold night I had two crewmen within three hours of finishing three years of training and joining an ops flight. Both were 'retreads' and coincidentally both had come from ground trades at Odiham. Dylan was an ex-engineer, and Stu was ex-RAF Regiment, in which he had been attached to 27 Squadron.

I waddled on to the aircraft wearing just about every item of clothing the military had ever issued me and carrying a flask of hot coffee. I took a seat where I could monitor both of them but would be out of the bitterly cold air flowing in from the cabin door.

After an hour and a half we landed in a dark field in deepest Somerset to change crews over. Traditionally, instructors would go through the debrief before telling the students how they'd fared. Tonight was different.

As Stu sat frozen in the door, I tapped him on the shoulder and handed him a mug of steaming coffee and a Mars Bar; he was physically shaking with cold as he accepted both and smiled like he'd won the lottery.

'Congratulations, mate. Welcome to the Chinook Force,' I said flatly.

His smile stretched from ear to ear, but I could see he was cold and tired, probably close to hypothermia.

'Go and take a seat down the back,' I added, then called, 'Dylan, you're up, mate,' as my second student unhooked his harness and made his way forward up the cabin.

Again, his was a good performance, especially given the temperature, and an hour or so later, I was handing Dylan a mug of coffee and welcoming him to the Force.

I was doubly happy with the two of them finishing strongly, as although they didn't realize it at the time, both were to be posted to C Flight.

By Christmas 2009 I had settled into the training officer role and had almost completed my dissertation, so it was with a clear conscience that I went to exchange drinks at the Officers' Mess and clocked off for the holidays. As I slept in the following day, C Flight on 27 Squadron were back in Bastion, finishing their TQs and starting out on operations.

* * *

By early January I was back at work and had submitted my dissertation to the university; and as I waited for the results I had started converting the latest pair of instructors on to the Chinook. January was always a fairly slow month as people filtered back from leave, and desks were empty since people were either deployed to the desert or off conducting winter training.

By late January we were carrying out some staff training when news came through from Afghanistan, and it wasn't good.

Chomper had been carrying out an IRT shout to evacuate a number of wounded soldiers, when the aircraft had been hit several times. One of the rounds had hit him in the flying helmet, travelling through it to cut deep into his forehead before being deflected by his NVG rail. With several systems out and the aircraft becoming difficult to control, Chomper had flown the casualties back to Bastion with blood running down his face. As if things couldn't get anymore 'Boy's Own', there was a film crew onboard who captured the whole event, along with Mike Brewer, the host of 'Wheeler Dealers'.

All's well that ends well, but it reminded us that things can turn ugly pretty damn quickly, and secretly we all knew we'd been riding our luck for some time. Eventually, something would end badly; it was just a matter of time.

March arrived with the news that I had been awarded a distinction in both coursework and dissertation and would graduate with an MSc in May. I was particularly pleased because I knew how much of the dissertation had been written between IRT shouts.

I also attended a physiotherapy rehab course in Aldershot to get my knees back into shape. The three weeks of intense physio were tiring, but also humbling, as there were a number of soldiers there recovering from blast injuries sustained in Afghanistan. Treating my knees, however painful, suddenly felt a little indulgent alongside a guy who had suffered most of the bones down one side of his body broken in a roadside blast.

One thing that did stand out was the response of those who had been injured and picked up by Chinook; I was repeatedly thanked, unnecessarily in my view, by guys who were dealing with life-changing injuries. Any of the aircrew answering to 'Tricky 73' would have given you the same answer: 'We were just doing our job.'

The summer passed quickly. Macca and I had found ourselves on the display crew and spent several weeks practising a quite complex role demo after work: dropping underslung Land Rovers, fast-roping JHSU hookers and other sample tasks.

For crowds at airshows used to seeing the more traditional Chinook displays of high energy manoeuvring we were probably a bit of a disappointment as we puttered in at 80 knots dragging an ageing Land Rover; but I can assure you that the same enthusiasm was there.

At midsummer I was in the Sergeants' Mess one lunchtime having coffee when I was joined by Bob, who had recently replaced the Ruffler as Senior Crewman on C Flight. We chatted for a while as I caught up on the progress of some recent students, including Dylan and Stu, before the subject inevitably switched to Afghanistan.

'So you must be deploying in a couple of months?' I asked.

'Yeah, October,' he responded with a pained look.

'Everything OK?'

'Um, yeah. Amy had planned our wedding for early December before I got posted to C Flight.'

'Oh, I see,' I replied.

Bob was going to have to disappoint either the Squadron or his future wife.

'That's not going to work,' I said. 'Can you get a stunt crewman?'

'Very few for the senior crewman role,' he replied.

He was right; there was always someone willing to go out to Afghanistan, but very few capable of the senior crewman role.

'You don't fancy a guest slot back on C Flight?' he asked.

Up to that point I hadn't actually thought of it, but I had always been a great advocate of people on the OCF and in HQs deploying regularly to keep a handle on the real world.

'Not sure they would have me, Bob.'

'Trust me, they would, Mick,' he replied, sensing the answer to his prayers was close at hand.

'Let me have a chat with Ginge. If he's happy to run light, I'm in. Why don't you warm up OCC on the idea?'

'Deal,' said Bob and set off with a spring in his step, as I settled back into the *Telegraph*, wondering what I'd let myself into.

Chapter 15

Thanks, Bob

Camp Bastion
Operation Herrick
November 2010

I arrived at Bastion in the early hours, stepping off the ramp of the C130, which remained running, and enjoying the warmth of the engine efflux until the cold hit me when out of range of it. I collected my baggage and as I left, the obligatory next-of-kin form filled out, I was met by Bob.

'All right, mate. How was the flight?'

'Shit, as ever,' I replied.

'Good, good,' replied Bob, laughing.

I climbed into the Land Rover and he drove around the camp and drew up at the new Tier 2 accommodation, helping me up the stairs to the second floor with my baggage. As he opened the door he put a finger to his lips.

The corridor was silent and in darkness, and we walked halfway down to a door with a sliver of light showing through the gap at its base. He opened the door and ushered me in. The room was split in half by a couple of wardrobes, with a bed in each half. He pointed to the far bed, already made and with a laundry bag at its base.

'You're over there,' he whispered as I put down my bags.

Within minutes I had undressed and was in bed fast asleep.

The next morning, I had a shower and dressed. Bob had already gone, so I headed over to the dining facility for breakfast and then up to the IRT tent. The IRT crew now had a new tent up near the flight line, but the old tent served as a crew room and was still home to all the aircrew.

As I walked up I passed a few of the guys and stopped for a quick chat; they seemed in good spirits. Outside the IRT tent the boss, Rich, sat smoking a cigar, nodding as I approached.

'Hey, Mick, good to see you, mate.'

'Thanks, Rich, how's it going?'

'All good, been a fairly quiet det [detachment] so far. Tasking aircraft are airborne, IRT crew had a quiet night.'

'Cool. I'm going to grab some coffee. You want one?'

Rich shook his head and settled back in his chair, puffing away on his cigar as I opened the door and walked into the tent, flicking on the kettle as I passed.

'*Bonjour, mon ami*, 'oo will buy my beautiful onions?' I shouted in an exaggerated French accent.

'You're still a dick,' laughed Frenchie.

'All right, Waldo? Managed to survive being crewed with the RPG magnet?'

'So far, so good,' replied Waldo, smiling.

Stu pulled out his earphones and walked over to shake hands.

'All right, Mick, good to see you. You know you're crewed with us,' he said, motioning towards Frenchie and Waldo.

'Whoa, whoa, whoa, sweet child of mine. Bob never mentioned anything about being crewed with Frenchie.'

'Unlucky,' laughed Frenchie.

'Talking of Bob, is he flying this morning?'

'Nope, he's over in operations,' Stu replied. 'Want to take a wander over?'

I nodded, and we left the tent and went over to operations. As we walked, Stu brought me up to speed with the deployment, which seemed fairly quiet compared with the chaos of the previous year. As we entered operations I saw Bob leaning over the bird table with one of the pilots, conducting some mission planning. He looked up and glanced at Stu and me as we approached.

'Hey, mate, welcome back,' he offered, as we shook hands.

'Yeah, well, I didn't have anything else on,' I replied.

Bob and I walked over to the bird table, and Bob talked through the large map of Helmand and explained what was ongoing, where the hotspots for enemy activity were and what tasks were on the horizon. Then we left operations and walked into the old IRT tent (now known as the Rec Tent) for coffee, as I brought Bob up to speed on the comings and goings back in the UK, and he did the same for the detachment. As we chatted, the crews came and went, saying hello or throwing out banter, mostly a bit of both. I was uniquely qualified to step in for Bob since, apart from knowing most of the flight from my time on C Flight, I also knew the brand new pilots and crewmen from their time on the OCF.

'As you've seen, Frenchie's on IRT at the moment and will be rolling off in the morning for a break,' Bob explained. 'I've got you and me flying with Lurch for the next two days to get TQ'd, and then you'll join Frenchie.'

I nodded. Despite the banter, I was pretty happy about flying with Frenchie.

'When do you fly out?' I asked

'As soon as you are TQ'd, Mick' he replied. 'No pressure, mate.'

'I'll try my best not to fuck it up,' I quipped, and we both chuckled.

Bob walked me through the usual arrival admin and then we headed to lunch. Quite a bit had changed, and we had now moved from the tents into tier 2 accommodation, which effectively consisted of containerized buildings. I was sharing a room with Bob and so would have the room to myself once he left.

The next day, we carried out tasking around the AO, with Bob watching me so he could sign off on my TQ. I noticed there was a load of new FOBs in the green zone, scattered across previous no-go areas. The other change was the naming of FOBs to reflect a more Afghan focus, with places such as 'Shawqat and 'Shazad'. We followed up with a night check, and I was TQ'd.

The following evening, I drove Bob around to the airport for his flight back to the UK. He was trying not to look too excited about getting back for his wedding, but failing miserably. I dropped him off and hung around for a short while until they called the passengers through security.

As we shook hands he said, 'Mate, I really appreciate this.'

'No worries. I needed a holiday anyway,' I laughed.

'The guys are all in good order. Hopefully you'll have a quiet time and I'll see you back in Blighty next month.'

'Go on, bugger off. I hate long goodbyes,' I replied, and he headed off towards the X-ray machines, lost in a throng of camouflaged passengers.

I climbed into the Land Rover and drove back to the block, climbing into bed and dropping off to sleep almost straight away.

The following morning, I woke early and had breakfast, then walked up to the Rec Tent with a mug of coffee. As I passed the neat rows of tents, one of the pilots waved as he walked towards me.

'Hey, Morts. How's it going?' I asked, thinking it was a social greeting.

'Um, Mick, we need to talk about Eyeball,' he replied nervously.

'Eyeball?' I asked 'What's up with Eyeball?'

Eyeball was one of the crewmen. He was fairly experienced and was on his second or third deployment to Afghanistan.

'He's lost the plot, mate. He's shouting and chucking ammunition around in the back of the aircraft.'

'OK. Thanks, Morts. I'll tee up a replacement and see what's up with him.'

'Already done,' chipped in Trigger, who had joined us. 'The guys are bringing him back here.'

I nodded and headed to the tent, sitting outside whilst I had a smoke. Morts was a good captain and genuinely concerned. It didn't sound like Eyeball at all.

I was crushing out a cigarette as the Land Rover pulled up and Eyeball climbed out carrying his kit. As if by magic, everyone vanished, giving us some privacy.

'All right, Eyeball,' I said quietly. 'Come and have a seat.'

He sat down and I looked him over, instantly recognizing what was wrong. I could tell by his eyes that emotionally he was running on empty.

'Morts told me you've had a bit of a hard morning,' I began. 'Want to talk about it?'

'Sorry, Mick. I just lost it a bit.'

'That's OK, mate. We all get like that from time to time.'

He sat hunched in his seat, staring at the floor.

'You look like someone who needs a break, Eyeball.'

'I'm fine.'

'Well, I want you to take today off and rest. We'll talk about it again tomorrow?'

'You're not grounding me' – a statement, not a question.

'No, I'm not. But you're running on empty, and I'm taking you off IRT for a while.'

'That's bullshit. There's nothing wrong with me.'

'No, there isn't. But you do need a rest, and once you're back to normal you can go back on IRT.'

He wasn't happy and he looked at me for a few seconds whilst he thought it through and nodded. Trigger helped him with his kit and took him back to the accommodation.

As he left, Morts came and sat down next to me.

'Thanks, Mick.'

He was obviously uncomfortable about raising concerns over a mate.

'No worries. We'll see how he is over the next few days. Any idea what triggered it?'

'Yeah, mate, now I think back, we've picked up a lot of double amputees in the past few days. He will have probably seen some heavy shit in the back.'

'OK, thanks, Morts.'

As Morts got up and walked back into the tent, one of the other crewmen, Sooty, slipped into the seat next to me.

'All right, Mick. Bit of an issue. I got shot in the eyes with a laser last night.'

The targeting of aircraft with lasers was an increasing problem, but I couldn't help thinking Bob must be chuckling as he sat at Brize Norton waiting for his transport.

'Go to the hospital and get checked out,' I told him.

'OK. What if there's an issue?'

'We'll deal with that when we get to it, Sooty.'

'Right. OK, Mick,' he replied as he headed off towards the hospital.

My coffee was stone cold by now, so I made a fresh brew before heading over to ops. I could see the next few weeks would be a challenge.

We trained aircrew to deal with aircrew stuff; they had spent years in training learning how to put out fires, get out of a helicopter sinking underwater, deal with system malfunctions and a very long list of other potential problems. In many ways this worked, and in all the times I was under fire I can honestly say I was always far too busy following a drill or reacting in the prescribed manner to be scared.

Unfortunately, the nature of warfare in Afghanistan was different, and we were yet to develop a system that prepared a twenty-five-year-old to have arterial blood spray up the side of his face from a triple amputee being kept alive in the back of a helicopter.

All of us have a horror story, some memory that instantly transports you back to the desert; for me it was the kids on stretchers after the bomb blast near Sangin in early 2009. We've all dealt with it in a different way, some more successfully than others, but Eyeball was just emotionally drained by then; he needed some time in the relative normality of just flying around Afghanistan getting shot at, without the added stress of dealing with life-changing injuries.

The night of 9 December was punctuated by stretches of poor weather. It was a low moon period anyway, and a strong wind from the south-east was sweeping in as a dust storm and reducing visibility. The operations room was silent, apart from the signallers at their radio sets scribbling notes as a 'nine-liner' came through. A soldier had been shot in the head at FOB Jackson in Sangin and needed immediate extraction for surgery.

Initially, the headquarters had launched the FLIR-equipped MH60 Pave Hawks, call sign 'Pedro', but they had got as far as the perimeter only to turn back in the face of extremely poor visibility. We'd been called to operations and stood at the bird table with the high-readiness Apache crew.

'What do you reckon?' the operations officer asked Frenchie.

Although 18 Squadron had gone to the trouble of developing an SOP for a similar set of circumstances, it was unclear whether the weather would preclude even that; in essence, an Apache would fly ahead of us sweeping the route with their FLIR, and we would follow their infra-red anti-collision light, at a few hundred feet and completely blind to the ground. As SOPs went, it was last-gasp and fraught with risk.

'Yep, let's go and give it a try,' replied Frenchie.

'OK. The only glimmer of good news I can give you is that FOB Jackson has IR mortar illumination,' the operations officer added.

IR mortar illumination is a flare that can be launched into the sky to provide light before descending slowly on a parachute. The twist was that these particular flares were invisible to the naked eye and would only provide illumination to NVG users. The Taliban would have no idea what the mortars were doing. It might be handy trying to get into Sangin in low illumination, assuming we could get there through the low visibility of the sandstorm.

With that, we headed out to the aircraft and started up, sitting on the pad for a minute or so waiting for the Apache. As the gunship took off past us, Frenchie lifted and fell in about 200m behind it. It was an awful night, and as we crossed the perimeter fence at 300ft we were blind to everything apart from a flashing light from the Apache. It was uncomfortable to say the least; if we lost the Apache we would have to pull up and divert to Kandahar. At that height, if Frenchie lost concentration and allowed even a gentle unchecked rate of descent, we would hit the ground and spread ourselves across the desert in a matter of seconds.

I pulled out a map from my flight bag and started plotting a route to Jackson, informing Frenchie of any masts or high ground and their height and distance from our track.

'Thanks, mate,' replied Frenchie.

Somehow we managed to keep pace with the Apache and dropped into the Sangin Valley, the GPS slowly counting down the distance to the FOB. The valley was pitch dark, and although we knew from the GPS where the FOB should be, it was just a black hole of shadow. Waldo counted down the distance, as Frenchie gripped the controls and guided the aircraft towards the gloom.

'Widow 45, this is Tricky 73, request IR mortar illume. Over,' I heard, as Frenchie transmitted to the JTAC.

There was a crackle of static, then a reply.

'Tricky 73, standby,' the JTAC replied.

By now the GPS was at zero; we should have been overhead the FOB.

'Guys, I can't see a fucking thing here. I am going to descend slightly and see if I can get some references.'

'Copied,' I replied.

'Everybody keep your eyes open.'

Suddenly, as Frenchie came to the low hover, small trees and the ground emerged from the gloom, if little blurred. At the same time, the radio erupted.

'Tricky 73, Widow 45, firing now,' called the JTAC, and there was a burst above us, bathing the ground in light.

'OK, I know where we are, coming right,' called Frenchie, and as we manoeuvred we saw the camp open up. The area we had come to the hover over was Wombat Wood, and I exhaled a lifetime's worth of stress as Frenchie crossed the perimeter wall and came to the hover over the landing site, with Stu talking him on to the ground.

'Clear ramp,' called Frenchie with relief, and I dropped the ramp and let the MERT off to collect the casualty.

We all sat for a few seconds in silence while we gathered our thoughts.

'Frenchie?' I said into the intercom.

'Yes, mate?'

'I'm fairly happy we were inside the envelope there, *mon brave*, but only fucking just.'

'Yeah, agreed.'

I told Stu we'd swap over in the cabin, and as I made my way up to the front door, we passed in the cabin; his face was white.

As I plugged back into the intercom, the MERT were bringing the casualty back onboard. They placed the stretcher on the floor and, by torchlight, began working on him. We were just getting ready to lift, when Bastion came over the radio. There was an Estonian patrol on the far side of the valley from us with a second casualty, also with a head injury.

I looked at the MERT paramedic, who was on the intercom and had heard the message.

'Any thoughts?' I asked.

'OK with us. We can cope from a medical perspective,' he replied.

Next to speak was Frenchie: 'Guys, what do you think? Do we give it a go?'

As a crew we agreed to give it a try, and within seconds I felt Frenchie pulling power and lifting. The mortars were still putting up illumination as we flew across the river valley towards the rising ground.

Fairly happy with the light levels and visibility, we had made a risk-based decision based on the conditions and the urgency of extracting a soldier with major head trauma. I quickly changed frequency to the Estonian patrol, having quickly scribbled this down during the update from operations.

'Lima Zero Five, this is Tricky 73, inbound to your location figures two for CASEVAC.'

'Tricky 73, this is Lima Zero Five, we hear you. We have one T1 casualty, we are glad to hear you,' replied a thick Eastern European voice.

At that point the mortar illumination ran out and we were plunged back into darkness, only too aware that there was steeply rising ground ahead of us.

'Fuck! Fuck! Fuck! Climbing!' called Frenchie as the power came in and we climbed hard.

WHOOP! WHOOP! WHOOP! The low-height warning blared.

'I'm at max power,' called Frenchie, the warning still blaring. We all held our breath and waited for the impact, as our lives flashed before us.

The warning sound continued for longer than I'd ever heard it, and just as I was convinced I was taking my last breath, it stopped and we cleared the ridge. All of us exhaled with relief; we must have missed hitting that ridge at high speed by the smallest of margins.

'Mick, we're not getting in there as it stands. I'm going to head back to Bastion and drop this guy off whilst we plan this out,' said Frenchie.

It was the right decision; we'd stretched our luck almost to breaking point already tonight and we needed to figure out a plan that didn't involve fumbling around in the dark during a dust storm.

'Yeah, mate, I'm with you. I'll update Lima Zero Five,' I replied, switching back to the transmit switch.

'Hello Lima Zero Five, this is Tricky 73.'

'Tricky 73, send.'

'Mate, we have a problem and are routing back to Nightingale at this time. Sit tight and we'll be back in a short while.'

'Tricky 73, you cannot leave.'

'Lima Zero Five, we'll be back shortly.'

'Tricky 73, we can hear you above us. We are ready. If you leave now, my friend will fucking die.'

'Lima Zero Five, we WILL be back. Out.'

I really felt for the guy on the ground, but we'd come far too close to losing thirteen people only minutes earlier. I'd remember that conversation for years to come.

We fell in behind the Apache and fought our way through the blackness and low visibility to Bastion, speeding over the fence and landing at Nightingale, where the ambulance collected the casualty. The MERT stayed onboard as we headed for the refuel site.

'Tricky 73, this is Zero. Sitrep. Over.'

The Commander of the Helicopter Force was on the radio. Frenchie quickly gave him a summary before adding our intention to head back to the ridge.

'Tricky 73, you've done an awesome job this evening, and I am not saying you won't be going back out, but I want you to shut down and come in whilst we come up with a plan.'

We taxied into the spot and shut down, then headed over to operations. As we entered, all heads turned to look at us as we squinted at the bright light. Sunray motioned us over to the bird table, where he gave us an update on the Estonian patrol.

'They are moving the casualty to FOB Jackson by road as we speak. Can you get back in there?' he asked.

We considered it for a few seconds; we'd already got into Sangin that evening, albeit uncomfortably and with a detour to Wombat Wood. However, they had used up all the mortar illumination on our last visit.

'Ah, might have a solution,' offered one of the operations staff. 'They have some in FOB Robinson they can put up. It might just give you enough light.'

FOB Robinson was an artillery firebase on the high ground overlooking Sangin. If they put up illumination, it might provide enough light to get us in.

'OK, we'll go and flash up the aircraft,' said Frenchie.

As we turned to leave, the Apache crew followed us out; we'd be relying on them to get us to Sangin, and our lives were literally in their hands.

Fifteen minutes later, we were departing Bastion into the dust storm, again fixed on the light of the Apache as it swept the route ahead of us. It was still an uncomfortable experience flying blind at only a couple of hundred feet, but we'd already crossed that particular Rubicon once that evening.

As we dropped into the valley we heard the Apache on frequency with the JTAC at FOB Robinson, and as Waldo counted down the distance to run we saw the first illumination rounds going up from FOB Robinson. Although much further away this time, they did provide enough definition to make out the FOB, and we made it in without waking up the Taliban at Wombat Wood.

With relief, Frenchie lowered the collective as Stu dropped the ramp for the MERT. They went off to take over responsibility for the young Estonian, returning a few minutes later with a stretcher. We weren't hanging around, and with the Apache circling, Frenchie lifted into the hover and we headed back towards Bastion.

As we crossed the perimeter, Waldo armed down the aircraft for the last time that evening, and Frenchie kept the speed on as we raced up the runway, flaring at the far end and turning finals for the Nightingale landing site. Again the ambulance was waiting, and the MERT went off to the hospital with the casualty as we repositioned back to the parking area, stopping to refuel before taxiing in and shutting down.

There was a noticeable silence as we pulled off our helmets, each of us pausing for a moment to reflect on what had been an eventful two hours. For me, the transit through the dust storm had been uncomfortable, but I had complete faith in both the Apache crew and Frenchie and Waldo. However, the blackness of the ridge as the height warning seemed to go on for an eternity had given me a bit of a pause for thought.

As we arrived back in the tent, Stu and Waldo began to argue over who was making the tea; some semblance of normality was returning.

As we sat there with a brew, Frenchie looked at us and, with a humility that surprised me, said, 'Thanks, guys.'

I don't think I was the only one who believed that ridge was going to be our final resting place.

The following day, we handed over IRT and were tidying up some of the accommodation ready for the arrival of A Flight, when the boss asked if I had five minutes.

'Mick, the OC caught me this morning. What the fuck went on last night?' he asked.

It was clear he was under the impression we'd bent the rules.

I outlined what had gone on, and his face changed as I ran him through the decision-making that had gone into the two pick-ups.

'Look, Rich, Frenchie did a pretty shit-hot job last night,' I added.

He nodded. 'Yeah, sounds that way. Can you do me a favour and just write a quick account of what went on?'

'Yeah, no worries, Rich. I'll have it done by end of play today,' I replied, unaware of the chain of events which last night and my account would set in motion.

That afternoon, I sat down and wrote down my account on two sides of A4, signing it at the bottom before dropping it off with Rich.

Chapter 16

Frenchie the Bullet-Magnet *Extraordinaire*

Early morning the following day, and we were airborne again. We had a run to an FOB to the south near Marjah. We dropped down into low level a few miles out and tracked down a river valley on the run-in, remaining fast and low.

As I manned the minigun in the door I saw an adobe compound up ahead on the west bank of the river, with a black figure sat on the roof.

'Mick, keep your eye on the compound coming down the right. There's something about it,' called Frenchie.

'Seen. Yeah, I know what you mean,' I said, confirming his suspicions.

On the roof was a tall, black-robed figure with a turban talking into a mobile phone. He might as well have worn a sign saying 'Taliban'.

I trained the gun on the figure as we drew level; a look of obvious hostility passed across his face as he watched us fly by. As we drew level with the building I kept the gun trained on him. Then, in my peripheral vision, I spotted a second guy behind the compound pointing an RPG directly at us.

I flicked up the guard and, quickly targeting the guy and allowing for speed, wind and gravity, put the sight over his centre mass and moved my finger to the 'Send' switch.

'RPG, right 3 o'clock, gunner next to compound,' I called.

In the microseconds it took Frenchie to react and make the control inputs, the gunner must have looked up the barrel of the minigun, because he lowered the RPG and placed it on the ground. He was obviously familiar with our ROE (rules of engagement) and knew that once he no longer presented a threat I could not legally engage him.

While the gunner was lowering the RPG, my head was busy being forced through my boots as Frenchie racked on the bank and manoeuvred. I flicked the guard on the minigun back down.

Clear of the threat, I debriefed Frenchie on what had gone down. I had done the right thing, since if I had fired once he had put the RPG down, it would have been an illegal killing, and probably, for all we knew, been captured by the gun tape of the Apache. This was the era of Stan McChrystal's 'courageous restraint', and footage of an 'unarmed' Afghan getting flat-packed by a minigun could have easily seen me in court.

The most annoying aspect of this incident was in the debrief. As I described the sequence of events, the intelligence officer, the same one who briefed us each morning, nodded.

'That fits. We've been getting intelligence that a Pakistan-trained anti-air team had moved into the area.'

Dwell on that if you will ... Someone had gone to the trouble of disseminating that intelligence and passing it to the Intelligence officer for the Joint Helicopter Force, the most targeted aerial unit in Afghanistan. And we only discovered that little nugget after we'd stared down the barrel of an RPG. During Coalition operations in Afghanistan twenty-seven Chinooks were shot down by hostile fire, a similar figure to that for all the other types of military aircraft put together. Yet we didn't need to know there was an anti-air team on our patch?

Two days later, we were flying again, although as the A Flight guys were arriving we had shuffled some of the crewmen around and Stu had been replaced by Dave Wright. We were tasking in the province, re-supplying a number of the FOs across the green zone in the Nad e Ali district, along with C3PO's crew in the other aircraft.

As we'd briefed, the intelligence officer had given us a threat assessment for each of the sites we would be going into that day. After our previous interaction with the anti-air team, I remained sceptical, still feeeling it was all chicken bones and dice, but as he finished I asked about the last line on the tasking sheet which he'd skipped over.

'That's a grid we got from 1 Para. We don't know much more, but I have been told it's benign,' he told us.

Not much to go on, but if he didn't have any more, that was fair enough, and I guessed 1 Para would probably have been busier dominating the ground than assessing it.

We had been airborne for a few hours and were sitting at height over the green zone as C3PO descended into one of the many FOBs. Suddenly, one of the Apache gunships peeled off and dropped height as the radio net erupted. C3PO's aircraft was taking heavy fire on their run-in. I could just imagine him saying, 'Oh my!' as the tracer passed him.

The Chinook made it on to the ground and sat within the FOB as the Apaches suppressed the firing points; after a few anxious minutes there was relief as we watched them lift, accelerating to pick up speed before climbing to height and joining us.

Having taken a few rounds, C3PO would route back to Bastion, while we would continue to our last serial on the task sheet with the Apache, dropping a 4-ton underslung load of ammunition, fuel and hexamine to the grid provided by 1 Para, before heading back to Bastion to join C3PO.

We tracked slightly to the north and identified the general area of the grid, smack in the dense vegetation of the green zone.

'OK, dropping into low level,' called Frenchie as we started a steep descent, rolling out at about 80ft and trailing the netted load beneath us.

It was a beautiful spot, almost like jungle, with irrigated paddy fields and clumps of dense bush. But something felt out of place, and as we approached a dusty road running left to right a moped with a rider and passenger slowed beneath us.

BANG! BANG! BANG! BANG! BANG!

Several rounds hit the airframe, and there was a loud thump from the cockpit, accompanied by a loud 'Fuck!' from Waldo. One of the rounds had smashed through the cockpit, passing within an inch of Waldo's left leg then making for the delicate flying controls in the forward pylon.

We needed to jettison the load so we could manoeuvre, and I looked back to Dave to tell him to jettison, but he had already done so, lying on the cabin floor with the release handle raised. Good man, Dave.

I scanned the area with the minigun, but there were no immediate targets, and by now Frenchie and Waldo were assessing our predicament.

'I've lost all power,' called Frenchie. 'Entering autorotation.'

That was not good. Ending up on the ground here, surrounded by angry Taliban, would not have a happy ending, however you spun it. I stuck my head into the cockpit and looked at the torque gauge. Frenchie was right; all three needles were at zero. But I also noticed the outside temperature gauge was blank.

'Mate, you've lost instruments, not torque. Look at the OAT!' I screamed, as Frenchie lowered the collective.

He lifted the lever and confirmed he still had power, but as he did so the aircraft was rocked by a large explosion which blew me off my feet and left me on my arse between the cabin and cockpit. As I sat there for a second trying to figure out what was going on I heard Frenchie calling that he had power and was manoeuvring.

That was good news, but I was still trying to figure out why I was sitting down. I got up slowly and went to the cabin door, which was slightly buckled and heavily scored with burn marks. We'd been caught by an airburst RPG quite close in.

Frenchie transmitted, 'Mayday, Mayday, Mayday, Ultimate 22. We've received several rounds and an airburst RPG and sustained damage to several systems. Recovering to Bastion,'

I climbed around the minigun so my upper torso was outside the aircraft and in the heavy airflow, and assessed the damage. Above us, the panels on the forward pylon which housed the gearbox and flying controls had all been blown open by a pressure wave. Down the right hand side of the aircraft there were creased panels, scoring and burn marks in the aircraft skin, and we had no instruments.

Frenchie had the hammer down and we vibrated and shook at a rather alarming level as he guided the damaged aircraft out of the green zone and across the short patch of open desert to Bastion. Once we were over the desert and out of the Taliban's playground I felt a little better, but relief did not really wash over me until we crossed the fence and came to the hover over the runway, all of Bastion's emergency vehicles there to meet us with lights flashing.

We landed and taxied into the parking area, Frenchie steering for the nearest spot.

'Ultimate 22, we have an exercise ongoing, and due to a suspect IED we need you to park further away.'

'Ground, Ultimate 22 cancelling our Mayday. We aren't playing, and I'm parking here,' replied Frenchie to a silent thumbs-up from the rest of the crew.

We shut down and were inspecting the damage as Gammo pulled up. The round that had passed through the cockpit had severed all the wiring looms to the instrument panels and come within millimeters of taking out Waldo, before striking the forward gearbox. Another round had hit the starboard engine, and yet another, one of the rotor blades. Several rounds had hit the airframe, including one that had struck the area Dave Wright would have been occupying had we not been carrying an underslung load.

The airburst RPG that had blown me off my feet had resulted in a range of damage and blown-out panels, leaving dents, scoring and burn marks down the entire right-hand side.

We stood there in silence for a few moments surveying the damage, as oil and hydraulic fluid slowly dripped into growing puddles on the ground.

'There's a spare aircraft available if you want it,' joked Gammo, lifting the mood.

'Thanks, mate, but I think we're done for the day,' I replied quietly and walked up the ramp to collect my kit.

It was time to head home.

* * *

Over the next few days life continued at Bastion as we prepared to hand over to A Flight and head back to the UK in time for Christmas. I got the guys to tidy out all the accommodation and restock the fridges, and it was great to see the new guys arrive, complete with Santa hats, to take over. The handover was made easier by the fact I was handing over to my old mate Galvo, and between us we managed to make the transition as seamless as possible.

There was one funny interlude, when we were asked to drop an old Humvee out on the range near Bastion, for the Apaches and us to use as a target. It was a 30-minute job, so I tasked the standby crew with it. Unfortunately, in the transition, someone had crewed Gammo and Barry together, and entrusting a task to the pair of them made me a little nervous.

'For once, no fucking about, guys. Just pick it up and take it to the range,' I told them sternly.

'No worries, Mick,' they nodded.

A couple of hours later, I had finished lunch and walked out of the DEFAC to hear the sound of a Chinook passing low over the camp. Like everyone else, I looked up, to see a Humvee swinging below the aircraft; down its side some comedians had sprayed, 'Cockpiss, Partridge'.

I laughed, but called them in anyway when they landed. Both gave a full account of how the graffiti had already been on the vehicle when they picked it up. They might even have got away with that line if I hadn't known that Gammo was a huge Alan Partridge fan.

As the A Flight guys rolled steadily through their TQs, one by one we handed back our Mark 60 jackets, morphine and other equipment, boxing up flying helmets and handing weapons back to the armourers to be bundled up for the journey back to the UK.

From an administrative point of view, leaving Afghanistan was almost as tedious as arriving, with weapon-cleaning and handing back of morphine, controlled documents and other bits of kit; there was a fixed number of NVGs and LCJs in theatre, so as replacements were trained, those leaving needed to hand their kit back.

There was a fair amount of sitting around drinking coffee as we counted down the days to our flight home, and it was during one of these sessions that we learned some bad news: the Tristar fleet had been grounded after cracks had been found in the tail sections. We were a day or so from flying home, and the entire air bridge between Afghanistan and the UK had come to a grinding halt, just a week before Christmas.

I went down to speak with the movers, hoping I could find us another exit plan and a ride home. As I walked into the portakabin that served as an office, the sergeant was on the phone.

Cupping the phone for a second, he said, 'Give me two minutes, Sir, and I'll be with you.'

'No rush,' I replied, and he gave me a strange look.

As he finished the call he turned to me, and it was then I recognized a face I hadn't seen in many years; Paul was someone I had worked for in Germany many years earlier.

'Bugger me. Hello, Mick – I didn't recognize you, mate,' he said, as we shook hands. 'Must be twenty years.'

'About that, Paul. How you doing?'

'Yeah, all good, just another month to push. What can I do for you, mate?' he enquired.

'We're booked on the Tristar on the 17th,' I replied, and he pulled the kind of face a mechanic pulls when he lifts the bonnet of your car to give you a quote.

'I guess you know about the sketch with the Tristars?'

'Yeah, not the best timing,' I replied. 'Any C17s going west?'

'Hold on, mate. Let me have a look.' He tapped away at a laptop. 'How many of you?'

'Twenty-eight, all up.'

'I can get you all on a C17 on the 19th out of Kandahar, mate. Does that work?'

'That's awesome, Paul. Much appreciated.'

And as he created a booking we caught up on events since we'd last seen each other as the base closed in Germany and we all headed back to take up new roles in the UK. With the booking made, I thanked Paul and went to update the guys; we'd need to start feeding people back to Kandahar on the C130 over the next 24 hours.

Within a few hours the first of the guys were on a C130 heading to Kandahar, baggage stacked on the ramp and headphones in, listening to music over the drone of the turbo-prop engines. The next day, the Boss and I followed them with the last of the guys, leaving A Flight to it.

We moved into our old accommodation block at Cambridge Lines, and the guys relaxed in the winter sunshine, drinking coffee on the boardwalk and recounting shit stories on some ageing garden chairs at the back of the block. Rich sat quietly with a book, smoking a cigar and trying to ignore the cacophony of laughter each time someone finished a story or delivered the punch line to a joke.

I checked with the movers at Kandahar, and Paul had been as good as his word; we were all booked on the C17 the following night. In mid-afternoon, though, Morts and Gordo turned up bearing bad news: the C-17 was now taking extra freight, and although we'd been offloaded to a later flight, it would be departing from Bastion. A few phone calls to the C130 guys, and we were on our way back to Bastion, retracing the route we'd taken the previous day, much to the amusement of Galvo.

'You can't stay away, mate,' he laughed. 'You can stay if you want to. I'll head home.'

The next twelve hours were touch-and-go, with rumour and counter-rumour about C17s and cancelled flights, but late at night we filed up the ramp of the C17 and sat up the front of the cabin on special pallets fitted with seats. There was a collective sigh of relief as the crew pushed the throttles forward and we lumbered down the runway and into the air, climbing rapidly away from any unfriendly locals who might be tempted to loose off shots at the massive noise of the huge jet as it rose.

We would be stopping for fuel at Minhad, an airbase located just outside Dubai, and from there would fly back to Brize Norton to join our families for Christmas; by now it was the early hours of 20 December. As we arrived in Minhad we were offloaded and herded into a transit lounge stocked with the obligatory water fridges and coffee urn.

After half an hour or so a small entourage entered, led by a Squadron Leader who walked to the front of the room.

'Shit! This isn't good,' I muttered to Rich.

'Problem?' he asked with a raised eyebrow.

'You don't send a group led by a Squadron Leader to tell you your flight's ready for boarding,' I replied.

Behind us, the other passengers, mainly from the Parachute Regiment, continued chatting, unaware that a bombshell was on its way.

The Squadron Leader cleared his throat, as the Sergeant with him yelled, 'Listen in!'

'Ladies and gents, I am afraid I have some bad news. Given the grounding of the Tristar, we have a backlog of passengers in Afghanistan. The C17 that was going to take you to Brize Norton will be turning around and going back to Bastion this evening. You will be accommodated here until we can make other arrangements to get you back to the UK. I apologize for the inconvenience, but it's a difficult situation at present, and I would ask for your patience. We will have you on your way as soon as we can. Thank you.'

As he walked out of the room, a dark cloud of disappointment filled the air while everyone absorbed the news. Behind us, the Paras exploded in a torrent of expletives, and although it wasn't anyone at Minhad's fault that our ageing air transport fleet was grounded, I did have some sympathy for them; they were travelling home on their seven days' R&R, and the clock was already ticking.

Buses arrived and transported us to an empty accommodation compound usually occupied by the Dutch military. Surrounded by barbed wire, the neat rows of white huts around a parade ground bore more than a passing resemblance to a prison camp. We settled in and made the best of it, finding coffee and gathering for a smoke under a sunshade, but there was a wide feeling of despondency, mainly because we had no idea how long we would be there; it could be hours, days or even weeks.

I unpacked a change of underwear and a towel and went for a shower; the area was functional and clean, and I'd just make the most of it. Emerging refreshed, I had another coffee and then lay down on a bunk bed and had a sleep, waking a couple of hours later.

As I walked out, squinting at the brightness, I saw Dave Wright and Max at a small table, setting up a game of Trivial Pursuit they had found in the accommodation.

'Joining us?' called Dave.

In the absence of anything else to do I nodded, took a seat across from Max and we began throwing dice and pulling out cards. It was, however, a bit of a struggle; Max is one of those incredibly bright people who struggle with anything less than the conceptual, and he didn't seem to have played the game before. He took ages to answer every question, going through periods of silence, gasps and facial contortions, before eventually delivering a wrong answer.

One question Max had was about who had reacted to seeing a picture of Jesus on a stained glass window, and after five or so minutes he replied, 'Jesus.'

'Pretty sure they didn't have stained glass windows when Jesus was about, and probably not ones with his face on them,' replied Dave, starting to become somewhat frustrated.

A few minutes later, Max was up again.

'In 1952, Nestlé invented the freeze-drying of which product?' asked Dave.

'Eggs. It's definitely eggs,' replied Max

'Coffee. Its fucking coffee, Max,' replied Dave.

We all had a chuckle, and ten or so minutes later, Max was in the spotlight again.

'Which is the largest museum in the world?' I asked him.

There were several minutes of humming and ha'ing before he clicked his fingers and smiled.

'The Natural History Museum,' he proclaimed.

'The Louvre,' I corrected him, replacing the card in the box.

'Shit, should have got that one,' said Max. 'I was there earlier this year.'

By now it had all become too much for Dave, who stood up and kicked the board across the compound before heading into the accommodation.

'I can't fucking take any more of this,' he shouted, looking at Max.

'Someone's over-tired,' said Max, as I collected the pieces together and recovered the board.

Later on, meals arrived and were laid out in one of the communal buildings. In the evening we heard lots of screaming coming from the shower block, and an ambulance arrived and took away one of the paratroopers. He had been showering when the mixer head had given way and he'd been badly scalded by very hot water.

It was two long days in the desert version of 'Tenko' before we learned we would be flying home the next day. As we rose the following morning, nobody needed to be reminded to be packed up and ready to go; everyone was dressed and sitting on their rucksack by 7.00 am.

The RAF had managed to charter a DC10 from Omni Aviation, an American civilian airline which carried out a lot of charter work for the US military, and we were soon aboard. The cabin crew were no-nonsense women, used to carrying the military; with no messing around, we were soon seated, and the plane lumbered down the runway and into the air.

We arrived at Brize Norton in the early evening, but fate hadn't quite finished with us just yet. The automated roller system in the hold had seized, and the containers with our baggage and weapons were jammed in place. It took almost three hours to free them and for us to reclaim our bags and climb on the transport back to Odiham.

We arrived back at the Squadron, handing over weapons as a handful of family members waited in the cold night with cars running, ready to reclaim their loved ones. As the guys began to bomb-burst, Roly appeared.

'Gents, OC 27 Squadron would like to talk to you all in the crew room,' he barked, to a general groan of disappointment. It was late at night on 23 December and six days after we should have been home.

We assembled in the crew room, many of the guys pointedly looking at their watches as the boss began a speech about how well we'd performed and how much attention our recovery of the Estonian had generated on the base.

With the speech over, the crew room emptied to the sound of car boots being closed and screeching tyres, as everyone headed home before anything else delayed them further. I was just going down the stairs when I bumped into Roly.

'Hey, mate, thanks a lot for everything you have done; not an easy tour by the sound of it,' he said.

'All good, mate,' I replied.

'I was pissed off to hear we almost lost you, as you covered for someone else, mate. What the fuck do I tell your family if something happened to you?' he added, the long-standing friend talking now.

'Well you didn't and you don't have to,' I smiled.

'Have a good Christmas, mate,' he laughed. 'You've earned it.'

As I walked down the stairs, leaving him behind, I had no idea how much that conversation would come back to haunt me a few years later.

Roly was killed when a Puma helicopter crashed and caught fire in Kabul on 11 October, 2015. He had been due to return home but had extended when one of the replacement crewmen was delayed in arriving. His death would come as a shock to all of us and remind us all that behind the bravado, training and the degree of arrogance required to convince ourselves 'it could never happen to me', we were all mortal and had chosen a profession that involved risk. That conversation on the stairs was the last one Roly and I would have.

As I walked out of the Squadron to head home I saw another familiar face. Bob shuffled forward awkwardly, aware of events since I had waved him off at Bastion for his flight back to the UK.

'I know this is insufficient, but I just wanted to say thanks,' he said quietly, handing me a bottle of my favourite single malt.

'It's OK, mate. Happy to call it quits,' I replied, grabbing the bottle before the Yorkshireman in him took over and he changed his mind.

'How did the wedding go?'

'Awesome. Amy sends her regards.'

'Cool. Well, listen, mate, as good as it is standing in the cold, I am going to head home.'

'Hop in. I'll give you a lift,' Bob replied, and I threw my bag in the boot and climbed into the passenger seat, gratefully soaking up warmth of the heater.

'Merry Christmas, mate,' he said as I climbed out a few minutes later.

'Yeah, Merry Christmas,' I replied, retrieving my bags and walking up my front path.

Chapter 17

It's Been Emotional

RAF Odiham
Hampshire
March 2011

On my fortieth birthday, a few months later, I was fortunate enough to be joined by friends for a curry in Odiham village. As I sat waiting for my chicken vindaloo to arrive, I nursed a pint of Cobra and looked around the table as Morris, DC and others talked and laughed. That was when I experienced an epiphany; what bound me to the Air Force was no longer the job or the challenge, but the people, and they would still be there regardless of whether I was at Odiham or not.

As the night wore on and the beers flowed, I decided that after twenty-three years the time had come for me to do something different. I thought it over during the weekend, and on Monday morning I went into work and gave in my notice.

With a series of clicks of a mouse, a career that had commenced in 1988 with my climbing on a train to Lincoln was over; 2011 was the peak period of defence cuts following the banking crisis, and notice periods had been reduced to six months. With leave, courses and resettlement, I had three months left in work.

My leaving bash from Odiham was in September, and as a small crowd assembled in a nearby pub for the traditional 'tequila darts' showdown, my phone rang. It was Rich.

'Hey, Mick, sorry I can't make it this afternoon.'

'No worries, Rich.'

'I have some news.'

'What news?' I was curious, and hoped Rich would spill quickly.

'The operational awards are being published in the morning. Frenchie has been awarded the Air Force Cross for the IRT task you guys did last December.'

'Awesome. That's really good news,' I replied, chuffed that Frenchie's efforts had been recognized but also aware that his French half would be insufferable.

'Have the tequila darts started yet?'

'Just about to kick off,' I informed him.

'Lucky I caught you then,' laughed Rich. 'Don't drink too much.'

'Can't promise that,' I said, and Rich laughed again and hung up.

It was mid-afternoon the following day before I was confident I'd be under the limit and legal to drive. C Flight were back in Afghanistan, so I couldn't call Frenchie. As I drove up the A34 I thought back to that night, and when I arrived I made a quick Facebook post on Frenchie's home page:

> Only four people know the magnitude of what went on that evening, and I am sure they will agree with what I have written below ...
> For having vision, but no visibility,
> for knowing the difference between utility and futility,
> for saying yes when others said no,
> for saying no when others said yes,
> for exploring the envelope but staying within it,
> for all these things, your AFC is very much deserved and I salute you,
> for not hitting the ridgeline that evening, I thank you.
> Well done, mate, I will raise a glass this evening.
> Not long to push, I'll see you all when you get home.

It would actually be the following February before we caught up properly; we assembled in London for the trip to Buckingham Palace to watch Frenchie get his Air Force Cross. As I arrived, Frenchie, Waldo, Stu and Gammo were just completing a trip down the Thames, and we headed to a pub near Westminster for a beer or three.

As Frenchie and Ali headed off for a civilized dinner, Stu and I stopped off at a pub near City Hall and finally ended up sipping Lychee Daiquiris in a bar opposite Waterloo Station, before going back to get some sleep.

The following morning, Stu and I met in the lobby, I in a suit and Stu in his No. 1 uniform, reserved for formal occasions; to be honest, it felt strange being out of uniform, but it still felt good being a civilian.

Frenchie and Waldo were staying at a swanky hotel on Park Lane and were finishing breakfast when we arrived. We joined them for coffee, and after a short while they left to finish dressing. Left alone in a Park Lane hotel, Stu and I did what any self-respecting crewman would do: ordered Bloody Marys and charged them to Frenchie.

As aircraft captain, Frenchie would be receiving the medal on behalf of the crew, an arrangement all of us were happy with, considering that if we had screwed up, Frenchie would be accepting the blame, possibly posthumously. For his part, Frenchie was acutely aware of the crew thing and made sure we were 100 per cent included in the event.

After taking as many happy snaps as possible at Buckingham Palace, we retired to an afternoon reception at the RAF Club on Piccadilly for a number of beers, before catching up with members of the squadron at a whisky bar off Trafalgar Square, over a bottle of Bowmore.

It was a good evening, and as I sat there with a Scotch listening to the banter and laughter of good friends, the moment was made all the better by the thrill of being alive to celebrate; we'd come damned close to spanking into that ridgeline all those dark nights before.

As the celebrations drew to a close, Stu and I capped the evening with another Lychee Daiquiri and a trip to Chicken Cottage on the way home.

Epilogue

I finally left the RAF in October 2011, after twenty-three years of service across every continent and all manner of operations, conflicts and minor skirmishes. The last decade, post-9/11, were the defining years that shaped and sculpted the person I was when I entered the grown-up world of civilian life.

One of the first questions people often ask is, 'Did you enjoy your time in the military?' and the answer is always yes. I met some fantastic people, faced down adversity with them and laughed as we did so. I am lucky that my memory blurs the bad times and emphasizes the good.

I do not suffer from Post-Traumatic Stress Disorder, and although I have close friends and colleagues who have really struggled to contextualize their experiences in Iraq and Afghanistan, I sometimes resent the relentless media image of all Afghanistan veterans being in perpetual mental anguish and ready to explode.

That said, it would be false to say that Afghanistan didn't affect me in any way; it did, and continues to do so. Like many who have been forced to confront life-and-death situations on a regular basis, I have a healthy disregard for those who wish to enslave us in trivia and expect us to suspend common sense; I distrust politicians, the media and 'experts', for I have seen too many of them either lie or distort the truth to suit their own objectives.

I entered civilian life down a well-worn path that many take with trepidation, yet I approached it with careful planning, a near-absence of fear and exceptional will to succeed; that's how I approached Afghanistan, and it was the only way I knew by that point. Like many others at the time, I have transferred skills learnt in adversity into the boardroom and excelled in the civilian world. In a very risk-adverse world, the ability to achieve through mitigation is a sought-after skill, and I found simple things such as doing what you said you would do were well received.

On an emotional level I have been less successful. Our family home was destroyed by fire a few years ago; for me, since nobody was home at the time and we were insured, it was more of an inconvenience than a tragedy. I struggled to empathize with my wife, who was traumatized by the event, and my lack of emotion opened up several fault lines within our relationship.

I continue to move on a regular basis, across continents, countries and states, and struggle to really put down roots anywhere. My life has settled into a never-ending cycle of change, adaptation and achievement which has very strong parallels with my time in Afghanistan.

Like many others, I was shocked by Roly's death in 2015; I had just arrived in Eastern Europe on business when I had a call from a friend informing me of what had happened. Roly was not only a popular member of the Chinook community, he was a close friend. Though never spoken of as such, his death confronted all of us with a reminder of our mortality.

Over almost ten years I had pushed these memories to one side, and it had reached the point where Afghanistan was like a distant memory, almost dreamlike. I once sat through a casual conversation about the war in Afghanistan and was almost surprised when I was asked for my thoughts as someone who had witnessed it at first hand.

COVID-19 reached Australia in March 2020, and like most people in the aviation industry I suddenly found myself with time on my hands. In a concerted attempt to spend some time away from the beach or the bar, I started writing and found I couldn't stop.

Luckily, my aircrew logbooks survived the fire, and I have made every effort to record events as accurately as possible; but in ten years memories fade, and I apologize in advance for any errors or omissions. Some names and call signs have been changed to protect both the innocent and the guilty, and anything best kept within the military domain has been omitted.

This book is about people, ordinary people, who just happened to find themselves doing extraordinary jobs. Each one was a volunteer, and none consider themselves anything other than fortunate. The term 'hero' is never used, and unlike the Americans, we do not live by a code; the highest form of praise accepted without acute awkwardness is probably 'good operator'.

Just as Iraq was replaced by Afghanistan, Afghanistan has been replaced by Libya and currently Mali. Like many veterans of Afghanistan, I watched the confused abandonment of Kabul with astonishment, anxious for friends and former colleagues in the country as the Taliban rolled through village after village. I was surprised, but not shocked; politicians and the media have a short attention span.

Glossary

4WD	Four-Wheel Drive
AK47/AK	Russian-designed 7.62mm assault rifle. Cheaply manufactured in large numbers by China, it was the Taliban's weapon of choice.
ANA	Afghan National Army
ANP	Afghan National Police
APU	Auxiliary Power Unit. An internal power generation system providing AC power and hydraulic pressure to systems required for starting the aircraft.
AWACS	Airborne Warning and Control System. In this case, a Boeing E3D aircraft acting as a communications platform.
C17	Large transport plane with jet engines
C2I	Conversion to Instructor
C130	Hercules transport plane with turbo-prop engines
CASEVAC	Casualty Evacuation
CB	Circuit Breaker
CFS(H)	Central Flying School (Helicopters). The RAF unit tasked with training and auditing aircrew instructors. Also referred to informally as 'the college of knowledge'.
Chalk 1	An allocation of troops and equipment to a formation of aircraft. Each 'chalk' number relates to a corresponding helicopter.
CIA	Central Intelligence Agency
CSE	Combined Services Entertainment. Live events to entertain deployed troops.
DFAC	Dining Facility
FARP	Forward Air Refuelling Point
FIBUA	Fighting in Built-up Areas. Usually refers to a training village where troops can practise fighting from house to house.

Flare	The act of raising the nose to decelerate an aircraft or arrest rate of descent, or a countermeasure burning at high temperature and dispensed by an aircraft to decoy heat-seeking missiles
FLIR	Forward Looking Infra-Red. A low-light camera providing an enhanced televised image.
FLYCO	Flight Operations Controller onboard a Royal Navy ship
FOB	Forward Operating Base
GMASS	Gun Master Arm Switch (make bang bang switch)
GMLRS	Guided Multiple Rocket Launch System. A GPS-guided rocket system, also known in the media as the '60-kilometre sniper'.
Green Zone	Irrigated area around the Helmand River, the thick vegetation providing a stark contrast to the brown desert
HALS	Hardened Landing Surface. A short strip for Apache running take-off and landings due to their considerable weight.
HQ	Headquarters
HRF	Helmand Reaction Force
HUMS	Health and Usage Monitoring System. Hardwired monitoring system on the Chinook which monitors performance of systems for engineering and technical analysis.
HUMVEE	US Army vehicle, known in civilian terms as a 'Hummer'
IED	Improvised Explosive Device (often referred to as a 'roadside bomb')
IFF	Identification Friend or Foe. A transponder which identifies you to air traffic controllers or air defence systems.
IP	Initial Point, a unique and vertical navigation feature used for the run into a grid or target
IRT	Incident Response Team
ISAF	International Stabilization Force (NATO)
JHSU	Joint Helicopter Support Team. A joint services team providing logistical support and proof that not all heroes wear capes.
JTAC	Joint Terminal Air Controller. Owner of the airspace within an area of battle, coordinating air transport and calling in airstrikes. Usually answering to the call sign 'Widow'.

LUP	Lying-up Point
M60D	Gas-powered, belt-fed machine gun
M134D	Electrically driven, belt-fed minigun with six rotating barrels capable of firing 4,000 rounds
MERT	Medical Emergency Response Team
MOG	Mobile Outreach Group of 45 Commando in the winter of 2006/7
MRE	Meal Ready to Eat. A US Army-issue ration pack.
NGO	Non-Governmental Organization (usually a charity)
Nine-liner	The request for casualty evacuation, pre-formatted and containing nine elements, including location, type and severity of injuries.
NVG	Night Vision Goggles
OAT	Outside Air Temperature. Shown digitally on a gauge within the Chinook cockpit.
OCF	Operational Conversion Flight. The unit which converts aircrew from the training system or previous types on to the Chinook.
Playmate	The other aircraft in a pair
QHCI	Qualified Helicopter Crewman Instructor. A Central Flying School (Helicopter) qualified rear crew instructor.
QHI	Qualified Helicopter Instructor. Central Flying School (Helicopter) qualified pilot instructor.
R&R	Rest & Recuperation, a soldier's short mid-tour break back in the UK
ROE	Rules of Engagement. The legal parameters under which military personnel may/may not open fire or deploy weapon systems.
RPG	Rocket-Propelled Grenade
SAFIRE	Small Arms Fire Report. A log of enemy contacts from which threat assessments are developed.
SAS	Special Air Service
SBS	Special Boat Service
SF	Special Forces
Singleton	Aircraft operating alone, rather than in a pair or a larger formation

Squirter	Someone leaving a target building or compound or running away during an assault whose intentions are unknown
Technical	Pick-up (usually a Toyota Hilux or Ford Ranger) with mounted weapons
TIC	Troops in Contact (a firefight)
TLS	Taliban's Last Stand. A bullet-riddled adobe building at Kandahar.
TQ	Theatre Qualification
TSW	Tactical Supply Unit. RAF unit operating Forward Air Refuelling Points.
WMIK	Weapon-Mounted Installation Kit. Refers to stripped down Land Rovers with mounted weapons and roll cage which were heavily used in early Iraq and Afghanistan operations but were very prone to mine damage.